LOVE, PLEASE
A MEMOIR OF DESTINY, LOSS AND HEALING.

SUSANA HAYMAN-CHAFFEY

authorHOUSE®

AuthorHouse™
1663 Liberty Drive
Bloomington, IN 47403
www.authorhouse.com
Phone: 1-800-839-8640

Published by AuthorHouse 2/11/2013

ISBN: 978-1-4817-0339-0 (sc)
ISBN: 978-1-4817-0338-3 (hc)
ISBN: 978-1-4817-0337-6 (e)

Library of Congress Control Number: 2012924288

Cover photos by James Klosty

Any people depicted in stock imagery provided by Thinkstock are models, and such images are being used for illustrative purposes only. Certain stock imagery © *Thinkstock.*

This book is printed on acid-free paper.

To Satoru,

The one I love more than myself and who changed my life forever.

and

For Christophe,

The light of my life, the miracle I have watched grow and have learned so much from.

TABLE OF CONTENTS

Preface   1
With Special Appreciation   3
1976   4
The Proposal   10
European Tour   15
Return to Tokyo   20
The Wedding   27
Back To New York   33
A Simple Life   40
Europe   44
Italian Sojourn   50
Performing Together   57
Here and There   63
Numbers   70
Christophe   76
Out of the Suitcase   81
Inventing Work   87
Japanese Country House   92
The Challenges   97
Japan in America   102
Grand Gestures   109
The Accident   115
Rituals   120
Family and Friends   126
Surviving   131
Friendships   137
Mama And Papa   168
South American Journey   172

Retracing My Steps	179
239 Central Park West	184
Fornacino Di Gre	189
Tuscany Summer	195
Italy and New York	202
Explorations	210
Demetrius in Tuscany	218
Poetic Acts	225
A Pool in Fornacino	233
Mahikari	239
Signs of Trouble	243
Tokyo	251
Saying Goodbye to New York	254
Friends Indeed	257
Destination Tuscany	263
Emergency	269
The Journey up the Mountain	276
Songs in the Night	283
Epilogue	291

PREFACE

I had wanted to write this memoir seventeen years ago but somehow always found a way to put it off. Then, one day in late September of 2010, while having lunch with my son Christophe, I was complaining about how useless I felt not doing anything serious in my life, and he suggested I finally sit down and write my memoir.

Many times we had talked about this and I said to him, with tears running down my face, "You don't understand I can't do this on my own. I need someone to help me." After lunch I decided to take a walk and get some fresh air and think about what he had said. I walked up to the small village at the top of our Canyon and by chance looked at the bulletin board where people pinned up cards offering their services. My eye fell on a pink card that said, "Writing Coach. Challenges starting your writing project? -- Finishing up? -- Stuck in the middle? -- Neighborhood writer, editor, instructor can help you realize your writing dreams. Call Lisa."

I immediately took that to be a sign and rushed home to get a pen and paper to go back and write down the telephone number on the card. It took me a few days to get the courage to call her. When I did a few days later, I started the conversation like this: "I'm a former dancer." She said, "So am I." I said, "I was married to a Japanese man." Lisa said, "So was I." We arranged to meet the next day.

We had one of those rare moments when you realize something bigger is at work; we were kindred spirits with many similarities in our backgrounds. She was someone I felt I could trust to help me. We agreed she would think about it and get back to me. I anxiously awaited her call which came the next day and, thankfully, Lisa agreed to take me on. It was the beginning of an extraordinary journey that lasted about eight months. She encouraged me when I was insecure, buoyed my up when I was down and supported me in so many ways that I could not have imagined. I am eternally grateful to her for being such a loving soul. I could not have written this without her invaluable help.

Lisa Mitchell is the author (with Bruce Torrence) of "*The Hollywood Canteen: Where the Greatest Generation Danced with the Most Beautiful Girls in the World.*" (Bear Manor Media)

With Special Appreciation

Patricia and Frederick Hayman-Chaffey, Satoru Oishi, Christophe Oishi, Shoichi Kiyokawa, Charles and Shyrlei Hayman-Chaffey, Nicolette Chaffey, Jeff Murray, Merce Cunningham, John Cage, Robert Rauschenberg, Jasper Johns, Julian Lethbridge, James Lee Byers, Takehisa Kosugi, Richard Nelson, Alex Gregory-Hood, Judith Pisar, Barbara Schwartz, Carolyn Brown, Jim Klosty, Sandra Neels, Meg Harper, Kathy Kerr, Martha Lohmeyer, Chase Robinson, Mel Wong, Robert Kovich, Ulysses Dove, Brigitte Lefevre, Benedict Pesle, Micheline Lelievre, Delphine Dupont-Midy, Steven Kolpan, Catherine Althaus, Peter and Caroline ffrench-Hodgess, Mr. and Mrs. Rogers, Janice Rogers, John Schneider, Nieves Mathews, Marianne and Bishi Mathews, Beatrice Mathews, Caroline Edwards, Sally Campbell, Jan Meisner, Ab and Tina Ten Dam, Joke, Mehlika and Anneke and Roel Ten Dam, Jerry Zanuik, Henrietta Alban, Demetrius and Rollodon, Nesta Brooking, Grant Muradoff, Olga Lepeshinskaya, Yuriko Kikuchi, Kitsuke and Ryu Oishi, Kimiko and Mitsuru Oishi, Gyohei Hayashi, Mrs. Hayata, Irving and Evelyn Marantz, Mady Marantz, Brenda Daniels, Brenda Marshall, Roberta Harrison, Aida and Max Tejeda, Pancho and Patty Bundt, Irene Borguet, Nicole Bouchet de Fariens, Connie Sayre, Dr. Gertrude Schaffel, Louise Attling, Jay Iselin, Ivo Bufalini, Anna, Carlo and Benedetta La Corte, Maria Luisa Tavasani, Christian Meneghini, Linda Montano, Marcia Barkan, Meg and Allan Pestel, Elisabeth and Dominique Pellerin, Carmella Rapazzo, Alan and Rosa Ritchie, Rosamund Otaviani, Rosarita, Rina Shenfeld, Rina Yerushalmi, Gilberto Motta, Vera Kumpera, Mercedes Battista, Micheline Flak, Hardress Waller, Anna Maria Reddi, The Borzi family and so many more friends and strangers who have touched my life in special and unexpected ways. To all I am forever grateful.

1976

I heard Satoru Oishi sing before I heard him speak. It was in the winter of 1976, when I was a soloist in the Merce Cunningham Dance Company. An English artist I knew invited to me visit the loft where Satoru was living and working. Hiroshi, Satoru's friend, had invited him to New York from Tokyo to manage his Simca Prints Company. They made silk screen prints for many of the foremost artists of the 20th Century. Two were Jasper Johns and John Cage, who were both part of Merce's Company. Jasper, was his artistic director, and John, his Music Director.

Satoru was up in an open loft area singing a hauntingly beautiful song for his friends. I remember how amazing he looked and how beautiful his singing was; he stopped while we were being introduced. With a charming, very appealing smile he asked me, "Are you wearing a wig?" His words, though, I found to be at odds with my perception of Japanese manners. I had recently, on a whim, had a permanent; so I found his question slightly disconcerting. However, I remember I liked Satoru's unique mix of fragility and strength and his slightly tilted smile. He was very handsome, but as a result of his comment, I thought no more about him. He would later prove to be the person who would change my life forever. Yet at that moment I was unaware of his extraordinary role in it. I have often thought that our destinies take shape long before we actually become aware of what is to come. We move forward often at a loss wondering why we feel a certain way, not knowing that soon everything will change and make sense.

In the spring, I left with the Company on tour to Los Angeles, Australia and Japan. It would be a long tour that I was very much looking forward to. After Los Angeles we went to Perth and continued to Sydney, performing at the spectacular Sydney Opera

House, the Adelaide Festival and Canberra and then on to our last stop, Japan. Excitement washed over me. Japan was the land that, growing up, I had heard my mother talk so much about. She had dreamed of going there sometime; I would be fulfilling her dream. We had a four-hour layover to change planes in Tokyo, before going on to Kyoto, our first stop. A press conference had been programmed that we would all attend, after which we were each put in charge of our baggage and check in to Kyoto. We had enough time to eat something so we all headed to the airport restaurant, looking forward to our first Japanese meal. It was a feast we all enjoyed, and a nice break between all the flying. I was the first to leave and went up to pay but, mysteriously, someone had already paid for me. I asked my companions if any of them had, but none of them was responsible. So I looked around me to see if there was a sign as to who might have given me this generous present, only to realize that a little magic had just touched me. It gave me the first inkling that something special was happening. On my way out, as I was searching where to go, an elderly Japanese gentleman, seeing me in doubt, asked if he could help. I told him I was looking for the Kyoto check-in counter. He, gently, with beautiful Japanese manners, took my suitcase and me to the counter and checked me in. I thanked him gratefully and he graciously bowed and went on his way. These wonderful events, in my first few hours in Japan, felt like what Carl Jung explains as "synchronicity."

I was so excited to be in Kyoto, that as soon as I had put my bags in my room, I ran out to get a feel for the city. As I was walking and window shopping, a very nice young man invited me to tea, in the tea house I was looking into. He said he would like to practice his English. We had a lovely conversation; he told me all about Kyoto, its history and temples. I was fascinated. As dusk fell, I had to get back to the hotel to which he kindly accompanied me. As I was walking into the hotel, Merce and John Cage were there with some journalists who had just finished interviewing them. They were on their way out to dinner, and asked me to join them. Since this was a very rare thing for Merce and John to do, I accepted immediately. We went to a marvelous restaurant for a wonderful meal. All this on my first day in Japan! I was stunned and wondered what kind of enchanted spell I was under.

The next morning, we had rehearsals in the theatre and, in the evening, gave our first performance. On the program was *Signals*, a very special piece Merce had choreographed for us. He made my first leading solo and a beautiful duet for Mel Wong and me, just two years after I had joined the company. It was a choreography that Merce created outside of the formal foundation planning and was homemade, as it were, so that he could do it quickly without restraints. He designed the costumes and the set, and John Cage composed the music. Rick Nelson, the company lighting designer, came up with special lighting and a ravishing orange spot for me. It was premiered in Paris at the Theatre Odeon on June 5, 1970. I vividly remember Merce and me sitting on two chairs, part of the set, waiting for the curtain to go up. He leaned over to me and said "Let's pretend we are in the Bois de Boulogne having a nice afternoon." He must have realized how nervous I was and used this suggestion to help me relax, something I was never really able to do, as the solo was so technically difficult. I loved the challenge of pushing myself to the limits of my abilities, not to become complacent. I wanted the solo to have a sense of danger, always feeling panicky before walking into my spot to start, and wishing it to end quickly, then regretting it when it did.

Carolyn Brown, who had been Merce's prima ballerina and muse for twenty years, since the inception of his Company in the 1950's, wrote about *Signals* in her book, *Chance and Circumstance* (published by Knopf in 2007).

This brilliant, highly charged theatrical work, with its six curiously bound bodies: six metal folding chairs: a slightly menacing stick: strange audible, rhythmic exhalations from the dancers: mysterious, dramatic lighting and magical music, resembled no other Cunningham choreography, and its first performance was a smashing success. Although Merce claimed that the dance was " really like a little traveling group of players that come out, place their chairs, sit down and do their parts," and that he " tried to think of something you could do in a very simple circumstance,"

but what actually happens on stage belies this simple explanation. "Signals" as I viewed it, seemed taut with psychological tension. The dance consisted of long solos for Merce and Susana Hayman-Chaffey: a duet of ultra cool, detached passion for Susana and Mel Wong; an intricate trio (or quartet) for Valda Setterfield, Douglas Dunn, Mel (and when a quartet, Merce), in which a slightly menacing stick was passed among the men, giving it a martial-arts quality; and finally a quintet (or sextet, with the addition of Louise Burns) that could appear sometimes playful, sometimes ominous. The costumes designed by Merce -- sweatshirts and pants, the legs, arms, and torsos wound round with tape -- added a mysterious gravitas to the proceedings. Although Merce claimed that the binding was merely for the purpose of delineating the body, those bodies seemed not only physically but psychologically bound as well. "Gravitas" describes Susana's very difficult solo as well: there was a regal, solemn yet voluptuous nobility about that solo as she performed it, although this quality did not transfer to others who assumed her part in later productions. Did I regret not being in "Signals?" Quite honestly I don't believe I did, but it did put me on my mettle. The solo Merce made for Susana was not one he ever would have made for me, as much as I would have wished it. It was choreographed for her particular strengths and unique qualities, and she performed it beautifully.

The Kyoto performance went fabulously well, and at the reception afterwards, Isao Domoto, an older, famous, Japanese painter, complimented me on my performance. I had felt his penetrating gaze on me, across the room, making me feel appreciated. Slowly, he had walked over to me and told me how much he had liked my dancing. We talked for a while and he invited me to go to visit his studio the next day. He said he would send his car for me; I don't know why, but I did not take him up on his invitation. Destiny works in mysterious ways, as I would find out later.

We returned to Tokyo, where we were to perform in the wonderful Kenzo Tange NHK television Hall in Shibuya. Since it wasn't far from our hotel, we walked. I loved looking at the structure, as architecture had always fascinated me. The performance was being filmed for television, so we all made sure it was the best it could be. As was my custom, I did not stay long after the performance, so I walked back to the hotel restaurant in the lobby, where I waited for the others to arrive. It was the end of a long tour, I felt sad reflecting on the fact that I had no companion.

Everyone having arrived, we started eating, when a little while later, my attention was caught by two gorgeous tall Japanese men walking into the hotel. One was particularly tall; the other looked like a Japanese version of Alain Delon. (I had worked with Alain Delon in Brazil, when I was there dancing on a weekly television program. He was a guest of the show, and ever since seeing him in person, I had fallen in love with him.) I told my companions at the table to turn around to look at the two handsome Japanese men, not realizing that they had been invited to have a drink with us by one of the dancers. The one that looked like Alain Delon was Satoru, whom I did not recognize from my brief encounter with him in New York. He recognized me immediately, came right over and introduced himself, asking if I remembered him. I apologized saying, "I am sorry, no," to which he responded, "You came with Julian to our loft when I was singing." It was to my relief, that we had a connection, as the electricity between us was overwhelming. He pulled up a chair next to me and ordered a drink; we sat and talked about the performance and how I was enjoying Japan. His English was very good, almost without an accent. He had a way of using very few words which he chose very effectively. I felt so comfortable in his presence and loved his way of talking. I just sat there drinking in his beauty, thinking how lucky I was. His beautiful smile captivated me and I could not help smiling with him during our whole conversation. We were very attracted to each other right away. Towards the end of the evening he asked me, "Will you come out to dinner with me tomorrow?" I answered, "We have an early start tomorrow as we are going to Sapporo for our last performances in Japan." "Will you promise to call me when you return, so I can take you out to dinner then?" "Yes, I will," I replied, at the same time realizing that all I really wanted was to go out with him right then and there.

On the day of our return, I found myself anxiously pacing in my room, gathering the courage, to call him. What if he did not remember me? What if I seemed too forward? All manner of insecurities besieged me; finally I picked up the telephone. He had been waiting for me to call and was so happy that I did. He invited me out to dinner that night; I brought along two of the male dancers in the company, who knows why? At the appointed time we were down in the lobby dressed to the nines. He arrived, breathtakingly handsome, and whisked us in a taxi to his private club, where we had a fabulous dinner. He and I talked, oblivious to my two escorts, who kept each other amused. Satoru paid the bill and suggested taking us dancing at a discothèque he knew, which we all agreed to. After dancing up a storm, at around two in the morning, Satoru whispered in my ear, that he wanted to sing to me. We took our leave of my escorts and went off to a Karaoke club. We were escorted to a comfortable couch with a small table in front for our drinks and Satoru fell asleep. I, not knowing him well enough to do anything, awkwardly just sat there, watching the show of people going up to sing. It was finally Satoru's turn and a waitress came up to get him. I gently nudged him and he jumped up and headed to the stage with the waitress running after him tucking in his shirt, which was hanging out. He bounded onto the stage, was given the microphone, and burst into the Rolling Stone's *Route 66*! A more unlikely choice I could not have imagined. He belted out the song, twirling the microphone with great abandon, to everyone's amusement and consternation. I thought to myself, *this is the man for me*! What a joy it was to realize my good fortune that by complete chance, I had come upon such an improbable soul the other side of the world! It was the last thing I expected. In fact, I had decided in my own mind, that I would just concentrate on my career and not worry about finding a life companion.

THE PROPOSAL

The long tour over, the Company was to return to New York. Satoru had invited me to see Kyoto and Nara with him, so I decided to remain. We had a two week break before I would need to leave Japan to return to New York for the taping of a CBS Special on the Company. The time was mine to find what my future was to be. The Company would all leave except Charles Moulton and me. I would be left in a strange, yet familiar, land, with a man I seemed to remember from some other life.

When I first met Satoru in Tokyo, he had just returned to Japan from New York and was supported by his parents, with a generous allowance, as I later discovered. I remember he spent it with great abandon, and it seemed he was always taking out bills from his wallet. He really took great and extravagant care of me. We spent a week between Kyoto and Nara and Satoru showed me an exquisite Japan. I was fascinated and enthralled, drunk with the beauty of it and with him. We spent days walking around Temples and Shrines, one more beautiful than the next, and since it was spring, all the cherry blossoms were in bloom. Such an exuberant display of petals everywhere! Our visits were always such a visual pleasure; the gardening was so exquisite. Satoru told me that a gardener would study the wind and light for a year or more at times, before he would plant a single thing. You can sense this, as nothing is out of place and every view is so inspiring. I loved the architecture, the gorgeous blue ceramic tiles on the roofs and the delicate shoji screens. In Nara, deer were allowed to roam the streets, free to mingle among the people. There we stayed in a Riokan, a typical Japanese Inn, so that I could experience an ancient Japanese custom. The rooms were very sparse with traditional tatami mats covering the floors and very little else visible. At night they put out a thick cotton futon mattress to sleep on with lovely sheets and quilt covers. They serve only traditional homemade Japanese food which is exquisitely prepared. It is very special and, of course, quite expensive as a result. As lovers, everything took on a mystical quality. I was always feeling how unreal it all was, yet also so natural. We could be together for hours and hardly say a word, but be constantly communicating; it was to be this way throughout our union.

The two weeks we spent together were an unforgettable dream. Satoru was teaching me about Japan and the Japanese way of doing things. I was learning at the hands of a master. He had an extraordinary, gentle quality, yet you could tell he was a very strong man. His name, Satoru, meant enlightenment and his last name, Oishi, could mean Big Stone or delicious; depending on the intonation. He was an enlightened big stone, an incredible combination that made him very striking to others. Immediately people were attracted to him, not only for his compelling good looks, but for this strange mix of gentleness and strength. I, on the other hand, was cool and aloof, yet a wildfire when excited or provoked. This strange mix was due to the fact that my English mother had Spanish blood and my father's was Scottish and Norman. In fact, my mother's ancestors had been on the Spanish Armada exploring the Americas. I inherited her love of wandering and her childlike curiosity. From my father, I got my strength and physical stamina. Satoru's mother was from a Samurai family, and had been very adamant that he understand the responsibility that that entailed. His father was from an artistic family. He was an Ikebana master (master of flower arranging), a Tea Master and a drummer in the Noh theatre. Satoru's mother was his father's second wife and held absolute control over her four children. She instilled in all of them the discipline of their noble Samurai blood. Satoru, being the youngest, was spoiled by both parents, which was not very appreciated by the rest of their children. He was chosen to continue the Tea Ceremony tradition, and, when he was in Japan, studied every day with his father. He had started very young, and would later teach the Tea Ceremony to students in New York.

The first documented evidence of tea in Japan dates to the 9th Century, when it was taken by the Buddhist monk, Eichu, on his return from China. The custom of drinking tea, first for medicinal, and then pleasurable, reasons, was already widespread throughout China. The Chinese author Lu Yu wrote, "The Classic of Tea", a treatise on tea focusing on its cultivation and preparation. His ideas would have a strong influence in the development of the Japanese tea ceremony, also called the Way of Tea. In Japan, it involved the ceremonial preparation and presentation of *Matcha*, powdered green tea known as *Chanoyu*. Zen monks were the primary influence in its development, the main principles being harmony, respect, purity and tranquility. The study of the tea ceremony and its Zen principles is the most effective way to bring the pupil to the understanding of emptiness, and thereby to spiritual awakening-the first step to "Satori," or enlightenment.

Satoru's father was a handsome, eccentric gentleman. He used to be chauffeur-driven in his motorcycle, with a side car in which he sat. I remember seeing him for the first time in a black fur coat, with a fabulous hat, walking with his silver stick. He was quite tall, which was, unusual for a Japanese man. Satoru was trained as an architect, as were his two brothers. He was the youngest of four and was born when his mother was past forty and his father was in his fifties. This proved to be a serious problem for him emotionally, as his class mates would make fun of him because his mother was so old. I remember him telling me that he was always in fights at school to defend his mother. He had also had diphtheria, a life-threatening infection, when he was very young. He remembered being carried on his mother's back and resting his head on her shoulder. They were very close, therefore he had great attention lavished on him. I, too, had nearly died when I was a child soon after we had moved to Spain; I contracted Typhoid fever and was rushed to hospital, and was in a coma for two weeks. There was something about the similarity of our beginnings that made us feel closer -- as if our young struggles for life had served to bring us to this moment in time.

One evening back in Kyoto towards the end of our week, Satoru and I were sitting in our hotel room, opposite each other on the floor at a low table, when he said he had something to ask me. I inquired as to what, and he said, "I would like to ask you to marry me; I would like to spend my life with you." I was a bit taken aback and told him, "I need to think about it a minute." Would you mind if I go for a walk?" He seemed peaceful enough with this, if a bit surprised. I must explain that Satoru was not the first Japanese man to whom I was attracted. My interest in Japan and all things Japanese had come from my mother. She had been fascinated with Japan since she had read "The Tale of Genji," written in the eleventh century by Lady Murasaki Shikibu. My first connection had been a serious relationship with a Japanese poet whom I met in New York when I was nineteen years old. His name was Shoichi Kiyokawa and he, too, had asked me to marry him but I had never wanted to get married, so we lived together for seven years. I had met him at a party given by a mutual friend where we were instantly drawn to one another and decided to live together. Our relationship was very interesting and creative but he had very high expectations of me, which I was not able to sustain. The pressure got to be too much and I finally had to admit that I could not continue with him. We remained great friends, however. That was why I needed to think about Satoru's proposal. I went downstairs and walked around the lobby a few times, and decided that, yes, I did want to marry him. I went up to our room and told him so. He took me in his arms and I felt so delirious with happiness. We then went down and had a wonderful dinner in the hotel restaurant. A stranger looking at us could have seen the magnetism that was bouncing off us. His looks made me weak at the knees; I could not get enough of them. The next day we returned to Tokyo where we stayed in a beautiful hotel, and the day after, Satoru took me to meet his parents.

I was worried about meeting them as I had heard a lot about them from Satoru. His mother, I felt, was going to be a difficult person to win over, as Satoru had more or less intimated that she had a Japanese girl in mind for her son. That first meeting, was, in a way, like what I imagined a job interview would be. After the introduction formalities were over, his father sat, gracefully smiling at me. His mother, however, went onto the attack immediately. She wanted to know about my work, my family, my plans and all manner of other things. I sat quietly trying to answer her questions as best I could. Neither of his parents spoke English, so Satoru had to translate for us. This was very stressful for all of us, and I really don't know if Satoru actually translated everything the way it was said. Suffice to say that it was a very tense and foreboding meeting. I liked his father immediately and I sensed he liked me as well. His mother, I think, was not very happy with me, more, I believe, because I was Western, than anything else. I must say that I was very relieved when it came time to leave. Poor Satoru! It could not have been easy for him, either.

That Satoru's mother was willing to let him marry me was only because he was the youngest, and she did not have the heart to refuse her beloved son. It was another thing that did not endear me very much with his brother and sister, who were of his mother's opinion. This was the mix into which I would enter. Not the most encouraging start to a new life! But I was in love and so was Satoru, and we had only thoughts for ourselves. We would conquer our world and everyone in it!!

EUROPEAN TOUR

Two days before I had to leave, we decided to go out to an Italian pizza restaurant. We ran into Charlie Moulton, and he reminded me that the next day was the first of May, the day we had to leave for New York. Shocked, we realized that one day had been snatched from us because I was mistaken about the date. In our blissful awakening, we had lost track of the days and our hearts sank down to the ground. The next day at the airport, busy with people going to all points of the globe, we were not ready to be separated, and we clung to each other. Reluctant to break the filament that had bound us together, we knew that too much time would pass until we were to be reunited.

I had the CBS taping to do and rehearsals for our upcoming European tour. We would be apart for more than a month, which seemed an absolute eternity. Since we had a week off before the tour started in Avignon, we had decided that Satoru and I would fly to Paris to meet. I would pick him up and we would spend two days together in one of the most romantic cities in the world. I arrived in Paris full of anticipation to meet Satoru at the airport and, as I was standing, craning my neck, looking for him, I saw him coming out with others all around him. He smiled that captivating crooked smile, and I wanted to laugh and cry at the same time, feeling so shy. The traffic was horrible, and it took us two hours to get to the hotel. Satoru did not feel well due to nerves and exhaustion. The weather was so hot; all records were broken that summer. After two blissful days in Paris, we drove down to Avignon in our rental car to spend a few days looking around, while waiting for the Company to arrive. I remember Satoru asking me, "Why are you driving so fast? Why don't you slow down to enjoy the countryside?" I answered, "I am concentrated on getting to Avignon to spend time together." In time, Satoru would teach me to slow down and smell the roses, and be less driven.

We checked into the hotel the Company had booked for everyone, and went to rent two motor scooters and off we went! The whole company would have scooters to get around from rehearsals to lecture demonstrations and classes, so we got ours early.

We would get up at sunrise and, after a delicious café au lait and croissant breakfast, would venture out to explore the territory. It was so much fun with the sun beating down on us. The heat and the beauty of our surroundings increased the marvel of our being together as we were free to roam and share our love. Passing pear groves, we would stop to ask if we could pick up some of the pears on the ground, and put them in our wicker basket. Then we would go to the open-air market and buy cheese, a baguette and a flask of local wine. All set, we would whiz off to find the perfect spot to have our fabulous meal. After which, sated and happy, we would have a nap under a tree. Rested and ready to be off, we would find a café/bar, where we would have a coffee or an aperitif and listen to music on the juke box. James Taylor had a song we loved that was called *"You've Got a Friend"* that became "our song". At dusk, we would get back on our scooters and return to the hotel. We would then get ready to go out for dinner at a local restaurant and sit across from each other, half-smiling all the time, as if we had some magic secret up out sleeves. We were in an enchanted place, where the air was thin and we were weightless, in a bubble floating.

The week passed in a flash. The Company arrived and our routine of rehearsing, taking class and teaching began. Satoru would come and watch when it was open to the public, and wander around exploring the city when it was not. In the evenings, we would all go to dinner together, after which some would go dancing, others to chat in their rooms. We would choose according to our mood. I remember one really striking moment when, after lunch and a nap, I left Satoru to go to the theatre to prepare for the performance that evening. I had told him he needed to wake up in time to come to the theatre to pick up his ticket in order to see the performance. The time arrived, and, when I saw that Satoru was not in the audience, I ran to call the hotel to see what had happened. Only to discover that he was still asleep, I was furious with him as I wanted him to see my *Signals* solo. He hurried over and got there just in time. The damage, however, had been done and after the performance, when we all went out to dinner, I told him he need not come, and left him at the hotel. Halfway through the dinner, he showed up dressed to the nines, with a huge bouquet of flowers that he had picked in the garden of the hotel. The whole table of twenty-four looked up at him and, to my enormous embarrassment, broke into applause. It was his *piece de resistance* that none of us forgot and smiled about when we brought it up occasionally. It was a convivial time, leading up to our two big performances at the *Palais Des Papes*, which was a magnificent outdoor amphitheatre, where we would give our last two performances in Avignon. My father, Frederick Hayman-Chaffey, the painter, who was travelling through Europe, stopped by to see us and met Satoru. We went out to dinner together and Satoru's meeting with him went much better than mine with his mother. They both got on well and we had a wonderful dinner. Frederick was against us marrying, but did not say anything then. He was involved with a young woman painter who, he had convinced my mother, should live with them. This was due to the fact that he loved my mother and wanted to stay with her but he also wanted to live with his girlfriend. So they had a *ménage a trois*, which I don't think was very much to his concubine's liking. I am sure she would have wanted to get married, but that was out of the question for my father.

The last performance in the *Palais des Papes* included my *Signals* solo, performed with a raging mistral wind that was so strong it buckled the marley floor we performed on. It was a miracle that I was able to dance at all, as the floor was like giant waves on an ocean. Satoru was there on time, much to my relief, as it was our last performance and we would be leaving the next day. He was to return to Tokyo, and we would continue to Greece, the next stop on our tour. Parting was so difficult, even though I knew I would be joining him in a month. The Company had wanted him to continue with us, so that we could get married on tour, and everyone could participate. He wanted us to get married in Tokyo, as his parents and family were there. I would have liked the tour option, but it was not to be, much to my disappointment and everyone else's. Athens was our next stop where we would perform under the Parthenon as part of the Athens festival. When we got to our hotel, a cable awaited me from Satoru. I opened it with trembling hands to read, "Love, Dozo" (Love, please) to which I responded with, "Love, Domo." (Love, thank-you)

The next evening we performed under the brilliant stars of Athens, on the stage set up just below the magnificent Parthenon. How incredible, that I was to be a part of all the history that had preceded us. I was so sorry that Satoru was not there to see the splendor.

We had two performances there, and then a few days off, which we would spend on the island of Hydra as guests of one of the Company's benefactors, who had a magnificent house on the island. Merce and John stayed in their palatial villa and the rest of the Company was put up on their boat anchored in the harbor. During the day we would all be taken sailing, getting off to visit small islands along the way. One evening, we attended a Greek tragedy performance in a lovely small amphitheatre. The last evening of the three days we had off, we were invited to dinner at one of the local restaurants and then on to a discothèque where we all went to dance, Merce included. I went up to him several times, inviting him to dance and, each time he refused. I was wearing what would later be my wedding dress. It was a costume that my father had designed for my first performance with my own group, the year before, on a hiatus from the Company. He had dyed some organdy fabric in soft pinks, purples and blues.

I was not to be put off and kept going up to Merce until he finally agreed to dance with me. It was one of the most unbelievable experiences I have ever had. He was extraordinary, and we danced for what must have been a half hour! At the end of each piece of music, he would hold me close while figuring out the beat and then we would launch into the movement. It came to an end when he let go of me with a kiss and went back to his seat. I was exhausted, but thrilled, as nothing like it had ever happened before. The next day, we returned to Athens for one last performance under the Parthenon.

The following day we left for Tel Aviv, Israel, where we had a series of performances after which we travelled to Dubrovnik, Yugoslavia for its summer Festival. That was the last stop on our European tour. It was there that I asked to speak with Merce, and with a heavy heart, had to explain to him that I would be leaving the Company. I was getting married and needed to be with my future husband. It was very sad and, in retrospect, I feel I left too soon, as performing had been my great love and I had not realized how much I would miss it. I had made my decision emotionally, without taking the time to really think it through.

RETURN TO TOKYO

I returned to New York with a heavy heart but happy to know that I would soon be joining my future husband in Tokyo. I made arrangements to sublet my apartment for six months and left my two dogs, Sireen, a small black poodle, and Taro, a little Sheltie, with my parents. Two days before I left, my father invited me to dinner at *La Grenouille* to convince me that marriage was not necessary. It is a beautiful restaurant and my father knew the *maitre d'*, who escorted us to a lovely table. Papa was a very charismatic figure, and always turned heads whenever he entered a room.

I adored him. We had a very lively dialogue throughout his life; he was the only person who was always one step ahead of me. He, being an artist, understood the sacrifices involved in pursuing a professional career. I remember that when I was ten years old, before I was to embark on my studies to be a ballerina—his sitting me down and saying that he would see that I had the best education, but I had to guarantee him that I would dedicate myself one hundred percent to my art. I, without a moment's hesitation, told him that I would. I kept my word and he did, too. I know it cost him a lot, as I had, what they call in Japan, a genius education. I went to ballet classes taught by extraordinary teachers in the mornings, and had private tutors for my school studies at home in the afternoons. It was a lonely existence, but it allowed me to pursue my career full time, and to finish my formal schooling two years ahead of time.

It was he, who, on a business trip to London in 1964, went to see The Merce Cunningham Dance Company at the Sadler's Wells Theatre, when they were on their first round the world tour. He returned to Rio de Janeiro, where we were living, and told me about seeing this extraordinary Company and wishing that one day I would be a dancer in it. I had not even started to learn modern dance yet, as I was a little ballerina dreaming of Swan Lake and Sleeping Beauty. He found out that there were Modern Dance classes being given at the Museum of Modern Art and we went to see what they were all about. We sat and watched three classes. The first was a Jose Limon class taught by Gilberto Motta; the second, a Brazilian Primitive dance class taught by Mercedes Battista, and the third, a Martha Graham class taught by Vera Kumpera. It was decided that I enroll in all the classes and start the next day. I never looked back, as it was love at first sight. I felt totally at home in those techniques and the ballet suddenly looked old-fashioned.

That was how we all moved to New York, so that I could go to study at Merce's Studio and try to get into the Company. Papa had me write Merce a letter telling him that I would like to go and study at his studio and to meet him when I got to New York. Merce answered that I should go to the studio when I arrived and he would meet with me. We moved to the United States in September of 1965. I would stay in New York and the rest of the family moved to Minneapolis, where my father had got a job as professor of Art at the University of Minnesota. As a consequence, we all got our Green Cards when we entered the United States. It actually took me until the end of 1967 to get the courage to go to Merce's Studio on Third Avenue and Thirty-Third. Not long after I got there, when the Company returned from tour, Merce called me over after a class he had taught and asked me if I would like to join the Company. To say that I was over the moon is to put it mildly; I was so excited I got dressed and ran out of there and grabbed a taxi to take me home. The traffic was terrible, and finally in the middle of the road, I paid the cabbie, jumped out, and ran all the way home, so that I could call my parents and tell them that I had made it into The Merce Cunningham Dance Company. I had fulfilled my fathers wish for me.

Joining the Company was like becoming a part of an extended family I loved the camaraderie, the company classes, rehearsals and the touring and performing. I was the youngest in the Company and everyone was very kind to me; especially Sandra Neels, who took me under her wing and became my best friend. I was in my element, as the theatre was magic, and I loved everything about it. I would return to the theatre at least an hour before everyone else, just to sit in the audience and drink in the atmosphere. To imagine, that in a few hours, all would be changed, with the lights, the music, the sets, costumes and us dancers. We would, for an hour and a half, maybe two, create a magic world for the audience.

So here I was all those years later, about to have a very special dinner with my extraordinary father. He ordered champagne as soon as we sat down, and got down to the business of convincing me to give up this foolish idea of marriage. He had not taken into account that I, like he, was very determined. I did not change my mind. Nevertheless, we had a fabulous dinner and ended up late in the evening, when all the other clients had left, with the *maitre d'* and several waiters all discussing the pros and cons of marriage in French. There was much laughter and I remember it as a wonderful evening, like only my fantastic father could produce. My mother stayed at home, as this was strictly a father-daughter affair. Mama was a compassionate and understanding person; I thank God to have had two such exceptional parents.

The next day, I was on the plane to Tokyo to embrace my future with my beloved Satoru. He was at the airport waiting for me, as handsome as ever, and I don't know why, but I always felt shy when first setting eyes on him. Instead of driving me straight back to his sister Kimiko's house, where we would be living while in Japan, he took me around Yokohama and then to a wonderful restaurant there. Satoru knew Tokyo like the back of his hand, and took me to hundreds of places, each special for something: a coffee shop where they played jazz, a Sake bar where they had every type of aged Sake. Each and every place had its specialty, and there seemed to be so many. He showed me a very select Tokyo, multi-layered and rich. I was so fortunate to have been able to see all that in 1976, because, as of the 1990s, so many of those very special places had disappeared.

At the end of the evening, we went back to Kimiko's and, even though it was late, she and her husband, Gyohei, and their four children, were waiting up for us. I had met her the first time I was in Tokyo, when I met Satoru and he had invited her to lunch with us. The children were very excited to meet their uncle's new bride-to-be, especially as I was Western. We shared a cup of green tea with them all, and then I was shown to the bedroom that Satoru and I would share for the duration of our stay in Japan. This arrangement was thought to be more practical for me, as Kimiko and her husband both spoke English. The next morning, bright and early, Satoru left to go and practice the Tea Ceremony with his father, then on to the site of the house that he was helping his brother, Mitsuru, build for an artist client of his. He had left without leaving me the address of where I was, so when I got up and found no one home, I wondered what I was going to do. I also had no telephone for him, as cell phones did not exist then.

I got dressed and decided to go out exploring anyway, hoping to find my way back by keeping track of when I turned left or right. I was fascinated with everything and walked a long way. A few hours later, I realized I had really wandered far and decided to get a taxi back. That was an amusing event as I did not have an address to give the taxi driver, just indications of right or left. I got the two words from my pocket dictionary, so it was migi (left) or hidari (right) and, incredibly, we got back to the house. Before leaving New York, I had bought a little English-Japanese book, thinking to say the phrases necessary to ask the questions I needed. Of course, when the natives shot back their answers, thinking I knew Japanese, I was totally lost. It took almost all of the six months we were there for me to even distinguish the beginnings and endings of each word. The four other languages I knew -- Italian, Spanish, French and Portuguese -- I had learned as a child in our travels around the world. I was not of the inclination to go to school and spend three or four hours slaving over grammar, and structural intricacies to try and learn Japanese. It takes knowing three thousand characters alone, just to read the newspaper. So I decided right away that I would have to pick it up by listening and asking. By the time we left, I was able to address people politely and go shopping on my own, but not much else. I never did learn the language, for which I am sorry, as communicating was always important to me.

Satoru returned at the end of the afternoon, and all his nephews ran to hug him, as they adored him. He was wonderful with children and you could tell he really loved them. That evening we had our first family dinner all together. Kimiko had cooked the dinner and it was family cooking, which I had not had until then. It was very delicious and fun to see the children enjoying themselves. I noticed that Kotaro, the eldest child and only son, was always allowed to choose first, and ate the most. In Japan, you notice how the male is so important, but it is the housewife who runs the home with an iron fist. Kimiko and Gyohei's house was a very modern Japanese home designed by Satoru's brother, Mitsuru, for them in Nishi Azabu, a very elegant part of Tokyo. I loved walking around there, as the houses were so beautiful and the shops exquisite. All the great dress designers had shops nearby: Rei Kawabuko, Isei Miyake and many others. Tokyo has the very best of everything from all over the world, as they have brilliant buyers who travel the globe to find the most beautiful things. I loved shopping in Japan, and my only disappointment was that I could never find their gorgeous shoes in my size, as my feet were so much bigger than theirs.

I, of course, did not spend all my time shopping; I had made friends with Mrs. Hayata, the lady who managed Merce's company while we were in Japan. She did not speak English but had a translator with her, and we both took an immediate liking to each other. So when I stayed the two weeks after everyone left, I had the opportunity to speak with her about my possibly returning to Tokyo. I asked her if she could help me set up master classes when I returned to Japan, to which she responded very positively. She asked me to let her know when I would be back so that she could start making arrangements for me. Upon my return I had Satoru call her and we met. She was an exquisite petite china doll, who dressed in western clothes with such impeccable taste, and I was always staring at her, she was so beautiful. She arranged many master classes for me and would pick me up and drive me to where the classes were held. I would teach Merce's technique without speaking a word of Japanese. This was possible, as Japanese students have a very keen sense of observation and would see all the details very quickly -- something western students don't do as well. I loved the classes and the students, and I earned a good living doing that. When Satoru had time, he would come with me and translate for me, but that did not happen often. I have such fond memories of Mrs. Hayata, who was so kind and generous with us. We went many times to eat out with her, to all sorts of wonderful restaurants. Tokyo is such a rich city for everything to do with food.

So we each had our work to do. In between, Satoru continued to show me the wonders of Tokyo and we enjoyed the company of his nephews and family. His father would have Tea Ceremony parties in different locations with very special invited guests. Satoru would assist him, as would his mother. Everyone would show up in their colorful kimonos and geta shoes. The shoes would be left at the entrance and always made for such a fascinating display of color and form. I looked forward to these occasions, as they were truly unique. I adored his father, Kisuke, who would always give me a present whenever he saw me. He was such a generous and charming gentleman. Satoru had inherited these traits from him and was a real tribute to his father. A very elegant and gentle soul, humble and gracious, Satoru was a unique human being, with whom it was my privilege to share my life. I was always introduced as Satoru's future wife and eyebrows would lift, as this was not the traditional choice of the son of a famous Tea Master.

To get the marriage underway, I had to go to the British Consulate to post the Banns and wait twenty days lest some British citizen claim he was already married to me. No one came forward, so Satoru and I were officially married by the newly appointed Consul in his office. After, he offered us a drink, which he got from a cupboard in his predecessor's office where the collection of liquor that remained was kept. Both the Consul and my brand new husband had quite a few drinks to celebrate. I, not being keen on whiskey, which was the preferred drink, just sipped mine. By the time we left, Satoru was quite tipsy and fell asleep in the taxi on the way home. Not very romantic, but what is a girl to do thousands of miles away from home?

It always amazed me how the Japanese in general could fall asleep almost anywhere. I would see them on the subway fast asleep, and wondered how they knew to wake up in time to get off at their stop. The subways were a challenge at rush hour, and I tried to avoid traveling then. Once, I was caught at that crucial time, and found myself having to change trains, when I was whooshed out of my train along with a teeming mass of people. From the other side, another group was coming at us, an American man amongst them, who, on seeing my panicked face, smiled, waving at me and said, "Fun isn't it?" I will never forget it! It was the last time I would ever get caught like that again. On the platform, attendants with white gloves help to push people on and off trains. This is unique to Tokyo and an extraordinary scene to behold.

THE WEDDING

At the beginning, living together had its challenges as we were from two completely different cultures and upbringings. However, since the moment we met and recognized each other, we were hardly two separate people. Love like that was so rare; we built a life together moment by moment. When we met, it was as if we had found each other again, after a long absence. This quality was always present, in the air we breathed; it became our friend, a constant in our lives. Sometimes we talked a lot, at others we hardly said a word. Yet we were always communicating, by looks, sensations, feelings. Satoru was not one for many words and once I asked him why. He said, "My father told me to think three times about what I wanted to say, and if it was worth saying after that, then I could say it." So each word he articulated had a weight which made it all the more important. It was like someone talking too low and you had to strain to hear what they were saying. Our exchanges were always lively, to do with the quality of life or differences of opinion. The first five years there were many, until we learned to adjust to our different cultures' imprints.

After our official marriage, it was time to plan our wedding, which we had decided we would have at the Meiji Jingu Mae temple in Harajuku, Tokyo -- a very large temple with huge, immaculately kept grounds. It is a favorite temple for Japanese and foreign visitors. Satoru had taken me to see it when I was there and we thought that it was such a beautiful place to get married. It was to be a Shinto wedding, following the rituals of that religion, because it was Satoru's family tradition. Shinto, from the Chinese, "Shintao," *The Way of the Gods*, is characterized by nature worship, ancestor worship, heroism and divine expression. Shinto has no founder, no written scriptures, and no religious laws. By the eighth century,

Shinto became the official religion of Japan, with the Imperial Family being ascribed divine origin. With the influx of Buddhism, Shinto teachings incorporated the Buddha as another of the divine beings of nature, a "Kami."

We were set to get married in the first days of January and we were very excited about the event. I had wanted to wear 12 kimonos and slowly shed one at a time, a ritual I felt was representative of shedding the past and coming to the union free of all constraints. This was vigorously opposed by everyone, so I got married in the costume my father had designed for my solo, in my own company's first performance in New York. This was the same beautiful organdy dress I wore in Greece, with a fabulous cape of the same material on top. Satoru would wear his black tuxedo, in which, I must say, he looked a bit uncomfortable.

As I had insisted that Satoru not accept his allowance anymore, and money was now in short supply, I catered our wedding reception myself. I had decided to serve poached trout cold with a cucumber sauce, steamed cold spinach, and rice balls for the main course, Japanese hors d'euvres and a special cheese cake with fresh berries for dessert. It all had to be cold, as I would not be able to do anything on the day itself. The day dawned clear and sunny, but was quite chilly and I had a fever of 102. I had been feeling a bit under the weather but hoped that I would be alright on the day. No such luck! So, feeling absolutely awful, I managed to get dressed and put a shawl over my dress under my cape, hoping to keep warm. Looking at the photographs after, I saw how miserable I was, feeling so sick. Nevertheless, the show must go on; I was not a performer for nothing. I used every skill I knew and smiled at everyone, hoping not to let them see how ill I was.

The guests arrived and the ceremony took place in the Shrine's beautiful surroundings. We were picked up in the receiving room by the monks and were led in a procession around the grounds near the chapel. The guests were now in tow, us leading, with the public who was there that morning witnessing the occasion. I wondered what they must have thought, coming upon this spectacle. We celebrated the traditional "San San Kudo," or, "Three times three," a lovely ceremony where the monk guided us to exchange three cups of

Sake, while another monk guided the family to do the same, thereby signifying the union of our two families. Following those exchanges, we offered twigs of the "Sasaki" sacred tree in worship to the gods. After which, we were married! None of my family was present, as my father had forbidden even my mother to fly over to attend. I was in this strange, yet familiar, land, sick and alone. I don't suppose one can start a life together any lower than that. I never told my mother about being sick or how much I had missed her, and never showed her any of the photographs -- a fact she never understood, but it was my way of protecting her from the truth.

The wedding ceremony over, we all returned to Kimiko and Gyohei's house for the reception. We changed our clothes and went to the big living room to receive our guests. I had set out a buffet table with the food and everyone went up to serve themselves. It had been hard work and I hoped that everyone enjoyed the food, which I think they did. Satoru, ever the charming host, was busy taking care of everyone, and was very entertaining. However, he neglected me in the process and Gyohei, realizing this, very generously got up and sang a lovely song for me. It was something I will never forget, as I felt so alone and abandoned. Feeling ill on top of everything, at around ten o'clock, I decided I had had enough, and went upstairs to our bedroom to change. I had decided that since Satoru seemed unaware of my presence, I would go and register at a hotel in protest. I quietly left the house, found a taxi and checked into the Tokyo Prince Hotel, without leaving a note as to my whereabouts.

At around two in the morning, after realizing my absence and checking hotels where he thought I might be, Satoru found where I was and came there to pick me up. The receptionist called my room to tell me he was out front and would I please go there, as they would not let him come to my room. I put on a robe and went out to meet him. He was furious, ordering me to get dressed immediately, and that I was to return home with him. I stupidly obeyed and we returned, only to have him get into bed and fall asleep! To say that all of this was not what I would have dreamed my wedding day to be is putting it mildly. And where did my soul mate idea fit in? In defense of the rapport, I have to say that the wedding day proved to be the one exception in an otherwise perfect union. I have often wondered about that day, and why destiny had created that experience, and I have never found an explanation that I could accept. I wish it had not happened like that, but it is not for us to ask, just to accept. Why could I not be more Zen? I realize my limitations and struggle to learn, when probably I should not struggle.

This brings me to a blinding moment several years later in the Tuscan hills. When returning home from the market, we were passing a village house at the top of the dirt road that led to our house down the steep hill. An old lady was in her garage holding up a rabbit, about to weigh it in preparation for killing it, and subsequently cooking it for the noon family meal. On seeing this scene, it hit like lightning, that we humans were in no different a position than the rabbit. We live our lives not knowing what will be the end result. It made me cry and laugh, the realization that we are all at the mercy of our own destinies. It was what I later thought of as a Shakespearian moment, remembering The Bard's poem called *"The Seven Stages of Man."* Sometimes I am hit by how tragic, and yet how magical, is this life that we live. Many are the times I have not been able to give myself a reason for what happens in the living of our lives. In a way, I have often thought that it is like Dante's *Inferno*, for who is to say that the life we live is not the inferno? Or that it is Death that brings the freedom from suffering?

The wedding over, I spent the next days ill in bed, trying to get better. Satoru continued his routine, except that now he also had a job delivering fish from the Skiji fish market to big department stores. We needed more money, to put some aside for our later return to New York. He drove a big truck to pick up and deliver the fish and sometimes he would drive by the house and take his nephews for a ride in it, something that really amused them. Skiji is the largest fish market in the world, with miles and miles of fish of all kinds and rows upon rows of just tuna, all going to restaurants and department stores. There were also small eating places where one could have the best fish meals around. My time in Tokyo was very rich and varied, and I learned a lot there. It was not always easy, but sometimes what is hard to come by, is worth it in the end.

Satoru used to say to me, he tried to start every day like it was a blank sheet of paper. He was very ZEN. Each day was an opportunity to write your life anew. Then, at the end of the day, you could be happy that you had done the best you could. As Daisetz T. Suzuki wrote in his preface to *Zen in the Art of Archery* by Eugen Herigel, "Man is a thinking reed but his great works are done when he is not calculating and thinking. 'Childlikeness' has to be restored with long years of training in the art of self-forgetfulness. When this is attained, man thinks yet he does not think. He thinks like the showers coming down from the sky; he thinks like the waves rolling on the ocean; he thinks like the stars illuminating the nightly heavens; he thinks like the green foliage shooting forth in the relaxing spring breeze. Indeed, he is the showers, the ocean, the stars, the foliage. When a man reaches this stage of 'spiritual' development, he is a Zen artist of life."

Satoru was on this quest and I, with him, tried as best I could to understand. He would say to me, "If you could do in your daily life what you do when you dance on stage, you would be totally free." I knew well what he meant, because I had studied technique for years to become a dancer. When I had achieved the technical skills to be able to control my body, then I understood that my freedom came from forgetting myself. I could then be an instrument for something much greater than the sum total of who I was. There I was free, able to just be movement, pure and clear, in other words, to step out of my own way. I tried to do as he suggested in my daily life and, at times, I was able to do just that. I suppose I have consciously tried to learn the technique of living, so that I could forget it, to be free. That was what we, as a breathing unit, tried to learn day by day. Satoru, born into that idea through his father, the Tea Master and Ikebana Master, had lived alongside the example on a daily basis. I had, too, following my father's and mother's examples from a Western interpretation. My father, as an artist, followed what all great artists have always strived for, the freedom to express, and in so doing, be free. My mother, on the other hand, was not an artist, but she understood more than anyone I ever met, how to be "childlike". I have always consciously tried to follow her example. It is the hardest thing for me, and I know that it is not often that I manage it.

My father also told me that nothing was impossible and so I have never been afraid to try anything. Here I have to mention that drugs have been the one thing I have never tried, because he and my mother gave me the security to know that I was loved and needed nothing as a crutch. I have been drunk on life itself, sometimes to absolute distraction, where I would cry from the absolute joy of living, of being ALIVE. So knowing that I could do that is all I have ever needed.

BACK TO NEW YORK

The building of the artist's house in Tokyo, where Satoru had been working with his brother, was coming to an end in the spring and we decided we would return to New York. We planned to make the city our residence, as I did not speak Japanese and, for both of us, it was the best place to pursue our careers. I still had my apartment, which I had sublet, and it would become mine again in April. Shoichi, having kept in touch with me, suggested he ask my father and Charles, my brother, who had formed a Plexiglas company together, to sponsor Satoru for an Alien Registration card, as my husband. We got all the forms from the American Embassy and proceeded to comply with all the pre-requisites. By the beginning of April, we would have everything, and so we bought our tickets for New York.

I was happy to be returning, as my two dogs, Sireen and Taro, whom my mother called her grandchildren, were anxiously awaiting us. I had missed them, as they were my faithful companions, always ready with wagging tails and wet kisses of love. I had never left them for so long and I really felt terrible. Departure day dawned and we took our farewells of our Japanese family, not knowing when we would be returning. I think Satoru's mother and father were sad to see him leave, and I am sure he would miss them. Mitsuru drove us to the airport and, as I looked out the back window to wave to his mother and father, I felt for them, having to see their beloved son riding away for who knew how long. We took our farewell of Mitsuru, checked-in and went to our departure gate. It was a long flight, and Satoru, as always, fell asleep almost as soon as we took off. He had this natural ability that I just never seemed able to pull off. It was a lot if I managed to sleep a few hours at most. On arrival at JFK, we went to the Aliens line, as I was already an Alien and Satoru, with the paperwork he was carrying, would be given his green card on entering. It was so impressive to walk through into an immigration office and walk out with a green card! Satoru was very happy; he had previously been entering with a B1 B2 visa, which was a business, multiple entry visa. My parents were waiting for us and drove us to their apartment, where we would spend the night before going down to my 10th Street apartment. Sireen and Taro were so excited to see me and curious about this new person who was Satoru. They would grow to love him as he them; many times I had to leave for work and he would be in charge of them.

This was the first time my mother was meeting Satoru and I am sure she was very curious about him. My mother Patricia, instantly took a liking to him as did Satoru to her. My father's reaction I liken to that of a bulldog to a new arrival on the block. Even though he had met him briefly in Avignon, you could almost see his chest puff up, planting his legs firmly on the ground. I was his princess, after all, and he had to see that this interloper was worthy. Satoru, in his Big Stone way held his ground, very polite and gracious with his beautiful smile. My father was momentarily surprised that Satoru had not cowered and slowly backed down. The male ritual over, the relationship between them was always as friends, and Satoru became a welcome addition to our family. My mother, who worked at New York University Hospital managing a Cancer Research Institute called Lemsip, had a wonderful rapport with Satoru. When I was away teaching, they would arrange to meet for a coffee or Satoru would take her flowers. I always appreciated this lovely ritual of theirs.

We had a delicious dinner of prosciutto crudo and melon, poached salmon and salad, followed by a great Pavlova meringue confection with fresh fruits in the middle and topped with whipped cream. I was introduced to it in Australia when we were on tour there, as it was the official cake for dessert. It was invented by an Australian chef for the Russian ballerina, Pavlova, on the occasion of her tour in Australia. I had told my parents about it, and they, avid chefs that they were, soon added it to their repertoire of specialties. We then retired for the night, and the next day, they drove us down to my apartment with our dogs. I had a very nice studio duplex-type apartment, with stairs that led up to the sleeping loft above half of the living room. I really liked it. It was modern and clean looking and very functional. My living spaces have always been very important to me. They had to be in safe areas, clean and modern. This one was on Tenth Street between University Place and Broadway, in Greenwich Village. It had the advantage for me, of being a pleasant twenty minute walk from Westbeth, where the Cunningham Studios were; Westbeth was once an operations building for AT&T that had been converted into artists' residences and studios. The Cunningham Company had the whole top floor with two studios, his and her dressing rooms for the Company, a student women's dressing room and three coordinating offices for the school administration. The Company offices were on the ground floor. My apartment was also right next to New York University and its young crowd, with lots of shops, restaurants and Washington Square Park, which was very pleasant. We took a few days to settle down and decide what our course of action would be. It was spring, my favorite time of year in New York, and the tender new light green leaves were sprouting on the trees and the air was fresh and slightly warm, with sunlight coming through the trees making patterns of shade and sun on the pavements.

Satoru called his friends at Simca Prints and we all met in the village at one of our hangouts for dinner. It was so nice for Satoru to have his friends in New York and to be able to see them socially quite often. I, of course, also had my friends and the Company members, with whom I had kept in touch. After a few days, I went over to Merce's Studio to say hello to him and the dancers. I took class and afterwards he asked me back to teach the advanced, intermediate classes and Company class when he could not. I was happy for this offer, as now I was a self-employed dancer, needing to find work to keep alive. This ensured me a modest living which I occasionally augmented with guest teaching abroad or at American Universities.

My first teaching job abroad was in Tel Aviv at the Bathsheba Dance Company, where Rina Shenfeld had arranged with the manager for me to be invited. Rina was the Company's Prima Ballerina, and we had become friends when I was performing in Tel Aviv with Merce's Company on my last tour. She had admired my dancing and asked me if I would be interested in teaching the Bathsheba dancers.

So I went over there for a month to teach the Company and also to give special master classes for the dance students at the Jerusalem Academy of music. I was given a lovely room in a friend's apartment and walked to the Company studios everyday. Three days a week, I would take a Sharut (a van with several seats that one could take with others) to Jerusalem. I would go right after company class and arrive in Jerusalem just in time to have lunch, then I would walk up to the Academy at the top of a hill over looking the city. I would teach my class and then go back in another Sharut to Tel Aviv, unless I stayed around to explore the city a little. Jerusalem was such a surprise. I had imagined it to be quite different, and was disappointed to see Coca-Cola signs and other publicity at the Stations of the Cross, where Jesus had passed on his way to his crucifixion. I had thought it would look more sacred, but such are the times we live in. I was also struck by how everyone points out that at least one family member had been killed in the wars. Also that only in Israel the fruit trees bear fruit twice a year.

I missed Satoru desperately; we wrote every day and talked on the phone once a week. He would keep me posted on his doings and how the dogs were faring, and I would tell him about my teaching. These separations, hard as they were, made us appreciate each other all the more. I have a lovely letter from Satoru written after he dropped me off at the airport, where he writes in his childlike way about how he got lost and Taro, our Sheltie, was looking at him, questioning, as if he knew they were not going in the right direction. I quote an excerpt here.

Dearest my baby Susana,

On the way back home I lost direction. I went to little hiking with Taro. Though traffic was very hard. I guess I turned too quick before Phillip Johnson designed Expo building. After forty minutes that I left airport I realized something wrong. Of course Taro instinctively felt something smell wrong, check up, he was telling me. But I said to him that don't worry Taro. This is a little picnic for us. Honestly I started worry, because direction was very new to me. Finally I got off at Flatbush Avenue. And long after I would see Brooklyn Academy next to me. I really appreciated that could see Brooklyn Academy. By the time, arrived at home, it was nearly twelve o'clock. But I must say, that was too much fun. But Susana I must say, when I arrived at home there was too empty to me without you----really.

I really miss you. Taro is absolutely lost alive without you. And also today I did picnic lunch which was fun. Susana we really miss you. Have a great class in your life. Love Satoru Taro. Kiss you.

These many years later, when I read the letter, it makes me smile as it is like a young child's writing. At the beginning, Satoru was not really looking for work, as I was earning enough for both of us and it was not really an issue. I returned and life went on as usual, until I decided it would be nice to take Satoru to see Mexico that summer, as I had lived there for a few years when I was a child. We went for a month, landing in Mexico City where we stayed for a few days to visit the sights. We went to the Anthropology Museum, one of the best in the world, and to visit an architect friend of my family's, Colin Faber of the British Faber family. He was the black sheep and was studying with Felix Candelas to be an architect. Since his family had disowned him he had very little money, and my parents gave him room and board at our house. He was also my father's chess partner.

I had lived in Mexico City with my parents when I was four and had gone to the French Lycee. My mother worked at the British Embassy as personal secretary to the Ambassador and my father painted during the day and was night watchmen there at night. He also had three exhibitions of his paintings during our time in Mexico. My parents were friends with the painters, Diego Rivera, David Alfaro Siqueiros and RufinoTamayo. They also counted among their friends the architects, Felix Candelas and Luis Barragan. Their working at the British Embassy gave them a very social life. I have photographs of them at receptions and at my father's gallery openings, all dressed up looking incredibly elegant. He was given one-man shows three times during our stay in Mexico. I remember that I always had my birthday parties in the Embassy gardens, with lots of children. My mother would arrange for Piñatas filled with sweets to be brought and hung between two trees. Each child would take a turn to hit the piñata with a long wooden stick, trying to break it open, so that all the sweets would spill out and we could all make a dive for them. The piñatas were made of Papier Mache, covered with colored tissue paper curled up covering the whole shape. My favorite was a shocking pink elephant. On the 2nd of June, 1953, there was a magnificent party held in the gardens for the Queen's Coronation, when we all got very dressed up; it was great fun.

I wanted to show Satoru Mexico "the people way", which meant taking third class buses and trains, eating at street stands and generally behaving as the locals. I felt it would be a more genuine experience. During our whole trip, Satoru was not sick once, as he immunized his system quickly by not doing as most visitors do, drinking bottled water and not eating the local food from stands. I had advised him to eat and drink normally, so that his body would adjust quickly to the food and water. He was brave and followed my advice. He always trusted me implicitly, as I did him. We asked the taxi driver on the way in from the airport to take us to a lovely hotel. It turned out to be near the Reforma and the Plaza Cinco de Mayo, which was central to everything. We would go across the street to Sanborns for exotic Mexican breakfasts, and start our exploring day. Mexico City is a rich historic capitol with many wonderful museums and buildings to see. It is also home to the Jai Alai, a Basque game that is played at the Fronton, a court where two players play against each other with a scooped out, round-shaped paddle that they hold and receive and throw the ball out of. One can bet on the game, too. It is very popular and beautiful to watch.

Colin showed us all the great architecture and some authentic restaurants. From Mexico City we went to Taxco, the little town up in the mountains famous for its silver, Mexico being the largest producer of silver in the world. Then we got a second class bus to Oaxaca, a colonial town where they make the black pottery, another to Acapulco, the famous American movie star resort, for the sea and beach, and then went to Palenque, the archeological ruins in the middle of the jungle. Palenque was extraordinary. We arrived in the evening and the station was full of families socializing and playing as it was the town's only real gathering spot. It was very colorful, with music blaring, food and souvenirs being sold, all lit with bare light bulbs, lending it a Spartan air. Much merriment was in full swing. We found a decent hotel and the next day went to visit the

Archeological splendor of Palenque. On arriving, you are greeted with signs advertising Campbell's soup with billboards just like Andy Warhol's iconic painting, in the middle of nowhere. It is truly a wonder that such incredible monuments could be built in the jungle like that. There is a team of workers whose only duty is to keep the jungle vegetation from inundating the monuments. In the heat and humidity, that is a constant job. Our last stop was Cancun which, in 1977, was just starting to be discovered. There were three big hotels and we chose a small boutique type right on the beach away from the others. We spent three days there discovering the Mayan King's summer retreat. The turquoise waters were warm and inviting, the sun hot and the air humid. We would retire to the coolness of our room after lunch, feeling the pleasure of walking on the cool ceramic floor tiles. Mexico -- the color of its folkloric past, its people, the vegetation, so rich and varied, everything brimming with life -- it is like nowhere else. It has always been in my heart, ever since my youth, where places leave a deep impression on one's spirit.

These interludes, out of the daily grind of working, served to keep our relationship fresh, as they afforded us quality time alone exploring other cultures. Living amongst other peoples of different backgrounds informed our souls and opened our minds to new possibilities. We were looking to expand our experiences, to integrate them, with future creative work. The artist is always looking, figuring out, and transforming information to serve the creative process. We talked about our experiences, digesting together what we were seeing. It was an open conversation that not only served our art but also our spirit together. I think I learned this from my parents who had started traveling when I was nine months old. It had left an imprint on my nature. In fact, I start to get restless if I tarry too long in one place.

A SIMPLE LIFE

A simple life was what Satoru wanted. I liked the idea, but slowly realized what it meant. To him it was extravagant concepts, independence from petty details, money worries to be put aside. I was puzzled; it was not my image of simple. Gradually wondering about it, I came around. Our visions were so different; I followed his example with an ever-present smile, thinking how the East was so inscrutable. Some years later, I wrote a little piece about our life, which I included in a prose poetry booklet, " Reflections on an East-West Relationship."

Times have been happy
Times have been sad
Times have been wild
Times have been frustrating
Times have been
A dream
A vision
A history
A responsibility
A state of mind
A way of living
An instant in our space
Our world
Do you have the time?

We were interested in the concept of devotion: where did art leave off and devotion begin? We tried to live life as art and art as life, wherein there should be no separation. It required a constant attention, a connection to the unconscious. Satoru would practice this by doing the Tea Ceremony every day and I would meditate for 45 minutes early every morning. Discipline was our taskmaster, yet it was worth the effort, as the rewards were so many. After these simple practices we would go for a long walk. We would walk all the way over to the East side, to a café in Little Italy where they made tasty muffins and good coffee. We would sit on the little wooden bench outside and talk, or not, depending on the mood that morning. This routine was rarely interrupted, as it was a way of sharing time and space in the fresh air while exercising our limbs. Our times together weren't only serious; Satoru had a wonderful sense of humor and made me laugh a lot, too. I remember when I did something he did not like, his saying, "I'm not amused." It made me laugh the way he said it. I was always more serious, but learnt slowly to acquire a quick wit, which I like very much about myself now.

When we returned from Mexico, I was invited to teach a semester at the University of South Florida which I gratefully accepted, as money was needed to keep us afloat. We were put up in an apartment belonging to the University, and bought a little Volkswagen Beetle to run around in for the three months we would be there. We took Taro, our Sheltie, as Sireen, our poodle, had passed away; Taro was delighted to be coming with us, instead of being left with grandma. I taught class every day, and Satoru gave Tea Ceremony classes to a group of ladies who had answered his ad in the paper. Teaching was always a pleasure for me; it was a chance to pass on all that had been given me by many exceptional teachers. The first thing I told everyone, when I was face to face with new students, was," You are each unique, special in your own ways, so I am asking you not to imitate what I show you, but to see the movements for themselves, and interpret them through your own bodies." It was so rewarding to see their faces when I said that. I had given them permission to be themselves. I learned early on in my teaching life that the words I would use in class did not always reach everyone, so I would find different ways to communicate, and eventually, my concepts could resonate with all the students.

I had been commissioned to choreograph a piece for the University, for the end of semester performances. I decided to do a collaboration with Satoru's Tea Ceremony as part of the piece. It was to be the first time we would work together. I used four women to represent a feminist point of view, to explore their relationship to each other and in society. It was to have a dream-like quality, with the movements very slow, as if the women were in a dream. Satoru was to be on the side of the stage, performing the ritual of the Tea Ceremony. The rehearsals were a wonderful exploration of discovery with the girls and Satoru's work. I had them all read *"Zen in the Art of Archery"* to help give them the mood I was looking for. I needed them to go to a place out of time, out of self, just to be moved by the steps. The work was well-received, which was gratifying to both of us. The semester over, we sold the little blue Beetle for $ 50.00 more than we had paid for it, and returned to New York.

These interludes out of New York were interesting, as they offered challenges to our modus operandi. I found it fascinating to interact with new students, as very often they were from the place I was teaching in and showed me a different way of thinking. The South is unlike the North, due to the weather and a more relaxed lifestyle. Many also came from other States, which gave me the opportunity to get a wider range of experience. Each came with a slightly different slant on things; it was enlightening and always very rewarding. I was a challenge to them, being English; they picked up on my accent right away and liked that. My demands for precision and punctuality, they were not so crazy about. I was a taskmaster, in that I was very inventive about putting steps together into combinations that used challenging rhythms. I remember a first year student coming up to me after class saying, "When you do the steps one by one I can do them, but when you put them all together I get lost." I laughed and told him not to despair, as in time he would learn how to string them together. He was an Anthropology student who was taking a Modern Dance class to be more limber. It turned out that he also studied Karate and, I think he told me, he was a Black Belt. By the end of the semester he had got the hang of the steps following each other and was vastly gratified. I loved these exchanges because they were fresh and amusing.

Satoru, with his group of ladies, had some wonderful experiences and made friends with their families. We were often invited to their houses for a meal. I found they liked Satoru's gentleness and his Japanese culture. They were always full of questions for him about Japan, his upbringing and Japanese philosophy in general. We would invite them to dinner where Satoru and I would make a home-cooked Japanese meal, which they always enjoyed. He also learned a lot about Americans this way; he liked their openness and jovial ways. Our students would always write us beautiful notes of appreciation for the teachings we had imparted, and for the humanity we shared. We really appreciated the notes and sentiments they expressed, and we treasured them always. To this day, I still have them. Many times these students would be inspired to come to New York to continue their studies after graduating; often some became friends with whom we kept in contact for years.

EUROPE

Before we left for Florida, we had given up our apartment on 10th Street as we were going to be away for three months and wanted to find something else. On our return to New York, we planned to stay with my parents. They picked us up at the airport, and back at their apartment, a beautiful dinner was waiting. My father's mistress, Toby, was still in residence, which always caused me to be a bit tense. I wanted to be accepting but I felt for my mother in that difficult situation. As usual, we were talking about our experiences in Florida and what was going on with them. I felt that Toby seemed to be having a condescending attitude by her responses to our conversations. I ignored it for most of the dinner, but as dinners at my house were always long affairs, towards the end, I could stand it no longer and made a comment. It had something to do with the Japanese way of accepting and being serene and how Toby could learn a lot from their ways of looking at life. Well! All hell broke loose! My father was outraged, and launched into a full-out attack, to which I, of course, responded in equal fury. The end result was that we were asked to leave, which, at the late hour of ten at night we did, after calling Merce's administrator to ask if we could stay at the studio overnight. We got a taxi with Taro and our cases and headed down to the studio in Westbeth. It had a magnificent view of the surrounding area and beyond.

I remember when Merce was choreographing a piece called *Torse*, with the most impossibly fast and incredibly complicated movements that he tried out in Company class; we were all reduced to tears. In desperation, we called John Cage, Merce's partner and Music Director of the Company, to please help us reason with Merce. To which he answered, "Don't worry. Just look out at the great view and it won't seem so hard". We did eventually struggle through, and conquered the steps, but it was uphill all the way. I had a really grueling trio with two of the men, which was so fast and had me weaving in and out of them, that, at times, I thought I would go crazy. I remember the first time we presented it to an audience at a Westbeth Event (these were informal performances at the studio before the public, where we performed whole pieces or parts of them and which usually lasted an hour and a half). At this one, we performed the whole of *Torse*, which lasted an hour, and I remember Barbara Schwartz, a Board Member, coming up to me after the performance saying, " My dear, you looked fabulous, like you were at a garden tea party." I almost burst out laughing as I had never been more terrified in my life! Not even *Signals* had such an effect on me!

At any rate, here we were, sleeping on the floor as best we could in the women's dressing room with Taro. The next morning, we were up bright and early and, as luck would have it, a Company member and a good friend, sublet us his small loft on 6th Avenue for three weeks, as the Company was leaving on tour the next day. So we thankfully moved over there and at the end of the sublet decided to go to Europe, for maybe a year, where I could find work teaching and we could get away from my father. We were very close and for him to take such an action was unforgivable to me. I had decided to completely cut off my relationship with him, so it was best we leave. Europe had always been appealing to me as I had a lot of contacts and friends there. We headed to Paris first, as I had, via telephone, spoken with Jacques Garnier and Brigitte Lefevre, the founders of the *Theatre Du Silence*, about them inviting me to teach their company. She was its Prima Ballerina and he the Director. They had both been stars of the Paris Opera Ballet Company and had left to form their own modern dance company taking Merce's example, as they were avid followers of his. They were delighted and invited me to go down to their company residence in the Maison De La Culture in La Rochelle, a picturesque seaside town on the east coast of France, about four hours from Paris.

We flew into Paris and rented a car at the airport and drove down to arrive the day before classes started. We had very little money, as most of what we had was spent on the airfares and settling bills and such in New York. We left Paris and drove straight down to La Rochelle, not sure if we even had enough money for the gas and tolls. We had no credit cards, so all had to be done with cash. This job was to save us for six weeks and give us a little cushion until I could get something else organized. For many years we were always going from hand to mouth, but that was the way things were and we accepted this state of affairs. It made me anxious, but I have always been an optimist, never letting anything stop me from doing what I needed to do. I have had the courage or, at times, I think, the stupidity, to have no fear. I have thrown myself into the wild blue yonder, managing to somehow land on my feet, my reasoning being that the worst that could happen was that I would land on my behind.

It was a lovely day and we set off down the highway and as we were nearing La Rochelle, we realized we had precious little gas left and hardly any money to pay for it, or the toll, before getting off. So we decided to drive more slowly, to consume less gas and started looking along the highway to see if there was any way we could slip off it to avoid paying the toll. The highways are well-designed and, of course, there was no way to get off. When we got to the toll station, I explained our situation and that I was going to be working with *The Theatre Du Silence*. The attendant had me fill out a form that made it possible for me to pay the toll in town when I got some money. Phew! That was scary, but we managed to slowly crawl into La Rochelle in the late afternoon and went straight to the company headquarters to see Jacques. I had to ask him if he could please give me an advance on my salary as we had no money left. He was very sweet and advanced me half of my salary and we were saved. He and Brigitte took us to the hotel they had arranged for us, and invited us out to dinner.

I had such a wonderful rapport with them. They had been fans of mine (and I of theirs) for quite a few years, and always invited me to teach their company whenever I had time from Merce's work. Brigitte became the Minister of Culture for several years and then was made Director of the Paris Opera, where she is still working.

My residence began, and our lives took on a pleasant pace. I taught the company every morning for an hour and a half and then I would have the rest of the day off. I occasionally went to watch rehearsals, to give advice or suggestions and to see what the dancers needed to work on in class to strengthen their techniques. It was early summer and the weather was glorious, so we took advantage and explored the area which was lovely, with its beautiful sea and the fresh, delicious fish. The hotel was very comfortable and the breakfast *café au lait* with croissant, baguette, butter and jam were a sinful delight every morning. It is almost my favorite thing about staying in hotels in France. I loved having Satoru with me, as so many times I had to travel far away without him. I hated those times, being away from him; they were always so lonely and empty for me. It was heavenly having him near and sharing our thoughts and feelings together. He always took his Tea Ceremony things with him so that he could practice every morning, while I was teaching. He was such a fine person, and his presence had a very steadying influence on me, so that I was able to be more serene and calm. As if being without him made me feel insecure.

One event remains engraved on my mind from that time with the company. Teaching in France was always a challenge as the French have a different idea of punctuality. This time I saw that the dancers were not all arriving on time, so, at first, I was waiting for everyone to arrive before starting class. This I allowed for a few days and then decided to give them a bit of their own medicine. I decided to walk in late with my dog, Taro. I made my entrance and noticed that they were all smiling and, puzzled, I wondered why and asked them what was so funny? They described how Taro was imitating me by marching angrily in behind me. It was so funny that they could not resist smiling. So much for my scenes! It did, however, have the effect of making sure that everyone was in class promptly from then on. When I told Satoru, he also found it very funny; it was the sort of scene he would never do, but it was the part of my character he cherished. I have to say that for the longest time, my temperament was stronger than my ability to control it. I am glad to say, he and my father both appreciated that about me. They were the two most important men in my life, who, coincidentally, shared the same birthdates, the 28th of January. They were Aquarians, as were my mother and I. The bond with my parents was always very strong; there was never a day that went by that they did not know where we were. I cannot adequately express how important they all were for me. Which was why, when my father threw us out, I had reacted the way I did. They were my reason for being, for everything I tried to achieve, for all I asked of myself.

Satoru and I were looking for the quality of our living experience, not for success or fame, necessarily. Those were was not the goals, although I had achieved them through my work as a dancer with Merce's company. I knew that success could leave you isolated and in a lonely place, which was why I left Merce when I did. My father had been in the same position many years previously, when Erica Brausen, the owner of the Hanover Gallery in London, who had made Henry Moore famous, had offered my father a one-man show at her Gallery. He sabotaged himself by deciding to undertake a journey from Mexico City all through Central and South America and South Africa in a Land Rover to prepare his exhibition. It was a three-year journey, embarked upon with my mother, myself, aged six, and my brother, Charles, aged three. We were the first family to do it -- and did so from 1955 to 1958, when there was precious little passable Pan American Highway available. In embarking on this huge project, he had not taken into account how long it would take, and missed the all-important date of his one-man show. Erica had invested much time and money promoting him and he would not be there in time. She never forgave him! And no one, myself included, ever understood then why he would do something like that. He did, however, write a book on that journey called *The Road Grew No Moss* published by Hodder & Stoughton in 1959. It was dedicated to me and my brother.

I have realized, these many years later, that he saw fame as a trap and had wanted his freedom above all else. I, having grown up with him, and seeing this, by osmosis picked up on it, and have tried to live my life as boldly as possible, not giving into fear or looking for fame. It seemed to me, and to Satoru, that the pursuit of fame, by necessity, kept you following the tried and true in your chosen field. It entrapped you, as it were, and that was fine for many people, but it was not for any of us. This was something we discussed a lot. Freedom to follow the unbeaten path was our goal, to live by the moment, to invent life day by day. There were no limits; only those imposed by ourselves. Since we never thought to be frightened by this way of doing things, we knew no better. Many has been the time when I have thought to myself, Thank God I never stopped to think about what I was about to do, because if I had, I probably would not have done it. I remember asking Merce, on the occasion of producing my first performance of my own work, if he had one piece of advice, what would it be? And he, without hesitation, said, "*Close your eyes and plunge*". I have been forever grateful to him for that; I think it is what I have consciously tried to do all my life. It is akin to diving into a lake of ice-cold water: you feel the cold for a moment but then you feel the absolute joy of the water all around you.

ITALIAN SOJOURN

Our time in La Rochelle over, we headed back to Paris where we sublet a lovely apartment on the Isle Saint Louis, a small island just behind Notre Dame. It had apartment buildings, boutiques, restaurants, cafés, two hotels and *Bertillon,* the absolute best ice cream maker in the world! Our apartment was right in front, across the street; we would look out our windows to see when the line was not so long and dash down to buy ice cream cones. Once we were settled, I set about finding my next job. I called the Modern Dance Academy, which gave me an appointment to go over and talk to them. I arrived right on time, and was ushered into the director's office. She was interested in my teaching her students, but did not offer the right salary. I told her I would think about it and call her back. The Cunningham Company administrator, Alice Helpern, had always stressed the fact that I came from a very famous company and should never sell myself short. With this in mind, I asked Satoru what he thought, and he, despite the fact that any money would have been welcome, insisted I turn it down. So that was what I did, even if I was a bit concerned about where our livelihood was going to come from. As luck would have it, Micheline, a faithful friend and Parisian student of mine, helped me arrange a studio and students to come and take classes with me. It was a temporary help, but at least kept us fed. After two weeks, when the series of classes came to an end, we decided we had better head over to Rome. Satoru spoke with his mother to ask her for a loan to tide us over for a month or two. She wired it over to Paris and we gratefully went to the bank to pick it up.

We left our apartment in Paris before our six weeks were over, and, to save money, sublet it to a friend for the balance of the time. We bought a little white Citroën 2CV with mold on the window frames, which Taro could stick his doggie nose out of. The windows were divided in half and opened sideways, not up and down. It was perfect for him, as the opening was not large enough for him to squeeze out of. It belonged to a student and was quite old, but we adored it and it was our faithful mode of transportation during our whole year in Europe. It had the most comfortable seats and made long journeys a breeze. It became a sort of family member. We crossed over the Alps into Switzerland and had a marvelous picnic above Lake Leman on our way to the Italian border. We arrived in Rome the next day, and, as arranged beforehand, stayed at my Roman dentist's office for two days until we found a sublet to move into. Giancarlo Arnao was a great friend, always willing to accommodate us when necessary. We slept there at night on a cot he had and left in the morning before the day's patients arrived.

Two days later, we rented a wonderful small penthouse belonging to an English lady who worked at F.A.O, the Food and Agriculture Organization, which was part of the U.N. It was in Monteverde Vecchio, one of the seven hills that are called the Palatine hills of the Eternal City. We had lived there, down the road, when my mother had worked in Rome from 1958 to 1963. She had headed the South American Department with Nieves De Madariaga, a very dear friend from my parents' Mexican sojourn. She remained a close friend until she passed away in 2002. She was the daughter of Salvador de Madariaga, the Spanish writer and Spain's Ambassador to France in the 1950s. I, especially, saw her more often than the rest of my family, due to my travels with Merce's company and my own travelling for work, after I left Merce. She could always be relied on to offer a place to stay; I would call her from different parts of the world and tell her I would be arriving and she never wasted time on the telephone but got right to the point. "When are you arriving?" she'd ask and tell me where I could pick up the keys. I loved her for her practicality and generous nature. When she retired from F.A.O., she gave up her apartment in Rome and bought a gorgeous house in Tuscany just outside of Cortona.

We moved in and I launched into my introduction of Rome to Satoru. It was my old stomping ground and I was anxious to show him my secret places, our old apartment, and magical Rome by day and night. Those first years we were always on the move for work to make a living, I was a fearless spirit; always ready to go where I could find it. Luckily, this suited Satoru as well; he was a good sport about it, which endeared him all the more to me. One day, we had driven the car into the center of Rome to go and see some sights, and, upon returning, found a note held in place by the windshield wiper, saying to go to the bar across the street, that they had something to tell us. It turned out that a garbage collection truck had hit our car and damaged it. The bar owner, seeing the foreign plates, outraged at the garbage people's negligence, had taken their license plate number and told us to go to the Commune of Rome (Town Hall) to file a claim for damages.

Since I spoke fluent Italian, we went straight to the address, found the proper office and the person in charge, and got instructions on how to file our claim. We had to get a body repair shop estimate, which we did forthwith, and, armed with that document, went back to officially file our claim. Within three days, it had been processed, and we were told where to go to pick up our money. The much maligned Italian bureaucracy, in this instance, worked to perfection. This was a small godsend, as our money was running out, and we had come to the end of our sublet and needed to find somewhere else to go and stay for free. So I called my friend, Nieves, who, by now, was living at her house outside Cortona in Tuscany. She was away in Poona, India on a retreat with her son, Bishi. Marianne, his American wife, whom we had not met before, answered. She was very charming and told us that she was staying at the house with their four children. When I asked her if we might go up there to stay with them for a while, she did not hesitate a moment and invited us up with open arms.

Our stay with them was an experience that I will never forget -- full of love, warmth and family fun. Every day was an adventure; we would go for long walks all together in that beautiful countryside. It was full summer and the air was perfumed with lavender and roses. We decided that we should put on a play in the fields and I was appointed director. We all wrote the script together. It proved to be a fabulously funny adventure where everyone's ideas were used and, somehow, we managed to come up with a serviceable play. Costumes were invented and made; make up was decided and rehearsals began in earnest. I, in my usual disciplined way, had everyone sign a little contract and stressed that rehearsals be attended on time. We rehearsed for two weeks and set the performance date. Invitations were sent out to all and sundry -- friends, shopkeepers, maids -- anyone and everyone we could inveigle into coming to this extravagant event. We all had the best time and I admit that laughter was rampant among us. We had a comedy on our hands, which we all found to be hilarious. Shakespeare, move over. We were going strong!

Marianne was in charge of the food and produced some really delicious meals followed by fantastic fruit crumbles that we all devoured in two shakes. We got torches for the lights and made a clearing for our make-do stage. The appointed day arrived. We were all really nervous, as we wanted the performance to go well and that the audience would laugh on cue. Well! We need not have worried; our public was very amused and laughed a lot at the antics. We were all thrilled and hugs and kisses flew around like there would be no tomorrow. Satoru, as my assistant, and I became the children's heroes and forged a lifelong friendship with all of them as well as with Marianne. In between all of this excitement, we went out to local pizzerias for dinner where bread would fly around the table at an alarming pace as we all had the time of our lives. The children were allowed to drink half a glass of wine each and us grown-ups more. I am not sure how grown up we were behaving after a few drinks, but a lot of fun was had by everyone.

One morning after breakfast, we were all out in the garden in front of the house when we saw Benjamin, the youngest, who was four at the time, trying to pee into the watering hose. We asked him what he was doing and he answered that he was putting water in so that we could spray the flowers. We all burst out laughing and he did not understand why, as his action was so logical to him. Children, for me, have always had the most extraordinary way of looking at things. How I wish that we could keep that innocence as we grow older! On hearing that none of the family or Satoru had seen the Siena Palio (a very famous medieval horse race around the Piazza Del Campo, the main square in Siena), I decided that we should all go to the one in

July that was only a few days away. Tickets were impossible to obtain, as they were almost all bought from one year to the next and cost a fortune. None of us could afford that anyway. So we decided we would stand in the main square with all the others.

The day arrived and we all piled into Marianne's and our car, along with some friends who had joined us. We were nine altogether and off we went singing on the drive over to pass the time, as it was a good one and a half hours distance away. We arrived, and, as usual, it was packed with people crowding down the narrow streets leading to the square. Seeing the masses and having young children in our group, I came up with the idea of trying to go up to the top floor of a building that would have a view over the square and knock on someone's door to see if they would let us see the Palio from their terrace. I tried several, only to be rejected. Not being one to give up, I found a perfect building right next to the start line, with a balcony and up we all went. I thought that if everyone stood behind me with hopeful faces, it might work better. I knocked and a nice lady came to the door, a bit taken aback by this motley group. I launched into my speech about my friends coming all the way from the United States just to see this fabulous pageantry, and would she be so kind as to let them watch from her balcony? She hesitated only a second, and, much to our great joy, said yes! I left them all up there, and rushed down to buy ice cream for everyone and flowers for the owner. She was delighted and the children were in heaven! It was one of my best coups! This, needless to say, guaranteed my eternal popularity. Children have been my passion, their inventiveness, their curiosity and joy are a tonic for me and inspire the very best that I can be for them.

The Palio, which dates back to the Middle Ages, is one of the most impressive pageants in Tuscany. It is passionately felt by the Sienese people and takes place twice a year, once in July and again in August. Each neighborhood has a Contrada with its own coat of arms on its flag. The Contradas are chosen for each Palio by a drawing, with half running in the first Palio and the other half in the second. Everyone is dressed in their medieval clothes, in velvet with tights and hats and gloves. They must swelter in the heat, as it is full summer and the thermometer can easily reach 95 degrees in the sun. Even for the public, who is allowed to stand for free in the middle of the square, it is a feat, as to get a place you have to arrive very early. It is a teeming mass of people, all straining to see above each other's heads to watch this thrilling event. It is said that serious money is exchanged between Contradas to get to the finish line first. The start of the race is a choreography that works the excitement of the people to its zenith, with horses moving in and out of the start lineup. The jockeys ride bareback on their horses and many times get thrown as they careen around the square three times. To start the race, a shot is fired from a gun, and many a time there has been a false start, and everyone has to fall back into order behind the start rope. There have been instances when it has taken up to an hour before the race officially takes off. This time it took 40 minutes and they were on their way.

The ceremonies start weeks before, as each horse is blessed in its Contrada's church and all its followers crowd in to assist this ritual. Dinners are held in their streets for the horse and the *Contraioli*, (the name of the followers). The horses can only be of mixed blood, as it is thought that it is too much stress for purebreds. The track around the square is between the bleachers that are erected for the paying public and the main square. It is a strip wide enough to fit 10 or 11 horses abreast, and since the pavement is of cobble stones, it gets packed with the *tufo* of the surrounding hills (a soft sand-based earth that gets compacted), to create a soft floor for the horses to gallop on. Once the gun goes off and all the riders and their horses have departed together, the race is on! They gallop at full speed around the track. The horse that reaches the finish line first is the winner, whether his rider is still on him or not. The prize is a magnificent sculpture of Santa Caterina, the patron Saint of Siena all dressed in gold, mounted on a platform made of wood, with two poles on either side for the pole bearers. The Palio spends the whole year in the Church of the winning Contrada, and its flag hangs on all the flag poles of Siena for a year. The Sienese people live for these two spectacles and you see grown men literally cry when they lose! It is so absolutely heart-felt.

This really was the *piece de resistance* of the holiday for everyone, and I was so happy that I was able to have them all see it from a balcony above the square! We made our way with the teeming masses out of Siena to our cars, to head to the nearest pizzeria to have a pizza, as by now we were starving. It took quite a while for everyone to calm down and by the time we got home, we collapse into bed grateful, to be lying down. For Satoru, this was a very special pageant, and one that he and I always went to with friends every summer when we lived in Tuscany some years later. We stayed a few days more and then we had to head out to go back to Paris where I was to teach at the American Center for two weeks.

PERFORMING TOGETHER

With heavy hearts we drove over the Alps back to Paris, where I was to teach for two weeks before going to England. The American Center had invited me to do a workshop, teaching dance classes and a repertory piece of Merce's. I taught the students *Scramble* which Merce had choreographed for the company in 1967, with sets and costumes designed by Frank Stella. They were very beautiful and consisted of long, fairly thin, panels of bright colored cotton strips that were stretched between two metal poles on wheels. Similar to Stella's paintings, they were moved around the stage in performance by Merce. The costumes were also of one bright color, the same colors as the panels: red, blue, yellow, purple, orange, green, white and black. Merce was in black and Carolyn Brown in white, the rest of us in the other colors. I liked teaching the piece as it had solos, duets and group sections; it was very popular with all the students to whom I taught it then, and would continue to be so with other students over the years. At the end of the workshop, a performance was held of the piece and everyone who was invited loved the work. This time, Satoru also taught the Tea Ceremony to a few students he had found through a notice he had put on the bulletin board at the American Center.

After Paris, we were going to London to do two performances at Alex Gregory-Hood's Rowan Gallery. It was the gallery where my father had exhibited in England and Alex was a very good friend of his. I had written to him when we were in Europe asking him if he would host these performances and he had kindly invited us. I was to do a solo I had choreographed for myself on roller skates; Satoru was doing a piece of his to do with flower arranging and a wooden grid. Our friend, Shoichi, was to perform a concrete poem of his that entailed the lighting of a circle of a hundred candles while he was reading one of his poems. It would mark the first time all three of us would work together. Shoichi was working on his Conceptual Poetry piece in New York and would join us in England a week before our shows at the Gallery. My mother would also fly over to help us with whatever was necessary, and would then stay with us for a holiday after the performances. Shoichi would leave straight after, as he had things to get back to in New York.

At the end of our work in Paris, we had the problem of Taro not being allowed into England because of their archaic six month quarantine laws with animals of all kinds. I had thought of trying to smuggle him in, and even went so far as to buy fabric to make a pouch that I could wear under a dress I had. The pouch made, I tried putting Taro in it, hoping to look like I was pregnant. He, knowing what I was doing, was very cooperative and put up with being squeezed into the pouch. He was so sensitive that it was obvious he wanted to have this thing work as much as I did. Poor dear was so disappointed when I realized it was madness to try to smuggle him in. Just the day before, the British authorities had caught a couple trying to smuggle their dog in, fined them, and put the dog into quarantine for six months. You could see his eyes drop when I was explaining to him that I could not take a chance smuggling him in. So we asked my dear friend Micheline and her boyfriend to take care of him until we returned to Paris two weeks later.

These separations from Taro were always heart-wrenching, as he was like our child; no wonder my mother called him her grandchild. She had resigned herself to making do without the real thing, realizing that I was not ready to take that step at the time. Satoru would have loved to have a child from the beginning, but I was afraid of deforming my body and the actual birth process. My mother had always said that to create and give birth to another life was a miracle, but it took me four years to come around to the idea. I wanted to be completely convinced that it was what I wanted more than anything else, as I believed that to bring another human being into the world was a great responsibility and one not to be taken lightly.

We crossed the channel with our car and drove to my mother's parents' house in Hastings. She had inherited it when her father passed away a year earlier. It was a lovely house up on a hill overlooking the town and was on two floors with a garden in front and back. We got there before her and decided to paint the inside for her, as a surprise, to give it a fresh look. We bought the paint and quickly set to, as we did not have too many days in which to accomplish this. We went to pick up my mother and Shoichi at the airport and when my mother walked into her house she could not believe what we had done for her. The next day we all went up to London to meet with Alex Gregory-Hood, to set rehearsal times and discuss the logistics of having a performance in the Gallery. He was charming and could not have been more accommodating; he even invited us all to lunch at his club. We were so excited to be performing in such a well-known Gallery.

Rehearsal times set, we looked around London in the afternoon and drove down to Hastings in the evening. My mother was wonderful, as she got on well with both of the men in my life and we had a very happy time throughout the week we were all preparing for our performances. I rehearsed my solo in her living room and Shoichi refined his sequence and Satoru made the set he would be using for his creation. He had to make a big square of wood divided into boxes, on which he would move vases filled with flowers around in a choreographed design, while also moving in a slow movement sequence he had invented. It was so nice to be together all working on our projects; my mother took care of the cooking and our general well-being. In the afternoons, we would go in search of a nice place to have an English tea with scones, clotted cream and strawberry jam, thin little cucumber sandwiches and good strong tea.

Shoichi was a Concrete Poet with many of his poems published in prestigious poetry magazines. That kind of poetry is a way of visually conveying a poet's meaning through the graphic arrangement of letters, words or symbols on the page. He was also a very fine calligrapher and hand-printed all my performance flyers and programs, as well as the ones we sent out for our London appearances. He had a wicked sense of humor and, over the years, when we were travelling, wrote us the most amusing letters. He, with my mother, took care of things for us in New York when we were travelling. He and Satoru had a wonderful friendship, for which I was so glad, as I think it was very nice for both of them. They were great ping pong players and used to have wild games at our loft. We made him godfather to our son, Christophe, after he was born. When Christophe was old enough, Shoichi introduced himself to him with, "How do you do, I am your godfather, but you can call me God for short." I loved his sense of humor and his quick way with words. He had a very good command of the English language. I include an excerpt of one of his many letters.

My dearest (here I go) Susana-san, Satoru-san, and Taro-kun,

.......So, once again on the lam are you? At times I wonder whether three (I believe of you are jet setting (oh, how bygone it sounds!) or just jot-setting! Tantamount to three months worth of upset stomach of a hard-core paparazzi, just trying to keep up with you all. It was at the Isle Saint Louis address, if I remember correctly, where I'd sent my last letter, which no doubt shall go astray....It is not so much that I have difficulty finding space in my address book which is problematic, but that I tend to forget how many times I've asked how you are and how many are answered, let alone whatever else I've lied-cheek!-said. (Just kidding.) Well, as my grandfather used to say (I'm sure, I think, that is,) when in doubt, do doubt for Pete' sake---so.... How are you all?

Now, Susana/Satoru-sans, what I would like to know from you is 1 when in October? 2 any fund for performance available? 3 who are going to help us in terms of performers? And 4 whatever are you going to do with Taro-kun? (I guess the last question 4 also means when are you two going to be in England?) I'd like to know them so that I could plan ahead a bio-financially and my money earning work wise. You might not know them yet, but could you tell me when you might in that case? Thank-you very much. Also, it would be very nice if you'd write about your performance projects--- but it's up to you ("I won't squeal, honest")

Well, I'll write soon again, this is only APERITIVO. Ciao Bella-Bello and Taro!

With warmest affection,
Shoichi-kun.

I am very proud of the relationship that Shoichi and I were able to keep as friends. It was a testament to our deep affection for each other. He became an important part of my new family and was very much appreciated by Satoru and Christophe.

The day before our performances started, we went up to London in the late afternoon, after Gallery hours, and rehearsed our pieces, set up the lights and decided the order in which we would perform them. It was at the end that we all realized we had a really beautiful event planned. The gallery walls and floors were all white, which provided a brilliant background for the work, pristine, spare, and very stark. The performance was a great success, and we were all very happy. I loved my solo, as it was all on roller skates, and had the effect of making me move very slowly, creating sculptural movement with my body. It ended with me jumping up and down repeatedly making a loud noise. It was almost like a child having a temper tantrum, very difficult to execute, but I really liked the effect. The three pieces were very different, yet the two Japanese inventions were very close in aesthetics. I was the strange wild thing in between the two very cool interpretations of my colleagues. It was sad that those performances in London were the only ones we did in Europe. We did, however, perform them again at our loft in New York, when we returned.

Shoichi went back to New York two days after the performances and we stayed on with my mother in the country for another week. One day, we decided to show Satoru Canterbury and set off early in the morning. I was driving along those lovely English country lanes, when rounding a curve, I came upon a car that was blocking the road and swerved into the opposite lane to avoid it. The driver on the opposite side did not react by moving over to avoid me, so I, unfortunately, hit her and our darling *deux cheveau* got a nasty dent that bent the front tire completely out of place. That proved to be the end of our poor faithful car. When we had to take it to the pound to be destroyed, Satoru asked if we could keep the license plates. When asked by the clerk why, as she had to fill out her papers, he answered, "For sentimental reasons". He said it with such sadness and pathos, the clerk had to smile, as did my mother and I. Satoru had such a way with so few words, of making you feel exactly what he was expressing. That episode marked the end of our stay in Europe.

We returned home to New York a few days later with my mother. A year in Europe had come to an end, and it was time to start our work in America. It had been an eventful year full of challenges, fun and discovery.

Travel is a great eye-opener on the world around us, a teacher that makes you grow, when confronted with other languages, ways of thinking and the challenges that arise as a result. I have become more open, more flexible and tolerant of my fellow human beings. We, as a couple, also grew as a result of all the varied experiences thrown our way. That is not to say, that at times, in our wanderings, I would get tired, Satoru would quickly whip me into a café for something to eat and drink. I discovered that this ploy of his, he once explained to a friend, was because I would start to get irritable. Eating would immediately calm me down and I would be good to go. For years he had managed my moods in this way, and I had not realized his magic. He was full of actions like that, not only with me but with others. He was aware, caring and thoughtful. My thoughts about the benefits of travel, lead me to wish, there were a way to get schools to have more exchange programs for students to travel abroad, as part of their learning experience. Surely there would be less intolerance and racism. An open mind is a treasure to cultivate, for the future of our children and the world we live in.

HERE AND THERE

Back in New York, we had to find a new place to live, as we had moved out of our apartment on Tenth Street before we left for Florida. We found a wonderful one in the West Village on West 4th Street, a few blocks from Westbeth, where Merce's studio was. It was in a four-story townhouse, on the ground floor. We had moved our possessions over and were unpacking when -- I can't remember what set me off -- but I found myself jumping up and down on a cardboard box, furious about something. Satoru just sat there watching me, smiling. I slowly calmed down, seeing myself from his perspective, and had to laugh at the absurdity of my outburst. He had a way of helping me see myself from outside, making me realize what I was doing. Where he was very calm most of the time, I was very passionate. It had to be my Spanish blood.

No sooner had we moved into the apartment, than a few months later, we found what we were really looking for: a divine loft on Gansevoort Street in the meat packing district, not too far away. It was scary signing a lease for ten years, as it seemed like an eternity then. Now we had two places to keep and renting either the apartment or the loft, became the preoccupation of the day. Excited, we set about doing what needed to be done to make the loft habitable. It had been used by the meat packing company for the storage of their refrigerators and had just one toilet and not much else. It was 3,500 square feet with a 100 foot wall facing south, and ten huge windows looking out at the World Trade Center. They were all grimy with dirt from never having been cleaned in all the time the meat packing company had used it. We could hardly see out of them, or see the floor space in its entirety, but we could tell it was special. Part of my deal with the landlord was that he had to move out all the equipment and broom clean the space.

The first order of business was cleaning the windows, to which I appointed myself. Satoru was to get the floors as clean as possible, before we would rent a sander to sand them. We would both paint the walls and rope in anyone in my family and among our friends to help us. We found they were few and far between, but we were not worried. Enthusiasm got us over all drawbacks, and dreaming of the end result kept us going. After those essentials were finished, we set about looking for a plumber to do the future bathroom and kitchen. Then an electrician had to be found for the electrical outlets, as there really were none. These two tasks proved to be very interesting, as we got estimates from Russians, Mexicans and Chinese: we finally ended up with a Russian right out of the *Brothers Karamazov*, who managed to get a fairly decent job done for a moderately reasonable fee. Soon after all this, I was to leave for Paris where I was invited to teach master classes at the American Center for Merce. I was to be away for a month, but the pay was so high I could not afford not to go. So leaving Satoru to deal with the loft's renovations, I was off to Paris.

The American Center had arranged for me to stay in a hotel for the duration of my stay, which I did not like. I wanted to find a room to let, and I saw a note up on the bulletin board for a room to rent in an apartment near the Museum of Modern Art. I called up to see if it was still available. A very nice lady answered and we made an appointment for me to go over to meet her and see the room. Nicole was in her eighties, a beautiful, elegant woman with whom I immediately got on famously. We arranged right then and there for me to rent the room and I returned to the hotel to pick up my case and moved in. Our friendship was to last until she passed away many years later. She was like a second mother to me, always warm, full of amusing stories about her life. She was there, ready to hear my news when I returned and we spent many an evening talking about life. Nicole had received the *Legion D'honneur* from the French government for her work with the French Resistance movement during the war. She had married a count whom she did not love, an arrangement made by her mother for financial and status reasons.

She had met her true love when providing shelter for him after his plane had gone down in flames not far from her chateau. He was a British fighter pilot in the RAF, a handsome, wonderful man whom she adored. He, unfortunately, died in a flying mission and her 'amour de la vie' was lost to her. She had three beautiful daughters whom she protected from the Germans who had commandeered her chateau, by keeping a shot gun under her pillow, always at the ready. She had sheltered and fed Resistance fighters in her basement right under the noses of the Germans. She was an extraordinary woman; I grew to love her for her humanity, courage and her wonderful sense of humor. After the war, she had divorced her count and had to make a living for herself and her daughters. She made beautiful silk flowers and became very well-known for her flower arrangements for the Elysee Palace and famous Parisian homes. She also expanded into creating beautiful hats which adorned the heads of many society ladies. She made one for me which I still have. This trip to Paris would prove to be very important for Satoru and me. In my conversations with Nicole, we also talked about her three daughters. A seed was being planted in my mind and, slowly, I could feel myself starting to think seriously about creating another life.

Coincidentally, our Dutch friends Ab and Tina's son, Roel, and his wife Marianne, had just brought into the world a beautiful baby boy. Tina commented to me that when she took me to visit him in the hospital, my eyes had misted over. She later told me that, in that moment, she could see that I had made a decision to have a child myself. All my talks with Nicole were bringing me ever closer to the decision that now was the time to start. I wrote to Satoru about her and our conversations. He, in turn, wrote back about how happy he was to have my news and could not wait for my return. He also told me about his progress with the loft renovations, which were going ahead as planned. My dear mother would go over on the week-ends to help him paint, as would Shoichi. They were the only two that really took helping seriously. Satoru was so happy to have the help and the company, he wrote telling me how much fun they all had over lunch breaks.

On my return to New York, Satoru and I talked about my finally being ready to have a child. He could not have been more delighted and we embarked on a concerted effort to accomplish this. We had many passionate amusing moments. It took three months, and Satoru knew exactly when we had conceived, as he had awakened me out of a deep sleep and had gotten down to business. I had the same feeling, so we anxiously waited for the results when I went to have a check up. They were positive, which sent us over the moon with excitement. We called my mother and father, Satoru's parents and Shoichi, of course, and also told anyone else we ran into. My gynecologist was a wonderful doctor whom I really liked, with gorgeous blue eyes and a ready smile. I was very fussy about choosing a doctor, as all the examinations and emotional issues are so personal. I was very shy that way, unwilling to have just anyone. He was great throughout the process, and very supportive of me and understanding of my concerns.

During this time, we were putting finishing touches on the loft, so that we could start our performance and teaching there. The work continued, with me a little less productive, but nevertheless pushing to get the space finished. We had publicized our first performances at our new 'Center' for three months ahead and were also rehearsing for those. One day, about six weeks into my pregnancy, I was rushing all over the place to see about advertising, when I sensed some humidity in between my legs. I quickly found a taxi and went back home. I rushed into the bathroom, found blood and quickly rang my doctor, who asked me to go to his office right away. On examining me, he said that I must immediately stop all work and go straight to bed and stay in a horizontal position, or I would loose the baby. My mother quickly came down to us and insisted that I only get up to go to the bathroom, and then only on my hands and knees. My rehearsals for our performances came to an abrupt halt and put the performances themselves in doubt.

I did not want to cancel anything, as my doctor had said that once I had reached twelve weeks without anymore bleeding, the baby was safe. The three months would be up the day before our performances were to start. I decided that when I got the go-ahead, I would get up and do my solo. As it turned out, I was ready the day before. I performed with a tiny belly and no one was the wiser. I felt it was a miracle of timing and fate, as the most important creature in my world at that moment was our future son. We were unaware of his sex at the time, as we preferred not to know. In fact, a person who read my hand had said we would have a girl. I had started to buy clothes thinking of a girl, though I suspected Satoru would have preferred a boy, as his family had no male heir. He was very sweet about this girl prospect, but I knew it was not his first choice.

My pregnancy was a wonderful time of hope and fulfillment; we lived every day with joy preparing for this life-changing event. I had read somewhere that one should read beautiful books and hear music of all kinds. We did this avidly together, amusing ourselves with all sorts of books. We went to galleries and museums to look at paintings and sculptures. We went to concerts and our baby loved the music. He would start kicking at the first sounds and not stop until the music had ended. It was very amusing and we began to think he might end up being a musician.

Seven months into my pregnancy, I had been invited to teach in Paris again and this time Satoru and Taro came with me. First, we went to Italy for a short holiday to visit our friends in Rome and Tuscany. Nieves was living in her house in Cortona by now and we stayed with her for a few idyllic days, walking in the hills near her house fragrant with blossoming flowers, accompanied by Taro running about in absolute joy. On our return, we would sit down and have wonderful conversations with Nieves who was a great cook, making simple, delicious meals we really enjoyed. Her daughter, Beatrice, came over once for one of these lunches and invited us to go and stay at her house in Montalcino, forty minutes away. We gladly took her up on her offer and left to go there the next day. Beatrice and I had been friends in Mexico, so we went back many years. She had married a French painter and had three children so gave us many of their baby clothes, which we gratefully took back to New York.

Beatrice showed us around beautiful vineyards where the famous *Brunello di Montalcino* was just beginning to acquire its world famous stature. She suggested we buy liters of it as an investment, as it would surely be worth a lot more in a few years. She was absolutely right, but we never had enough money to invest in anything. She also took us to see properties to buy, as we would have loved to buy something, but this was only day-dreaming. Loaded down with baby clothes and beautiful memories of Tuscany, we returned to Rome to stay with Mehlika, Ab and Tina Ten Dam's youngest daughter. We had met the family in Rome in 1959, when my brother Charles had made friends with her in his new school. In the course of getting to know him, she realized that he had a very interesting family. She enthusiastically returned home to tell her parents about us and that was how our families met and became lifelong friends.

We shared many adventures with the Ten Dams over the years. One in particular was when we went on a family holiday together in Switzerland. We had rented a Swiss chalet up in the hills above Lake Leman and we decided to each leave Rome at six in the morning and meet there. Well, Ab being Ab, got his brood up at the crack of dawn so that they would be the first to arrive. Our fathers having been very competitive, this was to be expected. However, my father was not going to take advantage and leave earlier than the agreed time. He would, however, drive like hell to get there first. You can imagine our surprise when we drove in the driveway and found that they were already there. Our mouths dropped open and Papa asked him, "How the hell did you get here before us?" to which Ab had to confess that he left two hours ahead of schedule. Jokingly, my father told him that he was a rotten bastard, much to all of our amusement. They had four children and together we were always up to no good, which was great fun.

Every morning, we would drive down to the lake after food shopping and going to the farm next door for milk, just fresh from their cows. We would then all pile into our family Bentley with its leather seats, as Ab would not have any of us, in our wet bathing suits, clambering into his Ford with its plastic seats. My father being the eccentric Englishman that he was, could not have given a damn about the seats. As it happened, we took care to change from our wet bathing suits, before piling into the Bentley which caused much giggling. The lake water was freezing, and we would tip-toe in with great trepidation, knowing that we would get pins and needles as soon as we managed to get under. It necessitated swimming frantically to warm up which made us feel boiling hot. When we got out, we would be a deep red color from the freezing water. One day, my father swam up to a rock nearby and took off his bathing suit to sunbathe, when a motor boat raced by almost next to him. That earned them a good look at the crazy bearded Englishman, provoking whistle-blowing merriment, which set us all on shore into gales of laughter as Papa just kept on sunbathing. We had many fun adventures with them that are a cherished part of my upbringing in Italy

We stayed with Mehlika only a few days and then took an overnight train back to Paris. This trip had been a delight for Taro as well. The countryside visits had been a great adventure for him; he had run happy all over the fields with Beatrice's dog Balbo, at times disappearing in the wheat. We would see their heads only as they took leaps in the tall wheat, to see where they were going.

NUMBERS

We decided to get the overnight couchette train to Paris, as it was cheaper and simpler with Taro. There was a slight problem, however, as dogs were not allowed. Of course, I decided that this did not mean our Taro and slipped him into my trusty leather bag that was his usual travelling home. I had bought the bag in Buenos Aires on our 1968 tour; it proved to be a perfect bag for our little Sheltie, as the top had small openings at either end. He was comfortable in it and could sneak his nose out when he needed. He was an expert at this, as he had flown on planes to Italy and Paris, without anyone discovering him. We got to the station, put him in the bag, and he, knowing the routine, was on his best subterfuge behavior. We boarded the train at the appointed hour and installed ourselves, along with our fellow passengers. All was proceeding well; Taro was lying low, not uttering a peep. As evening approached, the conductor came to put the four bunks down for us. Mine was the first, as it was on top. When it was ready, I climbed up with Taro in the bag. Unbeknownst to me, Taro, being curious, snuck his nose out the side of the bag, and the conductor, looking around to see that everything was in order, noticed. He immediately said that pets were not allowed and that we would have to get off at the next station.

I pleaded with him; I was seven months pregnant and couldn't he overlook this, just this once. "No, no Signora, the rules are the rules," he said. The other passengers were not disturbed by Taro, but he would have none of it. The next station came and went and we breathed a sigh of relief. A few minutes after, the conductor came back with a colleague, who repeated that we would have to get off at the next stop. This went on for a few more missed stops, until there were four of them, who announced jointly, "Signora, we have decided that we have not seen your dog, have a pleasant journey, and good luck with your baby." This was an example of the Italians' great sense of humanity that I have not seen equaled in all my travels around the world.

We arrived in Paris early in the morning, and got a taxi to the hotel we had booked for our stay in the city this time. We had negotiated a good weekly rate, so that we would not have to disturb Nicole, who had offered to put us up. I felt it was too much to ask of our friendship, and this also gave us more privacy. I had two weeks of classes to teach and then we would return to New York. My students were a bit worried about my teaching them so far along in my pregnancy, but I was feeling great and not the least bit bothered by my expanded belly. I taught as if nothing were different, extravagantly demonstrating all the exercises, much to everyone's consternation. I loved being pregnant; it was a wonderful time of my life. The back-aches that plagued me when I was not pregnant never bothered me. I was in heaven. It was a delight to be an expectant mother in France, as on seeing me, the French immediately gave up their seats on buses and trains. Something New Yorkers never did.

We took advantage of being in Paris to buy baby clothes, as they had the most gorgeous selections, as did Rome, where we also bought clothes. It was to become my habit to only buy Christophe's clothes in Europe and Japan. He was a very well-dressed child, in an unusual and fun way. No one ever had clothes like his; we were often stopped by mothers who wanted to know where we had bought his outfits.

It was early summer in Paris, the new tender green leaves were sprouting on the trees and the weather was sunny and warm. We walked around a lot and would go to Gallery Lafayette's food department to buy delicious ready-made meals to take back to the hotel. When we felt extravagant, we would go to the fancy Fauchon for a special treat. We visited museums to stimulate my joy factor, which would influence my baby's DNA. I had read that we could shape our child's outlook, by immersing ourselves in beauty during pregnancy. We went to see Nicole, as she was the inspiration for my wanting to have a baby, to choose our child's name with her. Since Satoru and I were both of different nationalities, we decided that, diplomatically, it would be best to choose a French name in her honor.

She had invited us to tea one afternoon and we surprised her by asking her to help us find a name. It had to coincide with the concepts of Chinese numerology, that is, the numbers of the letters had to add up to one single digit, except for the numbers, eleven and twenty two. His date of birth would be his destiny. This, of course, we could not control. As it turned out, his birth date added up to an eleven, a very fortunate number. Nicole thought the best thing to do was to get her saint's days calendar, and we would choose from there. Pen and paper were produced, names were put down and the letter numbers had to be added up to see if they could be reduced to a one. The only male names that came up were Pacome and Christophe. The female names were Cerise and Paloma. When our son was born, we gave him the name of Christophe, which, we insisted with everyone, could not be shortened to Chris.

Satisfied with our choice, we all sat down to a lovely conversation about our future plans. This was also the first time that Nicole and Satoru met, and I was delighted to see that they both took an immediate liking to each other. We invited her out to dinner before we left, sorry to be leaving Paris. We had also been invited to lunch by Ab and Tina at their house, just outside Paris, one week-end. Roel, their son, and Marianne, his wife, were also there with Mathieu, their baby (who had been the other inspiration for my getting pregnant). We spent a glorious day with them, going after lunch for a long walk in the woods, picking wild flowers near their house. Our time in Paris was drawing to a close and we sadly had to say goodbye to friends and students. My work had always been appreciated in Paris, which was very heartwarming for me.

Ab and Tina kindly took us to the airport with Taro and our cases, wishing us well with our soon-to-be-born baby. Taro behaved magnificently, as usual, with no one being any the wiser to his presence. As always, my parents picked us up at the airport and drove us home, where my mother had prepared a great dinner for us. We were back at our little charming apartment on West Fourth Street waiting for our miracle baby to be born. I decided to stop teaching now, as there were only a few weeks left. My doctor's orders were to take long walks, which, as the summer was heating up, got more and more difficult to enjoy. Christophe was due in the middle of July, so we had a month to wait. One day, when I was walking near the Cunningham studio, I ran into Merce, who asked me how I was coping and I told him Christophe was late, to which he said, "I don't blame him. In this heat, he is better off in your womb." I always liked my impromptu exchanges with Merce. That summer turned out to be one of the hottest summers on record, and I was sure my dearly beloved must have sensed this, and postponed his arrival for two weeks. I was not unhappy about this, as he would then be a Leo, which I much preferred over a Cancer. A Leo went along with our astrological ideas, as Leos are born leaders. I had not put on any weight towards the end and the doctor was a bit concerned, but not alarmed. Since I was late, and walking was important, I remember us deciding to go and see the Picasso show, which had just opened at the Museum of Modern Art. At least there we could walk around in the air conditioning. As luck would have it, the weather was so hot, hovering around 102 and 104, and with all the visitors, the air conditioning could not cope. Being extremely hot inside, walking became very uncomfortable. I remember sitting down a lot to recover.

We decided to limit our walking expeditions to the very early mornings and late evenings. One night, we decided to take a walk to little Italy to have dinner at Il Cortile, a favorite Italian restaurant of ours. On our walk over, we were passing through Soho, when a lady taking the air on her balcony, noticed us and told us how beautiful we looked and wished us good luck. I guess it was an omen, as after dinner, on our return, my back started hurting and I was having mild contractions. Once home the contractions started coming more frequently. At around two in the morning, we called Shoichi, who would pick us up and take us to Lenox Hill Hospital where I was to give birth. He arrived promptly and drove us to the hospital. Satoru ran in and got an orderly to come and get me with a wheelchair. We were rushed up to the maternity ward so that the nurse on duty could examine me, only to find out that I was not dilated enough and we were sent home. The wheelchair was gone, so I was left to walk out on my own steam. Shoichi was very disappointed as he had driven in from his apartment on Long Island and would probably not be able to come back in later. He had an awful time getting up once he had gone to sleep, so it was very unlikely that we would be able to wake him when needed.

Back at our apartment, he stayed a bit but then went home. The contractions kept coming, but apparently I was not ready yet. By noon, I could stand it no longer, and Satoru called our doctor who told him to get me to the hospital. He ran out to find a taxi, and off we went. This time there was no wheelchair; I had to make my way up to maternity on my own in great pain. The nurse came to examine me and I was ready. My doctor was called and I was prepared. By now I had been in labor for twelve hours and the pain was intense. But I was determined not to make a fuss as I did not like screaming fits, judging them to be exhibitionistic. As a result, Satoru got his hand squeezed for dear life, for he was holding my hand the whole time. We had gone to Lamaze classes to learn how to behave with natural childbirth; I don't, however, remember anything about torturing your husband with hand-gripping pressure.

My charming doctor arrived and I was wheeled into the delivery room and was instructed to push down. This whole part, from the contractions to the delivery, was what had kept me from embarking on the baby-scenario. Here I was in the middle of this pushing down, trying to remember what my mother had said: "Think of it as a river in which your child is descending; it is a great miracle, relax and let it flow". River be damned, the pain was so excruciating; I had all I could do to keep from screaming in pain. We were expecting a baby girl, so when I saw Satoru's face, as our baby was coming into the world, I knew immediately it was a boy. I saw then, that what he had really wanted all along was a boy, as his joy was visible! I was happy for him and, of course, for myself. At 3:37 p.m. on July 30, 1980, our son, Christophe Oishi was born. He weighed 7 pounds 14 ounces and was 22 1/2 inches long, with the most beautiful long thin fingers. Our doctor and the nurses all said that he would be a surgeon or a pianist.

I had wanted to have a private room to spend the two days I would stay in the hospital, but, as luck would have it, there were none available and I was wheeled into a ward with twelve other mothers. My baby was brought to me and started nursing right away. What a feeling of fulfillment I had with him lying on my stomach, breastfeeding. Satoru called my parents and his, as well as Shoichi. Mama and Papa came over right away and Shoichi would come the next day. My mother was thrilled and I could see that even my father was, too, even though he had thought it was not a good idea. After my parents left, Satoru and I sat together quietly staring at our creation. Satoru felt that Christophe looked like a wise old man lying on me sleeping. In fact, Christophe, at times, seemed more like my father than my son. He is a wise soul, beyond his years. I feel privileged to have been chosen by him as the conduit into this world. Satoru adored him more than life itself. He was so proud.

CHRISTOPHE

A few weeks before Christophe was born, we were in contact with Satoru's family. His mother Ryu, his brother Mitsuru, and sister Kimiko were in Germany for Hiroshi's and Kirsten's wedding. Hiroshi was born before Satoru and after Kimiko. He had left Japan when he was nineteen and had gone to live and work in Germany. He, too, was an architect, as were all the boys in the Oishi family. They were in Germany at the end of June for the wedding and were planning to fly to New York for Christophe's birth. They were calling almost every day to get progress reports on the imminent birth. They had to wait two weeks in Germany before they got the good news. They flew out on the first plane and were guests of my parents at their apartment on Central Park West. Satoru and my parents went to the airport to pick them up and brought them to visit me at our apartment.

I returned home two days after giving birth. My father and brother sent a limousine to pick us up and take us home. Their Plexiglas Company had an account with the limousine company, so they sent a stretch limo with champagne and all the frills. When the nurse, who had accompanied us down with our baby, saw the length of this thing, she almost dropped Christophe. I had been in the ward with twelve other mothers and I don't think she imagined that we could afford such a thing. She was right, of course, we could not. We got into the car, and all of a sudden, I felt panicky without the nurse nearby in case anything went wrong. As a new mother, at first it is frightening, as you have no experience looking after a baby. We got home without mishap and I went straight to lie down on the couch in our living room, exhausted from the whole experience.

We wanted to show Satoru's family New York. Satoru would

take them around in the day and we would all have dinner at my parents' apartment in the evening. My father, being the exuberant, extravagant man he was, would have music blaring and would regale Satoru's relatives with presents of scarves he had tie-dyed himself. He would send them wafting in the air to each one of them. They were very amused by him, although I am sure they really did not know what to make of this strange person. They were very Japanese; emotion was something that was not expressed in their culture, particularly as they were a Samurai family. They smiled and laughed like they were enjoying it all, but I really don't know if they did.

The last night, I wanted to take them all to see the World Trade Center Towers, as it was a very important piece of architecture. Designed by Minoru Yamasaki, the famous Japanese architect, it was a very important symbol, in my opinion, of the openness of the American people: that a significant landmark, like those towers, were designed by a Japanese architect. So I wanted to take them to *Windows on the World*, the restaurant at the top of one of the towers. I called the restaurant to ask if I could bring my baby, who was four days old, and they said, "Of course, if he does not drink any alcohol." We were very amused by their nice sense of humor; it made me feel more relaxed. We all drove down and went up to sit with cocktails to appreciate that magnificent view of New York. I felt very proud to be living in such an extraordinary city. It was the place that I considered home for twenty-eight very important years of my life.

The next day, everyone left for Tokyo, and we settled down to the routines of taking care of a newborn. Waking up in the night for feedings, changing diapers, and then trying to fall asleep again became our routine. Christophe slept between us the first few months, as we felt more secure with him there. My father had made a beautiful crib that had wheels on the bottom, so that we could roll Christophe around with us wherever we went. It was magnificent, made in wood, clad with their Plexiglas; and sat on a pedestal of the same material. The base was white and the crib went from dark blue, slowly changing shades to lighter blue, into white. Inside was a mattress and down-filled pillows surrounded the sides. When Christophe was inside it, he was lying in clouds. We would put him in there during the day and he would sleep peacefully, knowing we were always nearby. He was never out of our sight, which I liked. Papa's idea was that a baby should be able to sleep under any conditions, with or without noise. We fully agreed with this idea, which later proved to be wonderful for Christophe, as he never had problems sleeping anywhere. Too often children are put in their rooms and isolated from their parents and any sort of noise. These poor children grow up unable to sleep unless the conditions are just right, feeling abandoned, having been relegated to their isolated nursery.

I produced a lot of milk and poor Christophe could not keep up with the production, so early-on I got breast infections due to the milk that lay stagnant. I got a breast pump, but I could not empty the milk out fast enough. One night, I was in such pain Satoru had to take me to the emergency room at Lenox Hill to have then remove the excess milk with their much more efficient breast pumps. It also turned out that Christophe was allergic to something in my diet, because he would get colic after feeding and would cry terribly. I was in touch with *La Leche League* to see what I could do to help him. Suggestions to get in a warm bath with him and many others had no effect. This awful crying jangled my nerves and made me feel desperate, wondering what I was doing wrong.

In one of my frantic calls to our pediatrician, he suggested, to make me laugh, that when I felt like throwing my baby out the window, I call him, so that he could be on the street to catch him. We were at ground level, so it was not very far. Another time, he suggested that I put a tiny bit of whiskey in his water. He had a good sense of humor and relieved many a very tense moment. This went on for a few weeks, until my pediatrician figured out that Christophe might be allergic to something I was eating, and suggested I try to start removing things from my diet. Chocolate was one of my favorite snacks and I started with that. Thank goodness! That had the desired effect. As soon as I stopped the chocolate, poor Christophe was cured of the colic, and our life settled down to normal. There were times when I really thought I might go out of my mind, as I could not stand the constant crying and my poor baby's pain, I felt so hopeless. My mother, being a proud grandma, took a few days off work to come down and help me, which I appreciated. She would cook for us and we would go for walks together for fresh air.

Satoru was already working for Phillip Johnson. Jasper Johns, whom Satoru had worked with at Simca prints, had put in a good word for Satoru with the great architect. His office had called him for an interview and had hired him. Their offices were in the Seagram building on Park Avenue. He loved working there and made me laugh one day, when he reminded me of when he had found work at the Plaza Hotel, washing cutlery in the third basement and had dreamed of becoming a bus boy. He wondered how many of his architect colleagues could say as much. I have to admit that I was the instigator of Satoru's forays into the humble work he had to do, to contribute to our living. First delivering fish in Tokyo and then working in the Plaza Hotel. Knowing that he came from the privileges that he had, I admired his great humility and stoicism in the face of my insistence, to take on even menial tasks. I have always done whatever was necessary to make a living and firmly believe that no matter what, the effort has to be made. This, of course, was not Satoru's experience, but, nevertheless, he trusted me and, without complaint, did what he had to do.

Working at Phillip Johnson was a great pleasure for him and, of course, his family, who were concerned about his career. I was very proud of him as well, as he was very talented. He made many good friends there with whom we would go out to dinner occasionally. His good friend, Nao, with whom I had seen Satoru walk into the hotel in Tokyo, came to visit us. He was now married to an Austrian girlfriend he had met when she was sixteen and they had two beautiful children. Nao was the heir to the Kikkoman family. He and Satoru had travelled with Jasper Johns and Hiroshi to Europe several times. It amazed me to think that Satoru had moved in very privileged circles and yet he was so humble, such a very unpretentious human being.

We both had the incredible privilege of working with the most important artists of the twentieth century. Satoru, on his side, had worked with Phillip Johnson, Jasper Johns, Louise Nevelson, Claes Oldenburg and John Cage. I, with Merce Cunningham, John Cage, Jasper Johns, Toshi Ichiyanagi, Takehisa Kosugi, David Tudor and Gordon Mumma. The last four were composers who worked with Merce. They were all in the forefront of their professions and influenced the art world of our century. You cannot go to a museum and not see their work, or to a concert and not see their names as having influenced the new generation of musicians. We were the generation that followed them, informed by their rigorous aesthetic and great discipline. We were products of that age, as such, changing the way in which we expressed ourselves. We would become more interested in the living process, as it related to art, not as a means to success. In the shadows, we quietly pursued our art/lives not looking for outside approval. Maybe this was because we had been a part of these extraordinary artists' expressions. It became unnecessary to become known, as we were secure in our own skins. They had all mostly come from ordinary backgrounds, from which they had struck out to make their mark on the culture and the world around them.

This became clear to us over time, as, of course, we did not consciously understand our reasons for doing things the way we did. The influence they had on us was so overwhelming that it was almost intimidating to think that one could come up with anything half as important. I suppose it was like in the Renaissance, it came about after a long period of seeming inertia. After the Renaissance, nothing as earth-shaking took hold of the collective artistic imagination for a very long time. When you look back at history, it has always happened in this way. Great periods of fertile imagination were followed by periods of concentration on other aspects of the living process. In Satoru and my age (I suppose we could be called the *baby boomers*), we were witness to the incredible advancement of scientific and technological breakthroughs. The computer age, the internet, the immediate interconnectedness of us all -- we, as human beings, were almost left behind, helplessly wondering where we fit into the scheme of things.

OUT OF THE SUITCASE

Satoru and I continued our daily walks after he came home from work in the late afternoons. Now we also had Christophe for company. He would sit in his stroller like a wise old man. People would stop us and say that he looked like a little Buddha, which I think was because of his deep penetrating expression and his chubby cheeks. We called them his *onigiri* cheeks (the name of Japanese rice balls). Satoru had looked exactly the same in his baby photos. At other times, they would say he looked like a philosopher. He looked dignified, even though he was a baby, observing the world as it passed in front of his eyes. This quality was something that he never lost. He inherited Satoru's good looks and a little something from me. He is a very beautiful mixture of us, not only physically, but temperamentally as well. We were very proud of him. When he got older, we were constantly stopped by photographers for publicity shoots. I agreed once, just to see how it worked, and he posed in a handsome knit suit, for a layout in McCall's Needlework & Crafts. I realized the pressure was too much, so I did not have him do this again.

I was happy to be taking the time off to appreciate Christophe, but also needed to work to contribute to our livelihood, as we now had one more soul to take care of. I was invited back to Paris to teach for the *Theatre du Silence* and to Eupen, Belgium, for a company that Kirsten, Hiroshi's wife, danced with. My mother took time off to accompany me, as it was my first foray out to work with Christophe. He was now nine months old and I felt it was possible to start travelling with him. He was still breast-feeding and would continue until he decided to stop, when he was a year old. Ab and Tina were meeting us at the airport; we would be staying with them during my two weeks' work in Paris. I was nervous about this endeavor, and brought along every piece of equipment I had for him: his stroller, four-wheel rolling seat, high table and basket crib. We were loaded down, and when Ab and Tina saw us come out with all this baggage, they wondered whether they could fit us, and it, in their car.

I would take the train into Paris, a half-hour ride, teach my classes and return home. I would leave a bottle of my milk for Christophe, along with a little mashed homemade food. My mother and Tina had a great time, and, I am sure, Christophe enjoyed himself, too. It was spring; the air fresh and warm, full of flowers in bloom. The French countryside was very pretty and there was a forest near the Ten Dams' house, where Tina and my mother would go and pick wild flowers. Tina was an avid horticulturist and would draw the flowers she picked. From Paris we went to Germany, where Hiroshi lived with Kirsten, and we stayed with them. They lived in Aachen, on the border with Belgium, a short drive away from Eupen, where I was to teach the company Kirsten was in. Mama and I established the same routine, which worked well. It was my mother's first time in that region and she enjoyed the countryside. I was also invited to give a series of talks on dance and Merce Cunningham in Brussels for the "International Congress on Dance Education." My mother and Christophe came with me, as we had been provided with an apartment for the four days of the conference. Brussels is a fascinating city, the main square a jewel of architecture. The chocolate was fantastic, and my mother and I, being avid chocolate fans, went to town.

This was quite an experience for me. My mother was a great help with Christophe, as it was his first experience travelling and adjusting to different places and languages. This was a very conscious effort on our part, as parents, to educate our child to be flexible in his habits and attuned to different situations and languages. It had been my experience, growing up travelling with my parents, and I felt it was a fundamental part of my upbringing. It had opened my eyes to other ways of doing things, other languages and different peoples. Christophe became a very good traveler, as the first four years of his life he was on the go with me a lot. When he became four, we decided that it was important for him to socialize with children his own age and we enrolled him in a little kindergarten on Jane Street, one block over from our loft on Gansevoort, in the meat-packing district of New York.

Christophe travelled with me more than once to Paris, and Belgium, and to Syria and Germany where we went once. After the first time, when my mother came with us, I went alone, arranging with the people who were hosting me, to have a babysitter for a few hours while I was teaching. Together with Satoru, we went on holiday to Italy, France, England and Japan. One time, Christophe went alone with Satoru to visit his family in Tokyo, a chance for them to have some time with one another, just the two of them. I took them to the airport and when it came time for them to embark and Satoru and Christophe moved away from me, poor Christophe, realizing that I was not going with them, all of a sudden got this panicked look on his face. He had thought we were all going together, poor thing, and he was not too happy when he realized we weren't. It turned out he had a wonderful time with his father, and his Japanese family, with five cousins all happy to play with him and make a fuss. They had a grand time in Tokyo, going to Disneyland, visiting shrines and parks and buying the most wonderful children's clothes. He and Satoru returned content with their first travel together, Satoru very happy to have been with his son and his family. I felt a little bit lost without them, calling them almost every day. They took lots of photos that I enjoyed seeing when they returned.

In 1982, we went to Syria, having been invited by the *Theatre du Silence* to teach them on tour, and to prepare them for my upcoming choreography, which they commissioned for the next year. Christophe was two and I felt he was old enough to come with me. I arranged for a baby sitter for when I was teaching, and took care of him the rest of the time. We watched rehearsals together; he was very attentive, concentrating on the dancers. Everything was going well until one evening, Christophe started throwing up and had diarrhea. I immediately had the staff call a doctor to check up on him. The doctor arrived and diagnosed food poisoning. I settled Christophe down after giving him his medications and when he was asleep, I ran downstairs to get bottled water for his drinking bottle. I could not believe what I saw: the hotel staff was filling empty plastic water bottles from the tap, which they then served us as bottled water! Right then and there I understood how Christophe had gotten ill. I had carried most of his food with me in jars, but water was impossible to transport in big quantities on a tour. We trusted that it was properly bottled, not dreaming that it was really tap water. So from then on, I only gave him fruit juice, and plain soda water.

Syria, apart from that incident, was an unforgettable experience. We visited the *souk* and bought some wonderful presents to take home. I have marvelous photographs of that enlightening trip. The Company also performed in the famous amphitheater in Bosra. It was built by the Romans in the 2nd Century AD, and despite being converted into a fortress by the Ayubids during the Crusades, the original theater has been miraculously preserved. It can accommodate up to 15,000 spectators and has a stage that is almost 148 feet long and 26 feet in depth. It was a very striking setting! We went to see Palmyra, 200 kilometers northeast of Damascus, which is often described as "the jewel of the desert," and was a passing point on the caravans traveling the Silk Road from the North to Persia. There are moments in one's life when you realize that you are a part of something really extraordinary and this was one of them. I was so thrilled to be able to share this with my young son.

As he had been traveling with me often for my work, he had become a very good companion and was never a problem. He did not like me to put him to bed. He liked to be near me and, content with the proximity, would just fall asleep on my lap or on my feet under the table when he got tired. I remember vividly the other people in the hotel, refugees, I learned, who would come up to us to ask us to tell the West what was happening there when we returned to Paris and New York. The whole area was in turmoil. I remember on our drive to Bosra, the missiles lined up along the route with military personnel and vehicles along the roadside. I don't really know why I don't remember being frightened by all we were seeing. If it were today, I would not have gone anywhere near there. I am thankful nothing happened. I often think that I, before having Christophe, had also witnessed extraordinary settings and events in many diverse countries. I have tried to understand the impact that these pilgrimages had on my mind, and how they affected my way of thinking and reacting to life. I have watched Christophe grow, looking for signs of these influences, yet it is difficult to quantify in any way, what the impact has been.

In May of 1982, Satoru and I invited Mama to go to Japan with us, for her to visit the country she had so much admired. We all went together to Tokyo with Christophe and stayed with Satoru's parents. We stayed there for a week and showed Mama that incredible city, with its temples and shrines. She saw the Kabuki and the Noh Theatres, the department stores that had floors for clothes, as well as two whole floors for food, a floor of restaurants, and the top floor for art galleries. This was unique to Japan, as there is nothing like that anywhere else in the world. Mama got on very well with Satoru's mother and they would sit and somehow have a conversation in sign language. By then, Satoru's father had passed away, so she never met him, which was a shame, as he was such an exceptional person. Satoru also showed her a Tokyo of charming places to eat all the varied foods it had to offer, the special sake shops, the coffee places. Gyohei, Satoru's sister's husband, took us all to his private Geisha club to see their special tradition of entertainment for their clients. It was an unforgettable experience. Mama was so excited about everything we showed her and I was so thankful that I was able to give her that experience. We took her on the 'Shinkansen' bullet train to Kyoto, and we stayed in a typical Japanese Ryokan Inn. It was the fulfillment of her dreams. She was finally living what she had read so much about in *The Tales of Gengi*. We went to Nara, the town where the deer roam the streets freely, and visited all the temples in both Kyoto and Nara. I felt so lucky to be able to do this with Christophe and my mother. Satoru was a perfectly attentive guide and it is a memory that I will cherish always.

As a present for having hosted her in Japan, Mama invited me to Hong Kong, where we went after Tokyo, as neither of us had been there before. Satoru who had to return to work, left for New York with Christophe. We went for four days and I had suggested Mama make reservations for the Peninsula Hotel, the most famous hotel in Hong Kong. They sent a Rolls Royce to pick us up at the airport and we had a gorgeous room at the hotel in which they had put a lovely basket full of fruit and a gorgeous bouquet of flowers. We visited all the sights and had a fabulous time, just she and I. We would take off sightseeing after breakfast and return in time for the Peninsula's famous afternoon tea. It was a very special time, one that we had never had before together. Papa called every day to see how we were doing, and his attention to Mama was very endearing. They had such an extraordinary rapport, so close and personal. I spoke with Satoru twice during our stay and Mama bought him a very elegant Tissot watch as a thank-you present for his kindness to her in Japan. On our return to New York, Satoru and Papa picked us up at the airport, and it was so nice to see both our men waiting to greet us.

The very next day, Phillip Johnson had invited the whole office to visit his glass house in New Canaan for lunch. The architects were allowed to invite their wives or companions, and so I got to go as well which was very exciting, as none of us had seen his famous house. It was a great privilege to see this estate, which comprised his Glass House, a gallery for his art work, and his new studio which had just been finished. He was very proud of his new addition, which was very special. He also had a pavilion he had designed that floated on his lake that one could walk onto from the shore. It reminded me a bit of part of Pompeii, and when I told him as much, he was very happy with my observation.

INVENTING WORK

When we decided to have Christophe, we had talked a lot about how to bring him up. Satoru had read in a book written by a Japanese doctor, that a child's ability to learn is strongest from birth to three years of age. It is the time when their brains are at their most receptive, so the more information you can give them, the better. Believing this to be true, I started with books, going to galleries, music concerts and, of course, traveling as we did. As my first order of business, I chose all kinds of volumes on art, sculpture, nature, astronomy, Greek myths and a cross-section of children's books. Once we were looking through an art book, when I came on a painting of Rauschenberg's and he started to laugh. It was very amusing; I really did not know what had made him laugh. Satoru also decided that since fathers generally do not have much physical contact with their sons, he would give him *shiatsu* massages every night when we put him to bed. I would sit on the floor and read, while he was having his massage. When Satoru had finished, he would lie down next to Christophe. Invariably, my reading would put them both to sleep. I enjoyed reading out loud and seeing them both asleep. I would continue for maybe a half-hour longer, believing that even though they were both sleeping, their brains were still absorbing the words.

This ritual was one that we continued every night for many years, the exception being when we had to go out or had friends over for dinner. Christophe was always a part of our invitations and would make himself comfortable and go to sleep when he was tired. It was usually on one of our laps or on a couch nearby. We realized that this routine gave him a secure and tranquil personality; he was not needy or looking for attention. We noticed the difference between him and other children his age. I don't mean to say he was perfect, he cried on occasion, but not often, and did not make scenes.

When he started to walk, we were very excited, as then we could start all kinds of other activities. Satoru was at work during the day and I would have Christophe to play with. Since we lived in a big open loft, I went to town inventing all sorts of games for him to learn the alphabet and math. I would draw letters on the white walls and write words and we would play with them. Numbers I tackled by playing hopscotch, saying them out loud as we jumped on them. He learned the alphabet and numbers very quickly this way. I loved inventing games and seeing the effect they had on Christophe. Nurturing him like this was a great joy for me, as it pushed my creative instincts; I saw his upbringing as a work of art. When he was old enough to have children over to the loft, they would all play with crayons, paint, and his toys. They were allowed to use the walls and surfaces to draw on and could run around our huge loft to their hearts' content. When their parents came to take them home, none of them wanted to leave; at times it took up to an hour for them to go. I loved those times. To see the joy and happiness of those young lives was such a privilege.

In 1984, when Christophe started to go to kindergarten on the next block, each parent would be called upon to help with the children one day a week. I always looked forward to my turn, as I loved seeing how the children all interacted with each other and I could make suggestions for things to do with them. His going to kindergarten meant that I had to stop so much travelling, as he would no longer be coming with me. Since Satoru was working, there was no one to take care of him. I had to come up with a solution to replace the income from my work abroad. It occurred to me that I had my grandmother's recipes for typical English desserts. Her lemon curd tart was a legend, and when I made it, was always a great hit with people. I decided to try making the tarts and go to restaurants to sell them. At this same time, my mother and Satoru's mother helped us buy a lovely piece of land in upstate New York. We bought twenty-five acres above the town of Accord in the Catskills. We wanted to eventually build a house there. We had really been looking for a ready-built house, but soon realized we could not afford that. So we had started looking for land.

The tart-making and selling was to generate income and a business that, in a few years, would allow us to build our dream house. We had a big kitchen with a professional Garland stove and I started experimenting with the various tarts. I then loaded my samples in my white Citroen DS21, and went looking for restaurants. I started with an Italian restaurant in Chelsea. I parked my car in front and got out with my samples, walked in and asked to speak with the owner. When he came over, and I introduced myself and my tarts and I invited him to try them, which he did. Liking them we agreed on a price and I walked out with my first order. I returned home and, having seen that the idea was possible, I contacted my lawyer and set up a company for my new business. I called it *O'tarts*, a pun on the English slang word *tart*, which meant prostitute. I was prostituting my art for financial gain. It amused me, and it was something I emphasized with all my new clients.

The first year, I supplied four restaurants with my tarts, and at the end of the year, when I had to do my taxes, an accountant friend came over to help me. She saw that I was spending too much on my supplies and not charging enough for my tarts. I had worked so hard, with such long hours in the kitchen, only to see that it was defeating the purpose. I was supposed to make money, not lose it. I broke down crying, so much effort and time for nothing. That was when, as she suggested, I changed the things I was doing wrong. I had to locate wholesale suppliers for my raw materials and to find wholesale cake boxes. It was time-consuming work, but absolutely necessary, if I were to make this enterprise a success. The last thing on my list was to look for more business. I decided to ask for help from my first client.

He was an Italian and I got on well with him; he introduced me to his food consultant, an English woman called Jane Garmey. He thought that she would be able to introduce me to other clients of hers and therefore get me more work. She liked my offerings and suggested I try also making savory pub food. She had a client who had two Irish pubs in the Wall Street area to whom she would introduce me. She suggested I make Cornish pasties, pigs-in-a-blanket, plus my desserts. I embarked on my pastry experiments, which, I am sorry to say, were awful. My pastry came out hard as a rock and I threw away more flour and butter than one could imagine. One day, a friend gave me a recipe that he said was fail-proof. I went home to try it and it turned out to be the solution to my problems. So I launched into my Cornish pasties and pigs-in-a-blanket samples, and went down to the pub for them to try my fares. They met with success and I was on my way to supplying their two pubs. It was a very good account and prompted my investing in a professional convection oven.

This was what I had needed to produce a decent income; however the work was back-breaking. I worked all hours God made, buying supplies, cooking and delivering. This work, though, was convenient, as I could do it at home and be with Christophe when he came back from school. He liked sitting on the floor when I was working, playing with dough and pots and pans. Our pediatrician had said from the beginning, "Don't waste money with lots of toys; use things you have at home, he will enjoy them more." His idea worked very well and we spent many amusing hours in this way.

I was still teaching at Merce's school and I took Christophe with me. He would entertain himself playing on the side of the studio with a few toys, while I taught. He would also watch, and at times, as I was passing by him, he would point out someone not doing the exercises properly. He became quite an expert, his powers of observation, acute. The students were very taken by him as well, especially when he would climb up the big studio portable stairs to get a panoramic view. Everyone would crane their necks, worried he might fall down. They soon became used to this and carried on normally. Christophe got quite a reputation at the studio and Merce was always very amused by him.

Jane Garmey also introduced me to her client, Channel Thirteen, New York's educational television station. The director, Jay Iselin, was a friend, and she set up an appointment for me to meet with him, as they did all their fund-raisings with breakfasts, lunches and cocktails. They had been using different caterers but were not so happy with them. Jane suggested they try using me exclusively to see how it worked. We set a month trial period, after which they would decide whether to continue. At the end of the month, they were satisfied, so we signed a year's contract and I became their official caterer. My contact there was called Selma, with whom I got on very well. I worked with them for two years, until I realized that, if my business were to really produce money, I had to move it up another level. It was then, in 1986, after two years of overwhelming work, that I decided catering was not my love or ambition and it was time to put an end to it. Since I was also teaching at Merce's, and choreographing my own work, I was burning the candle at both ends. At the same time I stopped the catering, we also closed "The Center," our experimental studio. We had started The Center together with Rina Yerushalmi to have a place to teach, dance, the tea ceremony and acting, and to experiment with these three art forms. We taught the students who enrolled and gave several performances. It was very time-consuming and did not give enough results to merit continuing, so we decided to close it in the end.

The catering decision was also brought on by the fact that in photographs we took at Christmas, I saw that I looked grey from exhaustion. In addition, we were also talking about building a Japanese country house on our land in upstate New York. I had come up with the idea that it would be a good business for Satoru to design and build Japanese country houses. The sample being one we would build on our land. Talk about jumping from the pan into the fire!

Japanese Country House

In the spring of 1986, we started on my brain child of Satoru designing and building Japanese country houses. Great in theory, except that we only had $ 5,000 in the bank and twenty-five acres of land. However, those little details did not give us a moment's pause. The idea included bringing master carpenters and plasterers over from Japan who would build these houses with the traditional art of wood joinery. No nails are used; the wood joints are interlocked like a puzzle. This was another of my crazy ideas to make a business, to produce an income for our family survival. I was always concerned with the problem of how to earn money, independent of employers and the constraints they put upon our ideas and time. An eternal optimist, I saw the world as my oyster, where anything I thought of could, and would, become a reality. God knows why I thought I was so omnipotent. I suppose my father telling me, "Nothing was impossible" at an early age left an indelible mark on my psyche. I have to admit that I was proud of this side of my character, but the demands it consequently made on me were a heavy burden to carry. Not that I would have changed a thing, were I to have the chance to do everything over again. Satoru, being the person he was, graciously thought about my plans and proceeded to see how he could fulfill his part in them. I loved him for his utter faith in my madness. This synergy between us was what distinguished us from the norm. In our different ways, we would meet the challenges that we willingly undertook, our utter innocence being our saving grace.

Satoru's job was to design the house and coordinate the Japanese side of things with his brother, Mitsuru, in Japan. My responsibility was to raise the money and organize all the various details involved. To this end, Satoru started on the drawings which went back and forth to Japan for his brother's suggestions and input. Needless to say, Satoru had never designed a Japanese country house, or knew about all the intricacies of such a project. Bless his heart; he too, having assimilated a bit of my insanity, never gave it a second thought. In this sense, we were both wildly off the wall, but happy as clams.

I went to my father for help with introductions to his bank managers, to see about borrowing money for this endeavor. He set up the meetings and accompanied me. The managers could not have been nicer, but the outcome was a simple, "Unfortunately, we cannot be of help, as the project is in the upstate New York, and the best solution is to go to a local bank to get a construction loan." As disappointing as this was to hear, it did point the way to proceed. One manager did, however, offer to give me a small credit line of $ 10,000 dollars, which provided me with the funds to get things going. Taking his advice, I got dressed up, got in my Citroen DS21, and took myself up to the country in search of a bank that could, and would, give us a construction loan. I stress getting dolled up, as it was my opinion that people in authority, especially in banks, take you more seriously if you look like you don't need the money you are asking them for. After several tries, I finally found one in Kingston that agreed to give us a loan, if we met their requirements. This part gave me pause for thought, as dealing with tax returns, bank statements, and such things always made me nervous. Did we have what was needed? And if not, how was I going to resolve the problem? It goes without saying that, of course, not all was as they wished and all manner of things had to be done to fit their standards. Not being one to be put off by these minor details, I set about collecting the missing parts in any way I could. It required some acrobatics and plenty of fudging, but the requirements were eventually met, and a modest construction loan of $ 60,000 dollars was agreed upon. All that remained was to find a lawyer to handle that legal part, and we were ready to proceed.

We had to arrange where we would all stay and how many carpenters and plasterers to bring over. Mitsuru, in Tokyo, was in charge of the Japanese construction company, who would coordinate the workers, the necessary tools, the pigments for the plasterers, and shipping the things over. Satoru was in constant touch with Mitsuru for the planning stages, while going to work at Phillip Johnson's every day. It was stressful for him, but he was enthusiastic about the project and proceeded without any complaints. In order for me to have the freedom to go up and down to the country, organizing this project, we had to have a live-in baby sitter.

I had made friends with the mother of one of Christophe's little friends who, coincidently, had the brilliant idea of going to Stockholm, Sweden to look for a live-in baby sitter for her son. Linda was a headhunter by profession, so she was a good judge of character and an ideal person for such a mission. On learning this, I asked her if she could also find one for me. She had heard from a friend that Swedish young women were very responsible, and therefore decided to put an ad in a Stockholm newspaper, inviting young qualified ladies between the ages of twenty and thirty, to meet her at the hotel where she was staying. The result of her journey was the arrival of Louise Attling, a wonderful young lady whom we all adored at first sight. On the appointed day, we picked her up at the airport and brought her to the loft. The first thing she did, was give us a lovely present of a fruit bowl, made by artisans famous for their glass work. It was truly beautiful; I jumped up and gave her a big hug, we were so touched by her thoughtful gesture. She lived with us for two wonderful years, and was not only Christophe's baby sitter, but also became my friend and work collaborator. She held the fort when I was busy fulfilling all the requirements of this project, and moved up to the country with us when the construction actually started.

I made many journeys up and down in my trusty Citroen, that to make things a little bit more complicated, decided to have its air conditioning go on the blink. In the middle of a scorching summer, all dressed up, I would find myself driving into town with the heating on full tilt, to draw the heat out of the engine, and all the windows open for air. My carefully coiffed hair was blown to the winds and my fancy clothes would get damp from perspiration. As soon as I got to the building where I had my appointment, I looked for a bathroom to fix the damage. I would show up at my all-important meetings with bank managers, et al, looking reasonably decent, if not to the standards that I had wished. This was when I also put into effect my acting skills, learned from my dear mother, travelling through South

America. I was witness to many an acting *tour de force* by her, when it was needed, to get us past impossible customs officials or other emergencies. How I had admired her! I had watched carefully, and now I was able to put my observations to good use. I knew she would be very proud of me, which consoled me for my efforts.

Our twenty-five acres was off a dirt road up in the mountains above the town of Accord, New York. We had gone up there often on the week-ends to spend some quality time, having a picnic and enjoying the country air. On one of these visits, the neighbors on the right of us, curious, came over to introduce themselves. They were Mr. and Mrs. Rogers, a charming older couple who had lived there for thirty-eight years. They were, as usual, fascinated with Satoru, interested in Japan and the Japanese, and his British wife with the English accent. We became very good friends and they turned out to be our guardian angels for all the time that we owned the land. We always called them Mr. and Mrs. Rogers, out of respect. They tried in vain to have us call them Jane and Paul, but we just could not get used to doing that. They were a treasure of useful information: where to get cement, where to buy the wood for building, which plumbers to call, as well as the right man to create the concrete foundation for the house and a myriad of other things. Satoru had designed the foundation to have a radiant heating system running through it, so that the floors would be warm to walk on barefoot. Since it was a Japanese country house, we would be leaving our shoes just outside the entrance, where Satoru had designed a covered seating area where outside shoes could be exchanged for Japanese felt slippers.

On the Rodgers' recommendation, I rented two small chalet-style houses on a golf course, one for us and Louise and one for the Japanese contingent. We found out that the Japanese were avid golfers, and to make their stay more enjoyable, I went out of my way to arrange playing opportunities for them. I felt it was crucial that they be happy, so that they would do their best work. The four carpenters would come first and when they were finished with the main construction, the two plasterers would join them to start the interior and exterior plaster work. It was estimated that the construction time would be fifty-six days to build a 2,000 sq. ft house. They would work seven days a week and take two days off during the whole time. This was because they were also farmers, and had to get back to their farms in time to harvest their rice. All this was decided in Tokyo and we went along with the instructions. Summer was upon us, the time set to start work on our project.

Satoru and I took two months leave of absence: he from Phillip Johnson and I from my various projects. Before the plasterers arrived from Japan, we had to have the house foundation ready and the tools they had shipped over, picked up. They sent over absolutely everything they would need: the instruments to plane the wood beams and supports, the marking inks, most of the hardware, the plaster pigment powders they would use for the walls and their all-important golf clubs. We stocked up on the Japanese food they would be cooking and eating, and the beers and whiskey they would drink at night after a hard day's work. The pre-arranged day arrived and we packed the car with all we would need, saw our sublet tenants into the loft and off we went up to the country. Just as we were getting into the car, I remembered to check the mail and found a letter from the bank. With trembling hands I opened it, sensing that it did not contain good news, only to read that our loan had been rejected. Here we were, everything organized and ready to go, only to find out that we had no loan! We decided to go on with our plan and drove upstate to our chalet, with me madly figuring out how the hell I was going to get us out of this mess. It was a tense drive up for all of us, except maybe Christophe, who, being so young, was not aware of all the implications.

It was the week-end and my hands were tied until Monday, when I could call the bank and demand an explanation. What could have gone wrong?

THE CHALLENGES

It took two hours to get up to our chalet; the weather was warm and sunny. We piled out of the car and Christophe and Taro raced into our new home to check everything out. We could see it met with their approval and that, at least, I tried to think of as a good sign. The lack of a loan I tried to think of as a minor setback. The house was an A-frame style with the main bedroom upstairs, where we and Christophe would sleep. Louise would sleep in the guest bedroom just off the living room. We moved in all the things we had brought up for our two-month stay, and prepared lunch, which we ate outside on our terrace. What a pleasure to be in the fresh air with the sun beating down on our white bodies. We had bought Christophe an inflatable pool which we filled with water so that he could splash around and keep cool. He ran in to put on his little leopard print bathing suit, and jumped into the pool with screams of delight at the shock of the still cold water. Taro ran around him, barking with excitement and made us all laugh at their sheer joy. To hell with it, I would find a way to fix things with the bank on Monday.

Bright and early on Monday morning, I showed up at the bank to see what had happened. Apparently there was a document missing and without it we could not get the loan. It meant my going back down to New York to see about getting it and returning to deliver it to the bank. I had to enlist the help of my accountant, and my father's bank manager, to prepare the missing paperwork. I managed to get this done in two days and raced back up to the country to the bank. With my stomach in knots, I sat while the bank manager went over the missing proof of income, waiting with bated breath, for his verdict. When he was finished, he looked up and said that it seemed in order and he would approve the loan. I felt like dropping to my knees and thanking him and God for this wonderful news. I could not get out of there fast enough to ring Satoru to tell him the outcome. I was like a child let out of school to play. I drove back home as fast as I could, trying not to go above the posted speed limits, which, in itself, was a miracle of self-control. When I arrived, they were all out waiting for me, and we laughed and hugged each other.

We had lost three days, but we were now officially starting. We slid into the car and drove over to our land twenty minutes away. A little while after we got there, as we were sitting on the ground looking at the building plans, Mr. Rogers came over on his tractor, with his straw hat on his head at a rakish angle, and his inevitable cigarette hanging out of the corner of his mouth. Seeing us on the ground he said, "Hell, you can't start like that. I have a spare fold-up table and chairs that we can go fetch and bring back." We all went to pick them up, brought them over, placed them on a level spot under a tree, and we were officially in business. The perfect spot had to be chosen to place the house, the entrance driveway decided upon, and the man who would do the foundation. Mr. Rogers suggested a reliable builder he had used before, whom we called from his house to set an appointment for the next day. Mrs. Rogers invited us to go back to lunch with them a few hours later, which we gratefully accepted. They lived in a lovely old early-American colonial house, painted a light blue with white trim, with boxes of geraniums hanging outside the windows. They had four grown-up children, a daughter who had been married to an Air Force test pilot, who, we later found out, had died while testing a helicopter. She had been left alone to bring up their four children. They also had a son who was an officer in the Army, and two mentally retarded sons who lived with them. Despite all these trials, they were two of the kindest, most generous people we had ever met. We loved them, as I know they did us. We became their extended family with whom, over time, we shared our histories and our daily trials.

Christophe, Taro and Louise all went exploring, while Satoru and I walked around deciding where to place the house. It was to be a passive solar house, so the placement was very important. It had to have the right orientation to the sun and must not have a north facing front door. In China it is very bad luck to have a door that is facing north. Many things in the building of houses in Japan have considerations that come from Chinese traditions as well. In our wanderings we came upon an old foundation almost buried in the ground. We could barely make out its shape. The land also had low stone walls in different parts of the twenty five-acres, which, we supposed, must have been to separate, or make boundaries for, their animals. These were originally lands that belonged to the American Indians. In fact, when we bought the land, a search had to be made to make sure it was not still theirs. While we were looking around, Christophe came racing over to show us a stone arrowhead he had found while excavating with his shovel in the ground. It was all we could do that first day to stop from jumping up and down with excitement like children.

Mr. Rogers came over to see how we were doing and became our official adviser and counselor -- a position he took very seriously -- and we were very grateful to him for his commitment to our dream. At one o'clock we all went over to their house for lunch, washed our hands and eagerly took our places at the table. Mrs. Rogers said a prayer of thanksgiving for the food we were about to eat, and then we all dug in. She had cooked a delicious meal and for dessert she had made one of her famous apple pies, cooked with Northern Spy apples that were grown only in that area of Upstate New York. They were really special for pies, and I became an avid fan, driving miles to find them and the juice they made from the apples. There were a few hours of daylight left to establish the right spot, and by the time the sun was setting, we had decided where the house would sit, and where the driveway would enter the land.

We had spent a productive first day, and, satisfied, we headed back home for Christophe and Satoru to have a quick game of golf in the falling twilight. I prepared dinner, which we ate outside under the stars, after which we all went gratefully to bed for a good night's sleep. We were up bright and early to have breakfast, and set off to the land where we would meet with Mr. McCord to discuss building the foundation, and, most crucially, how much it would cost. Satoru had designed a system of separations within the outer walls, where hollow copper tubes would pass hot water through to heat the floor above. It made the construction a little more expensive, but the result would be much more economical in the long run, as a radiant floor would require less heating for the house. The hollow partitions were to be filled with Styrofoam to keep the cold out of the foundation. Satoru liked the builder and wanted to use him for the job; they decided on how to proceed and how he would be paid. I was in charge of ordering all the building materials that were not included in the Japanese shipment. I set about finding, ordering and paying for them. The construction loan worked in phases. A percentage at the completion of the foundation, and so on, till the building was finished.

I had never done anything like it before, but that certainly was no reason not to plunge in, and do what was needed to make this project become a reality. The next thing we had to worry about was the wood that would be used to build the house. We settled on pine, since it was plentiful and economical. With Mr. Rogers' help, we found a wood mill not far from Accord up in the hills, where we visited to see the quality of the wood, and if they could supply us with what we needed. Satoru and I were both fascinated with this part of the project, as we were learning something new every day. Working with Phillip Johnson, Satoru was not involved in the materials or supplies of a building. He was part of the design aspect and then the supervision of the building project. Satoru was one of the team for the Maiden Lane office building down in the Wall Street area that Phillip designed. Later he would follow the execution of the Lipstick building on Third Avenue, and be in charge of designing the canopy for the restaurant on the ground floor.

The emotions we felt as this project began to take shape were many and varied. Each step brought a new sense of accomplishment, and at times, desperation, if things did not work out as planned. There were hiccups along the way, but we got over them and were all the more proud when we had. As suppliers came and went with materials, our project excited more outside attention. Soon, word got around about what we were doing, and curious onlookers would stop by to ask questions. A Japanese country house around those parts was an exception and merited a look. We met many people of the area and exchanged frequent conversations with them. All of us learned a lot, and formed a sort of Japanese-American camaraderie. In the evenings, we would return home exhausted, but Satoru always found time to play a little golf with his son. I would have Christophe come and sit on my lap after dinner to cuddle, and would ask him to promise me that when he was too big for me to hold him, he would let me sit on his lap, to which we both always laughed. Mummy could be so silly! How Satoru and I both adored him. Sitting opposite each other, we would look deep into each others' eyes, so happy to have created this precious life.

Japan in America

The foundation work went mostly without major mishaps, and was finished in ten days. The wood was delivered, and we were set to receive the first four members of the Japanese contingent. This part was very exciting, as it would be the beginning of the wood joinery work, which was much anticipated by all of us involved in the project. The carpenters and Mitsuru, Satoru's brother, who was accompanying them to America, were due to arrive at 7:05 in the morning. We decided we had to rent another car for the week Mitsuru would be with us, as we would not all fit in ours. Satoru picked up the car the night before, as he had to leave at the crack of dawn the next morning. On their way back up, Satoru, not having slept enough, and exhausted from all the preparing and worry, and distracted with talking to them all, side-swiped a car in a takeover maneuver and dented the front of the rental car. This, of course, caused some delay and excitement, but they eventually got up to the country. I saw the damage and asked what happened and Mitsuru told me, with a resigned air, of Satoru's mishap. Bags and cases were unloaded and dropped off, and everyone climbed back into the cars, to see the site where they would be working.

Mitsuru was only staying for a week, to check that everything got off to a good start. He brought a video camera, on which he had recorded their departure from Japan. There was a video message from Satoru's mother and father wishing him much luck and success, Mitsuru and company arriving at Narita airport, what was happening on the plane, their arrival at JFK, Satoru's meeting them. There were also some shots of the drive up. He had bought the video camera for Satoru to record the whole building process, which he did. In all, there were hours and hours of footage. We were so amazed to see his parents' message and every step of Mitsuru's journey over. The power of video became immediately apparent, and from that moment on, we were aficionados, and video-taped many events in our lives.

From the moment they put their feet on American soil, they were off and running. Jet lag seemed not to have affected them; they were determined, concentrated and motivated. They represented their country, and its long history of building traditions, and every minute counted. We drove over, and as soon as we got there, they jumped out of the car, and the race was on. We saw them disperse in all directions, and the next thing we knew, they each chopped down a small tree and proceeded to make their wood hammers. My heart stood still as I saw what was happening, not realizing their purpose. These hammers were produced in a matter of minutes and were an indication of how organized, focused and speedy they were. Next, they found a proper place to dig a hole for their toilet facilities, an important concern for them, so as not to lose time.

In the middle of all this, Mr. Rogers came over on his tractor, with his inevitable cigarette hanging out of his mouth. Shortly after, Mrs. Rogers brought up the rear, and, in her warm and friendly way, welcomed everyone with her famous apple pie, which we all had for dessert after lunch. Mr. Rogers was soon offering his little bright yellow Honda Civic, to drive back and forth from his house to our land. Their tools would be stored at his house overnight for safety, as well as their packed lunches. They wanted to be in charge of their cooking, with one of them as the cook for the group, and the others his assistants. They only ate Japanese food. We had bought the important staples from New York, like Japanese rice, seaweed, spices, and sauces. The meats I would buy fresh, when needed. You could feel the excitement in the air. I could not believe we had actually come this far, and our adventure was to become a reality! Christophe was fascinated, and immediately made friends with the workers, and ran from one to the other, looking at what they were doing. They set up four work stations by stretching bright blue plastic covers, held at each of the four corners, to provide shade and cover in case of rain. Each would cut and chisel their allotted wood beams, which, when completed, would be joined to make the structure. Those of us who had never seen this procedure, wondered how on earth they could know, exactly, the measurements for each joint. It was like putting together pieces of a jigsaw puzzle. I was sure they would need to make adjustments once they started to interlock them.

That first day, I made their lunch, brought it over with me when we went there and we all sat down at the table that served for work and eating. We had many questions for our Japanese masters. Satoru translated for all of us, a task that could not have been easy for him as he was constantly needed for one question or another. That first day was an absolute eye-opener for us, as would be all the subsequent days of the building process. At the end of the afternoon, we all went back to the chalets -- the carpenters to play a bit of golf with Mitsuru, Satoru and Christophe, and Louise and I to prepare a Japanese dinner for us all. I remember that we cooked curry rice, a Japanese stew with meat and vegetables, thickened with a pre-prepared solid sauce called Golden Curry Sauce Mix that came in a package. It is added with water to the meat and vegetables, and cooks together for about forty minutes. It is served with white rice and eaten with a spoon. It is delicious, easy to use, and much appreciated by all of us. We followed it with a fresh salad, and fruit for dessert. Boy! Did that taste good, after our long day of excitement. By then, the carpenters were tired and drank their after-dinner glass of whiskey, and off to bed they went. Mitsuru stayed with us and we made him comfortable in our bedroom, while we made a bed on the couch in the living room.

We all slept like logs that first night and everyone was up by six a.m. for breakfast before heading to the site for the day's work. This routine was repeated, almost without variation, throughout the building process. Mitsuru stayed his week, to see that everything went off smoothly, and then Satoru drove him to the airport for his return to Japan. We could not have undertaken the project without him. We were eternally grateful for his invaluable help and support. He would continue to be our liaison between the construction company and the carpenters and plasterers when they arrived. When Satoru got back, he had to return the car to the rental company. I drove behind him with our car, and my mother, who had come over to visit us for the day. I have to say, the car really looked much the worse for wear. It now had a dent, the seats were dusty from the carpenters' ins and outs, and Taro's hair was all over the seats. You would think it had been through a war zone, it looked so bad inside and out. I was quite uncomfortable returning the car in such a condition, but due to the constant rush, with no time for anything else, we were not able to clean it up. Satoru came out of the rental place and told us, in his inimitable way, that the poor man almost fell in dismay at how the car looked. He said, "My God, what did you do to the car? It was brand new when you picked it up!" The way Satoru recounted it made us burst out laughing.

Deliveries came and went, inspectors showed up as scheduled, money was released at completion of each building phase, curiosity seekers came and went. Christophe was everyone's assistant and ran from one person to the other, amusing himself. His favorite pastime was driving the yellow Honda, sitting on the drivers lap, steering the car in the desired direction. Days were long, full of work for everyone. I was constantly on the phone ordering or going for things they needed. Day by day, the wood joints took shape. It was a proud day when the master beam was completed and set. A Shinto ceremony was held for the placement of it, and rice was put at the four corners of the house, for good luck. It was a solemn moment, significant for its roots in an ancient tradition. We were witnessing centuries of craftsmanship, handed down from father to son. There was a grace and beauty to all they did, from chopping wood, to cutting the shapes, to planing the wood beams. When each joint was finished, you could run your hands over it, and feel the smoothness. The artisans would be surrounded by the curls of shaved wood, which we would gather, and disperse over the land as fertilizer, as it would eventually disintegrate.

My parents would come over at the week-ends to see our progress, at which times we would have a long table set up for lunch where we would all eat the food they and we brought. I fondly remember those lunches, as they were jovial and fun, very relaxing and reassuring, for me, especially. My parents' presence was always a very welcomed warm reminder of their love for us. They were the foundation on which I stood tall, with confidence and pride. I don't know what I would have done without them. They were my sun, my moon, my everything, as were Satoru and Christophe. I could not have loved them more! Or have been more thankful for their impact in my life. Everything I did was in some way for them. They gave my life meaning.

When we first started going up to our land, before all this began, we had gone exploring the area and had found a wonderful restaurant called The Dupuy Canal House, which was owned by John Novi, a famous New York chef. It was a lovely, New England-type house, with pane windows and several rooms with fireplaces, where dining tables were set for lunches and dinners. John had a large wine cellar, with many different types of wines. People would drive two hours from New York, just to be able to eat his famous food. We went there one evening for dinner, having heard of his reputation, and had a truly stupendous meal. His wine steward was a large, rotund, charming man with curly black hair and a jovial, welcoming smile, named Steven Kolpan. We all immediately took a liking to each other and became fast friends. After dinner, he took us into the immaculate kitchen to meet John, so that we could complement him on his sumptuous meal. It was the beginning of a long and warm friendship with both of them. Steven, we would involve in our project firsthand, because his other profession was as a video artist. He would document our house project, and a video film, called "Premises" (Jo Ken), was the result. Steven would also be present at our group lunches, showing up with bottles of incredible wines, to which we all fell upon with joy. Everyone in our group was a wine aficionado and much appreciated Steven's contributions.

The wood joints finished, it was time to start fitting them to make the structure of the house. It was a magical day; what I referred to as the day of reckoning. I could not wait to witness this incredible feat. I have to say that it was the most amazing sight I had ever seen. The fact that each joint, when interlocked, fit exactly was nothing short of a miracle! Not one nail was used, and each piece was nudged into place with the wood hammers they had fashioned out of the small trees. This took a few days in all, and then came the walls of pine plywood, the windows, floors, ceilings, and room separations. Satoru had designed a reflecting pool that ran between the living room and the master bedroom, with a bridge over to the bedroom. Above it, there was a glass window that ran the same width as the pool, and in the day, the sunlight would reflect on the pool. It was very beautiful!

The kitchen was an extension of the living room and opened onto it. The dining area was next to the kitchen. My father and brother provided the cabinets in their Plexiglas material; they were a beautiful white, as was the counter that divided the space.

The time for the plasterers to arrive was approaching, and the shape of the house was becoming defined. On the ground floor was the living room, the master bedroom, the kitchen, the master bathroom and a Japanese Tea Room. The floor of the Tea Room would have Japanese Tatami mats, and all the windows and door openings would have Shoji screens for privacy. There was a second floor, where there would be two more bedrooms and a bathroom between them. We ran out of money for the upstairs part, so it was left unfinished. On the living room side, where they had made benches along one wall in front, they built a fire pit like in traditional Japanese houses. Around the edge, they made a frame out of wood, to put plates and such on. It was a wonderful touch and a great conversation piece.

The house came together like magic, every piece interlocked, and the art of beauty took shape in its design and execution. The wood was like velvet and it was a pleasure to run ones hands over it, to feel how smooth it was. The area over the living room and kitchen was all open with a very high ceiling, the master bedroom, bathroom and tea room had normal height ceilings, as the second floor was above them. Satoru had designed a beautiful bench outside the front door with a roof for shelter from the sun and rain, where one would take one's shoes off before entering the house. This was so Japanese, and reminded me of all the tea houses we had visited when we were in Japan. It was time for the carpenters to have their day off, and they chose to have Satoru take them to visit New York. He took them to all the important sights: the World Trade Center, the Empire State Building, the Seagram Building, Wall Street, Fifth Avenue and the Chrysler Building. He ended the day by taking them to Chinatown for dinner. They got back late, very happy to have seen the Big Apple!

The following week, Satoru would drive down to New York to pick up the two master plasterers, who were arriving in from Japan. Everyone was excited about their arrival, and the work they would be doing. He managed to go down and return, this time, without any mishaps, much to our relief. They, too, like their colleagues, wanted to be taken straight to the land to see what they would be dealing with. It was exciting to see them reunited with their friends, going over all the things that still had to be completed. They had brought fresh supplies of their favorite Japanese cigarettes, which were very much appreciated. Big-time smokers, this was very important, as, by now, they were dangerously close to running out. We had a party for everyone at our chalet that evening and afterwards, exhausted, everyone went to bed to recover.

The next day, bright and early, the work started again, this time, with six men, busy doing their assigned tasks. All the inside walls were to be done in the special Japanese plaster with the earth pigments. Each space had its own color, just as is the custom in Japan. They were very subtle shades of beige, olive, burnt Siena, and mustard. For the outside, we used American cement that was waterproof, in an off-white color which went well with the exposed wood frame of the house. The pace was fast as before, and it was quite a feat for me to keep up with all the various requests for one thing or another. Satoru was in his element, busy all the time, but happy to see his masterpiece come to life. I vividly remember his tilted smile when he was happy about how something looked. The Rogers were a blessing all the way through, helping in emergencies and unexpected events, of which there were many with a project such as ours. I recall one time when we took the entire Japanese contingent and Louise to the Dupuy Canal House to have a dinner out for a change. We arranged to leave Christophe with the Rogers. When we took him over to drop him off and Mrs. Rogers came to the door, the first thing he asked her was, "Do you know how to clean bottoms?" in case he had to go to the bathroom to do number two. We all laughed and he looked at us, with surprise on his face, not understanding what was so funny about his simple request. I took him in my arms and squeezed him with love!

GRAND GESTURES

The plasterers' work was very different from the carpenters. They were also not as friendly, as they had come later, and, I thought, probably felt they had missed the excitement of the beginning. Their work, nevertheless, was fascinating and whenever I had time, I would watch them weave their magic. My last big assignment was renting a U-Haul truck to go down to Queens to pick up the Mexican terra cotta tiles that would cover the living, dining and kitchen areas. I left bright and early, a bit worried about doing this on my own, but steeling myself to complete my task. The drive down was no problem; finding the place was a little more complicated, but with a lot of stopping and asking, I eventually found the place. I must say I was stunned to see how many flats there were, and they barely fit into the truck. As they were being loaded, I could see the truck's body lowering perilously close to the wheels, ending up with very little space between. I was going to have to drive very slowly in order to keep moving forward. Slight inclines were murder, and since it was traffic time, driving was nerve-racking. Every swirl of wind rocked the van from side to side, and I felt at any moment it might tip over. I said my prayers many times on the way up, asking, Why, Oh, Why, did I keep getting myself into such impossible situations! I admit to being terrified and was so relieved when I finally made it up safely. I was greeted with cheers by everyone when they saw what a feat I had accomplished.

The second day of rest was due and there was a big discussion. The men had all wanted to go to Niagara Falls, but there really was not enough time, as it would be a two-day affair. The carpenters did not want to take the extra day and the plasterers did. They were at an impasse, which did not help the already tense situation. It was resolved that Satoru would take them to a very nice golf course near Woodstock and, at the end of the day, they had a typical American meal of hamburgers and French fries. They ended by going to a pub, drinking and singing Japanese songs for the locals, much to everyone's amusement. They returned late, drunk and satisfied with their excursion. The last days of their work went without a hitch and we held the last Shinto ceremony to bless the house with sake and rice. It was a triumphant moment to which everyone involved was present: we, the Rogers, Mr. Mc Cord, the foundation man, and my parents. We had a big lunch laid out after the ceremony, sake was poured, and toasts were made till we all got drunk, and Satoru and the Japanese contingent sang their wonderful Japanese folk songs for us. It marked the end of an incredible adventure of learning, experiencing and believing. A beautiful expression of an old culture had been brought to life for all to see and feel. Satoru had created a beautiful testament to his heritage.

We had wanted to see the artisans off in style, and ordered a stretch limousine to take them to the airport from our loft, where we had all returned the previous day. We were up for the early departure, waiting for the limo. A half-hour passed and still no limo, so we called the company who told us it was on its way. The limousine never showed up. Satoru and I were so disappointed, but there was nothing to do except for Satoru to drive like a demon to the airport himself. He managed to get them there just in the nick of time, as they jumped out, grabbed their cases and ran like hell to Japan Airlines, while Satoru parked the car. He barely made it back in time to say goodbye and wish them well. I, in the meantime, called the limo company to find out what had happened. The driver had got into an accident and realized he would not be able to make it, so he returned to the garage and no one bothered to call us; so much for grand ideas and limousine companies.

It was time to return to our jobs and to make a division in our loft to create a one bedroom apartment that we could rent to pay for the building loan we had taken out. Since the loft was 3,500 sq. ft, we had the space, and it did not interfere with the layout. We were able to rent it almost immediately and assured ourselves of paying for the loan we had taken out. Flexibility and ingenuity had been our calling to fix all manner of problems. I thank the powers that be for endowing us with this ability. Christophe went back to school and it was time for Louise to return to Sweden. She had been with us for two years, becoming almost a family member. We would all miss her terribly, but understood that she had to get on with her life. To this day, we still communicate with her. She is married and has two children and seems very happy.

We loved going up to our new house at week-ends and it never ceased to amaze us that we had actually got it built. It was now time for us to start on our mutual project with Steven Kolpan to make our video piece on the house. It was to be called "Premises" (Jo Ken), and consisted of an interview by Steven of Satoru and his design concept, a water scene I had created as a purification ceremony for the house, and the result of the architectural project. This we worked at on week-ends until all the footage was complete, and then Steven concentrated on the editing and the completion of the video. He showed it at many video festivals and it was very well-received. We both loved doing the project and working with Steven. He was such a generous artist and human being, we felt blessed to have him as a collaborator and friend.

When sending the video around for video performances, this was how Steven described our collaboration:

PREMISES (JO KEN)
Is composed of choreographer/performance artist,
Susana Hayman-Chaffey, architect/set designer,
Satoru Oishi and video artist/critic Steven Kolpan

The work of the group encompasses the fields of
performance, architecture and intentional environment,
and electronic media. The three artists do not strive
for aesthetic integration, but rather try to stress
both the obvious and the subtle influences of the
cultures of Japan, Europe and the United States.

Video = Japanese technology in America

Architecture = Japanese tradition in America

Performance = European/American response
to Japan in the United States

Susana Hayman-Chaffey is a well-known modern
dance choreographer. As a dancer, Susana
performed with the world-renowned Merce
Cunningham Dance Company for eight years.

Satoru Oishi's work encompasses the traditions of Japan
and the corporate architecture of the United States. As
an architect for the firm of Phillip Johnson and John
Burgee, Satoru has been instrumental in undertaking
projects on a grand scale. As the founder of Zogo Design,
he designs traditional Japanese houses in the United
States. Satoru is also a master of the Cha-No-Yu Tea
Ceremony, and teaches this ritual in New York City.

Steven Kolpan is a pioneer in video and multimedia as an
art form. Since 1970 he has shown his work extensively and
taught in many colleges. His video tapes and installations
have been exhibited in the Americas, Europe and Japan.

Steven submitted the video to many festivals all over the world
and I presented it in Japan a few years later as part of an American
Japanese art festival held at Spiral, a performance space in Tokyo.

After the work on the video was finished, our week-ends up in
the country were always magical. We would go for long walks in
the surrounding fields with Christophe and Taro, who loved the
freedom of running alongside us. Since my parents had a house on
the opposite side of the Hudson, we would drive over to them for
lunch on a Saturday or Sunday, and then they would come over to
us the next week-end. We all enjoyed spending time together, as we
were very close. My father was wonderful with Christophe, always
introducing new ideas and questions for him to answer. Papa would
become a child and Christophe would become an adult, and it was
fascinating to see them interact together. Mama was always the
mother to us all, warm, kind, gentle, understanding.

As the months passed, we were becoming increasingly aware that
our mortgage payments and the credit lines we had taken to build the

house were putting us in a financial bind, even with the extra rental income. We realized that we would have to sell our lovely creation. We contacted the agent who had sold us the land, and asked her to list it with ten acres, so that we could keep the other fifteen for future projects. It was a sad decision, but one that had to be taken. She showed it to quite a few people and every time our hearts would rise in hopes of a sale. It took over a year, and as the second spring was approaching, it seemed she might have a buyer. She was a jeweler who, it turned out, had been married to a member of a very prominent family. She fell in love with the house. There was much negotiating back and forth with the price and the acreage, as she wanted the whole parcel. We stood firm on the land and gave a little on the price. We had put it very close to our cost, in order to sell it quickly, so we did not have much room to go lower. Finally, in July, the closing was set and we all met with the lawyers. In a matter of an hour, we were no longer the owners of Satoru's beautiful Japanese country house. We struggled with the sadness of loosing it and the relief of getting out from under a large debt we could not maintain. To console ourselves, we decided to go to Italy for a three-week holiday.

For some reason, my father was very insistent that we not go, as it was an added expense and he would have liked us to stay near. It was strange, as he never stopped us from travelling or going away on holiday. I was adamant, though, so we went as planned, in August for three weeks. Taro remained with my parents. We flew to London, as it was cheaper that way, and stayed with our dear friend, Catherine Althaus Addison, at her lovely house in Chelsea. Papa had met her when he was in England doing an article for *O'Cruceiro*, the Brazilian magazine he did stories for. She and her husband were charming and we spent a few wonderful days with them. We took a cheap flight to Rome and rented a car to drive up to Tuscany to visit Nieves, where we would stay for part of our trip. We had brought over our video camera to record all the events of the holiday, which provided us with a first-hand account of what we had done. At first, no one was too pleased to be constantly on video, but, after a while, they no longer noticed.

Nieve's son, Bishi, and his wife, Marianne, were staying on holiday with their children. Bishi's sister, Beatrice, came over with her family from Montalcino. It was a full house and provided a lot of enjoyment for all of us. We had large, rowdy lunches in the garden, everyone involved helping with some task, and I remember that period as being a warm time spent with great friends in a very loving atmosphere. Towards the end of our stay, Christophe woke up in the middle of the night crying, as he had had a nightmare in which his grandpa Maxi and grandma Tricia had died in a car accident. Maxi was the name my father had told Christophe he should call him. He did not want to be called Grandpa and so told Christophe that he should be called Maximilian, but Christophe could call him Maxi for short. We were shocked, but held him close and reassured him that they were fine, and there was nothing to worry about. The next day, on recounting this to Nieves at breakfast, she mentioned that I really should try to get more of a distance from my parents. She felt that I should be more independent. I tried to explain to her that I needed to be close to them, as I did not know how long I would share their presence. We had always been very close: my father designed the costumes and lighting for my own performances, and my mother was my publicist and all-around helper. She and I also had a telepathic communication, so it seemed absolutely pointless to think of life without them, though I knew that it was hard for people to accept that a family can have such binding ties. We were a unit artistically, as well as spiritually. As I was saying this to her, I started crying and cried on and off for the remaining two days we were there. I could not explain the terrible sense of loss I felt, as they were alive and well in New York.

From there we went to Venice for a few days to show it to Christophe. I cannot think of a more romantic city: the gondolas, with couples in love drifting on the canals, the beautiful bridges to walk over -- everything is truly filled with magic. Christophe loved standing in Saint Mark's Square, feeding the pigeons that landed on his hand to eat the corn we had just bought from a vendor. The churches, the art, the history, are a constant reminder of the greatness that is the story of Venice. We were in love with each other and that magnificent city. The boat rides from one section to another were always an adventure, which particularly delighted Christophe. The last day we rushed around looking for presents for my parents and the Rogers, then regretfully had to leave to go back to Rome for a day before flying on to London.

THE ACCIDENT

We stayed in London for a few days before flying back to New York. We almost postponed leaving to hear Seiji Osawa conduct the London Philharmonic, but good sense made us leave as planned. My parents picked us up at the airport on Wednesday and we had dinner with them that evening, planning to go up early Saturday morning to their country house for the week-end. We had also left our car in their garage while we were in Italy and had to collect it. On the way up, we passed what looked like a terrible accident, and we all thought how sad for the poor people involved.

The one-and-a-half-hour journey was filled with talk of our holiday and what had been happening with them. We had an extraordinary exchange about the quality of life, what Papa thought about his dealings with Nevemar (part of International Paper), and how he and my brother, Charles, would be concluding a licensing agreement for their Acrylic Surfacing patent. It was actually my brother who insisted they get the patent, as Papa was not of the mindset to protect that which they had invented, partly because of the cost. They had been working on this for years, and now they were at the signing stage. It had been a much anticipated event for their company, and would mean a big expansion of the product on the market -- with the added advantage of a whole other income level for them. They were very excited and anxious to get the contract signed. They had spent their lives worrying about money, making ends meet. This was their opportunity to live comfortably at long last.

We arrived at their house around ten in the morning, ran in to put our bathing suits on and plunged into the inviting pool to cool off. Christophe played with Maxi and Tricia, jumping in and out of the pool, seeing who could make the biggest splash. A lot of water ended up on the slate deck. Mama and I went in to prepare lunch, after which we all sat outside under an umbrella and had a delicious meal. My father talked about wanting to go ahead with Satoru's plans to expand their house, something that they had started thinking about during the building of our Japanese house. We were so happy to hear this as it was a confirmation of Papa's belief in Satoru as an architect. We showed them the video tapes we had taken of our holiday in Italy, so they were able to see their old friends, whom they had not seen in years. I was happy that we were able to bring them those memories, making a perfect ending to a beautiful day with them. The plan was that my father would leave early Sunday morning to pick up the head of Nevemar at JFK for their very important signing of the documents to conclude their agreement. Tired after a long day, Papa and Mama went to bed early and Satoru and I stayed up to talk a bit longer. My mother was going to stay with us and drive over to our neighbors on the other side of the Hudson. We were going to visit them to say hello and give them the presents we had brought back from Italy. At the last moment, before she went to bed, she had decided to return to New York with Papa.

We awoke around 7:30 in the morning and went about washing, dressing and having breakfast. Mama and Papa had told us they would be leaving at 6:00 a.m. Soon after, I called my parents' apartment in New York to see if they had got in alright. I got no answer, so I called my brother to see if he had heard from them, but he had not either. I felt a slight sense of worry, but not excessive, as I thought that maybe they had planned to both go straight to the airport, and, therefore, were not home yet. We thought we would wait a bit and hope to hear from them soon. This was difficult; I was getting more and more nervous as time went on. I called the State Troopers to see if any accidents had been reported. None had, but I was worried anyway.

I called Charles to say that no accidents had been reported, and asked him if he had any news. He had not heard anything, so Satoru, Christophe and I left to go over to the Rogers' house. When we arrived and I called him, there was still no word, so we gave the Rodgers the presents we had brought back for them and had a cup of coffee. We had not been there more than ten minutes, when the phone rang and it was Charles. Mr. Rogers passed me the phone. My brother said, "Papa and Mama had an accident and they both died instantly." I felt a terrible chill run all through me and let out an anguished, "No! It has to be a mistake!" My brother gave me the State Police's address so that I could stop by on the way down to New York to pick up their personal effects. Looking back to the day before, I could not get over what incredible luck we had, to exchange all the thoughts and plans for the future the way we did. Satoru, Christophe and I would forever be grateful, that even with the abruptness of their death, we had been mercifully granted that last perfect day. We had, without knowing it, said our last goodbyes to each other.

Their car, a big Lincoln Continental, had hydroplaned in the pouring rain. It seems Papa was driving too fast for the weather conditions and hit a stone on the side of the embankment that sent them sailing up into the air and smashed them against a tree. Some people in another car, who saw what happened, stopped to put out the fire that had started, and called the police. They told them that my parents had died instantly, and probably did not feel anything. I have tortured myself about whether they realized what was about to happen, what went through their minds and whether they felt any pain. But such thoughts are useless, as we will never know. After many years, I have tried to give myself some peace over this, and try not to think about it, but it is always just within reach. I only hope that they did not have time for anything, and that it was all over in a blinding instant. The absurd thing is that the stone they hit was the only one in a very large bank of grass, and, had they not hit it, they could probably have come out of it. Destiny and fate are the deciders and obviously, their time was up. God, oh, God, have Mercy on us who are left behind! It took me two years to accept that it was, indeed, their time, and that they had completed what they had come on this earth to do, how difficult it was for us to let go.

The weather was awful; pouring down with rain. All I could think of was that maybe on the way back down, the State troopers would realize there had been a mistake. We took our leave of Mr. and Mrs. Rogers, poor things. How they must have worried about us driving down. I remember gripping the wheel of our car, my knuckles white, straining to see the road through the sheets of rain.

A part of me wished to die somehow, and the other held on for dear life. We finally arrived at the State Police offices and were given my father's briefcase and my mother's bag. That moment was when it finally sank in, that they were gone. Fate had left us abandoned and alone. We would no longer have their protection, their concern, their caring. How on earth could I go on? They were the reason for my very existence: everything I had done up to then was for them. Now what was I going to do? The State trooper asked if we wanted to see their bodies, but, at that moment, it seemed morbid to want to do that, so we refused. However, we had to go to the hospital, where they had been taken, to pick up my mother's jewellery and my father's signet ring and watch.

As we drove up to the hospital, our neighbors' daughter, Janice, was waiting for us, as if a miracle had brought her there. The Rogers had called her and told her to meet us, as she lived not far away. It was an overwhelming relief to see her standing there waiting for us. We hugged and cried and the first thing she asked us was, "Are you going to see them?" When I said, "No," she said, "You must see them, so that you can accept that they have passed away, otherwise you will not be able to." She had lost her husband, an Air Force pilot, who had died while testing a helicopter, so she had not been able to see his body, and had not had closure. On her advice, we picked up my parents' things and went to the morgue, where they had been taken, but it had already closed. It was arranged that we would see them at the funeral chapel we had chosen in New York. I asked that nobody should touch them, to leave them as they were. We took our leave of Janice, forever grateful for her caring and advice. On the way down to New York, Satoru told me that around two or three in the morning, Mama had looked in on us, and it felt almost like she were saying good-bye. It makes me so sad to try and imagine what she was thinking or felt; and what had got her out of bed to come and check on us. There were so many things we would never know or understand. I have often wondered why she changed her mind to go down with Papa, instead of coming with us.

I don't think I could have borne the terrible pain I felt had I not crossed paths with so many extraordinary people, like Janice. They had enriched my experiences, taught me valuable lessons and shared unstintingly of their warmth and kindness. It was truly a miracle! Despite this difficult life lesson I had to experience, I still felt that it was a great privilege to partake of all that it meant to be alive. Yet, the anger inside about being abandoned was overwhelming, and I could not understand why I had to learn this lesson as well. But I had to believe that staying alive was also a miracle. I tried to breathe deeply to help the pain, but despite all the breathing I was trying to practice, the pain and absolute blinding sorrow would not go away.

I felt angry for them, as they had worked so hard all their lives and struggled financially with all the ups and downs. Now that Papa and Charles's company was finally going to produce an income on which they could live comfortably, they had been robbed of that satisfaction. My mother had reached sixty-five and could retire and finally have time to do what she wanted. She would not be alive to enjoy it. Papa was sixty-seven and he, too, could have taken it easier and enjoyed the fruits of his labors. How unfair it all seemed to me!

RITUALS

Janice gave us some homeopathic remedies to help with the emotional pain and the crying. One, I remember, was belladonna. Having always used Homeopathy and Homeopathic doctors growing up, I continued to believe in its power to help. It was truly a godsend at this highly emotional time, as just the deep breathing was not enough. We arrived back at my parents' apartment only to find my brother not there, but he returned soon after. I suggested that he also see our parents, as Janice had convinced me, when they would be at Frank E. Campbell's Funeral Chapel. We had dinner together and then went back downtown to our loft, agreeing to return to the apartment the next day. Our uncle Don and his wife, Paula, were arriving from Los Angeles, and my brother's girlfriend, Louisa was coming in from Rome.

The next day, as arranged, we went to the funeral home to see Mama and Papa. I remember my mother's eyes were open, as if she wanted to see us, like she was still alive. She was beautiful. Her hair was still damp and brushed back and it was so natural. Papa, unfortunately, due to the sliding sun roof being bent inwards with the impact, lost a part of his head. It was a terrible shock to see. All I could keep repeating was, "My poor babies," over and over again, as if, somehow, they had become my children. I was grateful to be able to see them, but the pain was overwhelming. My body and spirit felt like they weighed hundreds of pounds. As my universe had come crashing down on me, I felt crushed, lifeless, resigned to oblivion. I wanted to give up on life, but I knew I would have to go on, broken and crippled, for my husband and son. I remain to this day, so thankful that mama and papa were left as they had been found, and we could see them as they were. I remember how delicate the director and his staff were. I am forever grateful to them.

From there, we went to the airport and picked up uncle Don and Paula. It was good to have their presence: at least having my godfather (my father's older brother) there gave me a small feeling of security. He would be able to take charge and be a support at this awful time in our lives. When we returned home, I called Kenneth, my father's younger brother, to tell him the news and to give him the option of coming over for the funeral. I offered to pay for his flight and transport up to London to catch the plane. He wanted to come over, so I immediately called our dearest family friend, Peter ffrench-Hodges at the British Tourist Authority in London, and asked him to arrange the whole thing for me, which, bless his heart, he did in a flash, and got Kenneth on a plane the next day. He arrived the morning of the funeral and I was so glad that I was able, with Peter's help, to get him over.

The funeral took place on September 16, 1987, at 2:00 p.m. at the Frank E. Campbell Funeral Chapel on Madison Avenue and 81st Street. I had told my brother on the day of the accident to call them and arrange the funeral. I remembered that Irving Marantz, a great painter and sculptor friend of our family, had his memorial there. It was an hour service of remembrance, and, according to all who attended, a very moving and spiritually uplifting event, which is what both of our dearest ones would have wanted. We had ordered Birds of Paradise to be put next to Papa's casket and yellow Chrysanthemums next to Mama's. I had remembered that they were her favorite flower, as many years before, with the first monies I earned in New York, I had a standing order with a florist in Minneapolis to send her a dozen every Saturday.

We had decided to leave the lids open so that others, like us, could have closure. Papa's head, where it was hurt, had been put against the coffin wall so it did not show the damage too much. The question arose whether we would let our son Christophe see them or not, as he was only seven, but we thought that it should be up to him. He decided that he wanted to see them. He, with great calmness and aplomb, went over to them and laid a red rose, which Mehlika had given him, on each of them. I think it was the right decision.

We had wanted the funeral service to be a respectful mix of what their lives had signified and were. It should comprise laughter, tears, beauty, drama, poetry and, most of all, be human as they were. My cousin, Nicolette, sat between my brother and me, and Christophe sat between me and Satoru with Uncle Don sitting on Satoru's other side. Charles and I had taken our Homeopathic remedies against crying, as I felt our parents would not have been happy if we had. We sat in our seats holding hands, squeezing for dear life to keep from crying.

We started by playing Papa's favorite music -- Beethoven's 5th Symphony, for about five minutes. It was his "Piece de Resistance" to be played loud and clear, to stress a point, as an indication of his character. He was larger than life, explosive, fragile, intoxicating and, at times, deeply insecure; the consummate artist who carried all the perplexities of life in his soul. Don, his elder brother, and my godfather, was the first to go up and began by telling everyone that this was a " happening." He went on to describe a happening that Papa had orchestrated with other painter friends of his, in Rome, in the '60s. I remember that he was so nervous; he kept pulling his handkerchief out of his pocket to blow his nose. He was a film director and a really wonderful narrator with a fabulous sense of humor. Nicolette, his daughter, my cousin, and a wonderful actress, was wearing a soft grey dress with a gorgeous hat that had a beautiful feather on it and looked regal. She recited a poem by Yeats that Mama had sent her mother, Edna, many years before, when she had become ill with cancer. Once again, Don returned to the lectern and read Papa's words written on the occasion of his wife's death. It was an extraordinary piece that described his feelings on life and death. It was uncanny, in that it was as if Papa were there, saying the words through Don, for his own funeral.

We played a beautiful song by country singer Jimmy Dean called "Yes, Patricia, There is a Santa Claus." It was a song that Papa and I heard on the radio just before Christmas many years previously, when we were driving his car in Minneapolis where they lived at the time. It was so moving and such an appropriate gift for Mama, that we promptly went all over looking for it to give her that Christmas. When she opened the present and we heard the words, we all started crying. We loved her so much!!!! My father's play name for her was "Chief Sitting Pretty Face." She really was our chief! The lyrics spoke about believing, no matter what, and having faith, which is what we felt Mama always did with all of us. I wanted everyone at the funeral to be encouraged by the words. My mother, the eternal child, full of faith, full of curiosity, was at the same time, stronger and more organized than any of us. She was the glue that held us together, the arbitrator between us and the note of common sense when we would all fly off in different directions with ideas, thoughts, and conflicts. She always had the ability to bring us down to earth, and when we were grounded, lifted us up with that child-like side of her character. I have spent much time trying to imitate that part of her, and, sometimes, when I can pull it off, I think of her, and hope that she is watching with approval. It was a "tear-jerker," as they say, and there wasn't a dry eye to be seen after it. The tears were important, not for sadness, but for the hope that the words inspired and the belief they talked about.

I followed this by saying a few words that our lifelong friend, Nieves de Madariaga, had asked me to say on her behalf. The words were: "Federico remember? Once you drove us into the sea. Because you were driving, I knew it was all right. Now I know it is all right, too!" I recounted that she was referring to a week-end out of Mexico City in the early fifties, when they had rented a car to go to Tuxpan to be by the seaside. It seems it was raining very hard also that time, and Papa was driving along the sand. Nieves and Patricia warned him several times that he was driving too close to the sea, and he kept answering, "Nonsense," I am on the beach." As it became more obvious that they were, indeed, in the sea up to the doors, he managed to point the car in the right direction and everyone got out and pushed. That time we were all spared, and spent the next day drying out the rented car, and wiping the engine with motor oil so that the rental car people would not realize the car had been up to its gills in sea water. It was reason to have a great laugh and provided an unusual beachside activity.

Next, it was my turn, and I had decided to do the water ritual that I had created for our video film, "Premises" on the building of our Japanese country house in Upstate New York in 1983. It was a sort of purification ritual that both Mama and Papa had very much appreciated when I had performed it for them, and I thought it was appropriate for this occasion. I was dressed in a beautiful Rei Kawabuko black linen dress with a black silk turtleneck. It was a very slow motion ritual that gave importance to each and every action. On the lectern, I placed a large white bowl to my right, and in front, a beautiful Tiffany crystal flower vase, given as a gift to Satoru by his Tea Ceremony students, filled with water. I placed my hands at either side of it, resting on the surface. I lifted my hands to slide up the side of the vase until they reached the neck of it, where my hands surrounded it and lifted it in front of me; gradually I tilted my whole torso to the right and poured all the water into the empty white bowl.

After the last drop had fallen, I returned the vase to a space on my left, sliding my hands down its sides and, just off the surface, across to the white bowl, where they travelled up its rim. I then picked it up and brought it over my head and suspended it for a moment, while I said a silent prayer for Mama and Papa. I then, very slowly, began to pour all the water over my head and face. It was a difficult moment, as the water made it difficult to breathe till the last drops fell. I then rested the bowl in front of me, and slowly looked up and out at the people gathered there. At this point, I brought my right hand up to my lips and placed a kiss in it and curled my fingers to enclose it. I then reached out with it in the direction of the caskets, and slowly released the kiss blowing it away to sail toward them. The kiss action had been given to me by James Lee Byers, a conceptual artist friend, as a ritual I could perform when I desired.

To follow, my brother went to take his place and read some words he had written for our parents, and managed to do it without crying. I was glad for him, as I could see how difficult it was. Don returned and recounted another anecdote, which I cannot recall, and then thanked everyone for coming and asked if anyone else wanted to say something about Frederick and Patricia. Mama's boss did, and their personal doctor, as well. We then played a recording of "Amazing Grace" by the Scottish Grenadiers, as it was one of my father's favorite pieces and reflected our Scottish side, where the Hayman part of our name comes from. I am so proud of all of us for having had the courage and humanity to create a very beautiful event in honor of two extraordinary human beings.

The ceremony over, we said goodbye to all who had come to pay their last respects, and, with our close family and friends, piled into the four limousines we had ordered. They took us out to Riverdale to the Crematorium, and we said our last farewells to our beloved parents and sadly left to return to their apartment, for a buffet lunch we had prepared for everyone. It was all an enormous strain and very exhausting. As it is with our family, this was not without its drama, as three of my brother's lady friends, one ex-wife, Harley, one ex-lover, Natalie, and the present lover, Maria Luisa, were all there and none knew about the other. Charles had forgotten to assign a seat in the limousines for Natalie, and, in a panic, he came to ours and asked to squeeze her in with us, which, of course, was no problem: we were all used to this. At the apartment, Harley realized that something was strange, left in a huff. Maria Luisa, not knowing about Natalie, asked me who she was. I had to pretend she was just an old friend of the family, as she was threatening to take the first plane back to Italy. Natalie asked the same question and I repeated to her the same excuse.

This has been a recurring thing with my brother, always having us cover for him and his women. I suppose it could be considered endearing, although, I must say, I could have done without the extra drama that those entire goings on entailed. He has always been fascinating to women and he, fascinated by them, but unable to deal with the complications that came about by his games. His logic was that they were all adults and, therefore, should be able to cope; none of his women, however, ever saw it that way, unfortunately for him. In all fairness to Charles, he used to run interference for me with my father when we were growing up, when I was out with some boyfriend or other that he was not very happy about.

FAMILY AND FRIENDS

Mehlika had flown over from Rome, to represent her family, the Ten Dams, who had been our dearest friends when we were living in Rome. She had that rare quality of empathy that very few people ever achieve. I remember her quiet presence arranging, helping, and organizing, all unobtrusively and silently. I was unable to eat anything, or very little, for several days, and she just kept a cup of tea with honey near me to drink. She kept me alive with those endless teas, as they gave me the stamina I needed to hold up under the strain of it all. She later wrote us a letter from Rome apologizing for her silence, as she felt she did not want to intrude on our pain. Mehlika is an extraordinary, humble human being, whom it is my privilege, to call my friend still today.

We all stayed at the apartment, as Charles wanted us all to be together; I would have preferred to go home to sleep, but I respected his wishes. Don appointed himself cook and whoever was willing, became his assistant. I did most of the food shopping and helped as well. The morning after the funeral, we were all sitting at breakfast, I was in my father's seat and expressed my sadness at the fact that they had not said goodbye. Soon after I said that, we heard a huge noise out in the hall where the bookshelves were, where cabinets held our parents' personal papers, files, and other effects. We all went flying out to see what had happened, and found that one of the cabinets had burst open (we don't know how, as the doors had to be pushed inward for the catch that held them closed to be released), and out had fallen lots of loose photographs and a large collection of coins from all over the world. I bent down and picked up a photo of them both sitting in the garden of my mother's parents in Hastings, holding hands, smiling. We all got goose bumps, as it was clear that they had answered my plea, and were telling us that they were happy and together and not to worry. All the spilled coins signified that we were well taken care of in that way as well. It was to be the first of many manifestations I had from them during a period of two years, when I had needed to hold on to them.

It was decided that we would all go up to their house in the country on Friday night for the week-end, to plant all the bulbs my mother had ordered and were waiting to be put in the ground. On the way, we arranged to go and see the car and the spot where the accident had taken place. The car had been completely smashed, there was no escaping that, and, at the site, we saw that there had probably been many other accidents in that spot as it was on a sharp curve. We found one of mama's shoes and many other things that indicated others had met a sorry end there. We left several bunches of flowers. I was to go back there many times after with Satoru and Christophe. It was about a year later that the Taconic Highway Authority re-did that whole area and we could no longer recognize where it had happened.

We then proceeded up to the house to prepare and have lunch. Afterwards, all of us went into the garden to plant the hundreds of bulbs we had brought up with us. It kept us busy all afternoon, and, Charles and I had decided we would each use the house on alternate week-ends. We were privileged to see all the flowers bloom gloriously that next spring. It proved to be a very positive and tranquil week-end, after all the heart-wrenching pain re-awaked every time some dear acquaintance dropped by to express their condolences. That was so hard, as no sooner would I regain my composure, then someone else arrived and I'd be plunged into the abyss again. So the week-end was a much-needed healing respite, spent quietly with family and friends. On Sunday night we went back to the city, as the next day everyone, except Don and his wife, left to go back to their respective homes. We returned to our loft and resumed our daily lives as best we could.

The next few days were spent answering all the many notes sent to us, and I went out to look for a card that I could send to everyone that would, in some way, express something about my parents and me. I found what I considered to be the perfect card. It was the photograph of a little girl and boy beautifully dressed with their backs to us walking in a garden, and the title was, "The Walk to Paradise Garden." It seemed absolutely appropriate for the occasion. The photograph was a reproduction of an original painting by Eugene Smith. On one side of the two children were written the words:

> "A walk into the Paradise
> With you;
> The day is warm and fulsome
> The garden bright with splendor
> And in the dazzling light, your smile
> Commands
> Me not to ask more questions
> All I ever wanted is here
> Let it be enough, just now with you."

I folded it in two and wrote in the inside. It had the advantage of not being too big, so that I did not have to write a lot, as it was still very difficult to deal with the memory. I remember I photocopied everything I wrote and I am so glad, because I have been able to look back over the years at them, and realize just how much everyone cared and how I was able to respond to that caring. I include some of the notes, as, in a way, they express my pain at that moment in time.

From Tina Ten Dam: our very dear friend from our time in Rome.

Dearest Susana, Charles, Satoru and Christophe,

What terrible news! Ab called me this morning to tell me. I had difficulty coming through to you on the phone and when at last I got a line I was not capable of controlling my voice or my tears.

Such an unexpected loss of two loved ones at a time must be almost impossible to bear. I wish we could be with you to give moral support, if such a thing is possible in such circumstances. I am glad that Mehlika is going to join you. Being younger and fitter, her presence will be of more use to you than ours. We will be with you in our thoughts.

    Satoru told me that Fred and Patricia had died instantly, luckily for them. I think neither of them would have wanted to put up with a major handicap or a lengthy and painful recovery. They probably would have wanted to go like this, together in a flash, in the same way they had lived. I am thinking of all the things you will have to do. Charles is going to have an additional burden, having to shoulder the responsibility of the business alone. How is Christophe coping? Having had such a special bond with Fred and Patricia, it will be more difficult for him than other children who lose run of the mill grandparents. Give him an extra hug from me, poor thing. I wish you all the courage you will so badly need in these days. Mehlika will give us all the particulars when she comes back. All our love and sympathy goes with this letter. Take care. Tina and Joke

My answer inside the card:

Dear Ab and Tina,

Thank-you for your kind wonderful letter! I write a short note now as I cannot sit down and write much more due to time and the emotional problems involved. It has been total devastation. I feel as a handicapped person, as if I lost my sight or a leg. Having to re-learn everything again, having to come to terms with what fate has given us. The anger I feel, the sadness, the total and absolute pain of this experience. Mehlika has been extraordinary and we are so grateful for her presence here and her subsequent telephone calls. With all my love, Susana

Dearest Susana, Satoru and Christophe,

What can I possibly say, only that we love you all very much. That your video bringing all the love and joy and connection of your family to ours may have been the last image your parents carried with them- one of light, happiness and joy, amidst the usual quarrels and fracasos of family life. That you had the art to provide this gift must comfort you for all that was never said. Though I never met Fred and Patricia only that one evening- they are part of our family history, as so we grieve. And I know what wonderful and unique people they were from the daughter they created- Susana, may your beautiful child and husband comfort you- all our prayers will be with you in the days ahead.

All our love,
Marianne, Christopher and the children.

Dear Marianne and Christopher,

Thank-you both for your beautiful words on paper and on tape, they were very moving and gratefully received. It is still too soon to sit down and write without breaking down. So for now, just a short note to thank-you for your thoughts, it is a long road ahead and I feel weary before I even begin. We were so close so much in love with each other, our spirits were connected and I know in my mind that since that was the case why should the departure of their bodies be such an impossible obstacle to overcome? In reality it is never so simple to put into practice what you know in your mind and soul. I still want to hear their voices and kiss them hello and goodbye. But never again! It is so painful. All our love, Susana

---

SURVIVING

Our bright and tranquil loft became a welcome haven to get on with life under the new conditions that had been thrust upon us. I likened my existence after my parents' passing, as if I now lived minus a limb. I had the terrible realization, sitting in complete silence, that my life was irrevocably changed forever -- that never again would I be able to return to my innocence. The feeling of total and utter abandonment was overwhelming, at times, even suffocating. I found myself struggling for breath, trying to stay calm. I don't know how many times I got up to go and call them. I would pick up the telephone, realizing, yet once again, that they were no longer at the other end of the line, feeling a deep emptiness in the pit of my stomach.

I remember thinking it was important to do one thing every day, to keep at least one disciplined ritual. Before breakfast and the events of the day began, I took care to dress well and put on my make-up. It was my way of holding on, of reassuring Satoru and Christophe that I was getting on with life; that I was not giving up. It was an outside accomplishment that had nothing to do with the million broken pieces of my heart. As life would have it, there were practical things that had to be done. The will we found was an old one, dated from our years in Brazil in 1964, and was not reflective of the present situation; nor were the executors in America. So it was subsequently discarded by our estate lawyer. Mama had always told us that their will was in their file cabinet if we ever needed it. I was sure they had a newer will, but we never found it.

This unfortunate situation was responsible for a lot of heartache and serious problems between my bother and me. In order to deal with the situation, our uncle suggested that I inherit the apartment. I had found it and lived there with them for two years when they moved from Minneapolis to New York. When the building subsequently went Co-op, my parents had asked me if I had any objection to them purchasing it on their own. I was in agreement with them, as I had had nothing to do with their company and I should not have any part of it. This was because my name was on the lease, as I had done all the negotiations on it when we rented it in 1971. My then companion, Shoichi Kiyokawa, and I had done this to help my parents financially with their move to New York. They would not have jobs on arriving and we had all agreed that it would be easier for us to share expenses.

Before uncle Don left, Charles and I had a meeting with him to go over the details of Papa's and Charles's company, of which Don was a 10% shareholder. My brother had quickly put into action my participation in the company by giving me half of Papa's 40% share. Don suggested I help Charles with the day-to-day running of the company. So, for awhile, this was what I did. I would go in every day and assist with whatever Charles wanted me to do. This situation did not last very long, as we soon got into trouble with each other, and my brother one day announced that he no longer wanted me there. It was a bitter pill to swallow, but I was glad to be out of working with Charles. The uncomfortable situation with my brother lasted, in all, about four years and was a source of terrible stress for me, as I am sure it was for him, too. Our lawyer was very smart and suggested we write out our grievances to each other, which is what we did. We have a massive correspondence between us from that time.

We kept my parents' apartment in New York, which Satoru, Christophe and I lived in until we sold it, in order to sort out all their things, and for us to get an income from renting our loft. The house in the country was shared with Charles, with each of us using it on alternate week-ends. That situation also became a problem, so I suggested I sell my half to my brother and I would give the proceeds to go towards Christophe's schooling. I was certain that his grandparents would have wanted to leave an inheritance for him.

I noticed after the accident that I had developed a fear of driving, convinced that I would some day be in an accident myself. Christophe also had a problem that was brought to our attention by his not wanting to go to school. On trying to understand what was bothering him, it came out that he was afraid we would be in an accident on the way home and would also disappear from his life. We decided, with his teachers, that I would drive him to school and stay parked outside until it was over for the day, so that he could look out the window and check that I was still there. This lasted for about a week, until he felt strong enough and realized that I would not vanish into thin air. However, we decided to go and consult a child psychologist to see if he needed more help. We presented ourselves at the appointed time and had an hour session with her. She asked Christophe several questions as well as us. At the end of the session, her opinion was that we were doing the right things and not to worry; in time things would settle down, which was, indeed, what happened. His teachers were very helpful, and since we were a very close unit together, his concerns slowly melted away. We also never went out without Christophe and never left him in the care of a baby sitter. My fear of driving, however, lasted a good deal longer. I also discovered when I took my first flight away, that I had become terrified of flying, certain that a tragedy would happen on the way to my destination. These fears of mine lasted for almost two years. Of course they did not stop me from driving or flying, but it was a trial every time I did either.

Since I was plagued with the idea that something similar to my parents might happen to me, I had an astrologer friend of my brother's come to do my chart. He assured me, based on what he read in it, that I would die at a ripe old age surrounded by family and friends. Stupid, I know, but somehow, this helped to reassure me. Out of this session came a suggestion by him that he teach me how to meditate, saying that it would help me confront my fears more calmly. I was happy to try, and he gave me a lesson that day and came back for two more. We started with five minutes at a time and then I continued on my own. I got up to forty-five minutes a day. I would start when Satoru left to take Christophe to school, and in the quiet of our pristine space, I would make myself comfortable on our couch next to the window. I loved starting my day with this ritual, as it gave me a sense of tranquility. He had taught me to sit upright in a comfortable position and to fold my hands together resting on my lap -- then to imagine a white light and concentrate on the light. I was not to worry if my mind wandered; I should just let any thoughts that appeared float away like clouds.

After a while, I decided I had better go back to take a dance class, to use up a bit of energy and move my body. It was a comfort, but I started to feel some pain in my hip when I lifted my right leg. I continued going, but worried about the pain. So I asked Meg Harper, one of the dancers in Merce's Company with whom I had danced, if she knew of a chiropractor I could go and see. She gave me the name of her's, whom I went to see. After examining me, she said that I should really stop dancing as the hip problem would get worse and I could end up paralyzed. To say that I walked out of there in shock is an understatement. She had just got rid of my life's work, and future, in one fell swoop. So, now I had lost my parents, my dance career, had a terrible rapport with my brother, and was about to lose a good part of my inheritance. Not bad in the space of a month! Down-hearted, I dragged myself home and sat and stared at the walls. A ritual I proceeded to do on a daily basis for about a year, until, one day, I realized I could not sit down, lie down or walk without pain. I got so frightened by it, that I pulled myself together. I parked my body in front of our huge mirrors along one wall, and made myself go through the class exercises being careful not to lift my right leg to the point where it had hurt before. This I did on a daily basis and slowly cured myself of the partial paralysis.

Mehlika had suggested we all spend Christmas in Rome that year, knowing that it was going to be a very difficult time for us in New York, and we and Charles agreed to go to Rome. I remember it being a huge relief to be among friends, sharing old times together and temporarily forgetting the tragedy. Well, not forgetting, but concentrating less on it. Rome was beautiful, all decked out in its Christmas best and Mehlika had gone out of her way to organize friends' apartments in which to put everyone up. We were a very large group with all our families together. Meals were very rowdy and we did laugh a lot. What a relief! We threw away a lot of empty wine bottles and consumed great quantities of food. When out and about, we would get ice cream cones and drink steaming cappuccinos, such heavenly treats in Italy. Christophe had a wonderful time with the other children in the group, which was so nice to see. We stayed two weeks and really enjoyed the "time out."

We returned to New York in time for the start of school, Satoru went back to work, and I to my meditating and staring at the walls. I interrupted the staring to go for walks occasionally, when, since we lived near Merce's studio, I would sometimes run into dancers and friends. They would invariably ask how I was doing and my standard answer was, "I am learning to just live." They never knew quite what to say to this and would go on their way. It must have been hard for them, but I could not think of anything else to say, as I was indeed learning to re-invent myself. It was a painful, exhausting endeavor, which I did not take kindly to. The meditating became a very important part of my development and would lead me to go searching for other means of helping myself. Challenges such as those I was experiencing were opportunities to grow, if one could understand the tasks involved. As it turned out, the staring at walls was a way to go into my unconscious for answers to the complexities of life. I instinctively realized that I could only do that in stillness. Keeping myself distracted by working would have been my putting off the inevitable day of reckoning. Since we received money from Mama's insurance, and a few other things, earning money was not such a burning issue. I could allow myself this small luxury.

On alternate week-ends, we would continue to go up to my parents' country house, as I did not sell my share to Charles for about a year. In the spring, we were able to see all the bulbs we had planted in bloom, creating a profusion of color and perfumes. The house sat on a big parcel of land that ran along a river and we could hear it flowing past in the spring, after the snow had melted. In the summer, Christophe and Satoru tried floating down on a rubber raft; I would drive them up to the bridge where they could enter the river, and they would career down, screaming and laughing all the way to the house. In spots, it was not so deep and they would end up scraping the bottom on the river stones, hurting their behinds. When they got out, they would be holding their bums in pain. We would all laugh, as they looked so funny.

On the week-ends that were not ours, we would drive out to the Hamptons to walk on the beach to get a change of air. At times, we would take a friend of Christophe's and they would run and run with kites blowing in the wind. Sometimes we took picnic lunches and at others, we would choose a nice restaurant and have lunch. The sea air always made all of us hungry. These times became very important, as they provided a respite from the four walls and the confining city. We also took advantage of the country produce markets to buy fresh vegetables and fruits direct from the farmers. Everything tasted more delicious than the supermarket fare, and bought enough to last us the week.

For those first two crucial years, Satoru and Christophe were a solid foundation for me while I was trying to find a reason for my parents leaving us in such a shocking way. I was also preoccupied with the fact that I was not sure Mama and Papa had done all they were supposed to do. Satoru's and Christophe's quiet self-assurance and strength -- I might even say wisdom -- was reassuring for me. I remember Satoru's and my relationship taking on a very soft, caring feeling to it. At times when we were in bed, he would just take me in his arms and hold me gently, making me feel protected and loved. I held onto the sense of absolute love that we all had together. The experiences we went through, those first years, were opportunities to grow, to learn and to understand. Painful as it was at times, we came out stronger and, in many small ways, I became a changed person. So with their help, and that of many strangers along the way, I slowly started to re-create myself, leaving the old me behind.

That fateful day I had fallen off the track, as Joseph Campbell described in his book, *The Power of Myth*. He said that when you are in the right space, in touch with your unconscious, you are, as it were, on a track which guides you along. Up until that day in my thirty-ninth year, everything I had ever imagined or wished to achieve, I had. As if by magic! There was no sense of effort involved. I thought -- and it materialized. My life was like a dream; I had sailed along in a blessed state. It was like I had a guardian angel walking by my side, looking out for me. My parents' accident woke me up out of that dream and I found I was in a nightmare. My angel had disappeared and I had to find him again. So I had embarked on an adventure to find the hero in myself, without, at first, understanding what would be required of me. It would take me seventeen years in all to find my way back.

FRIENDSHIPS

That September of 1987 was also when we enrolled Christophe in the Fleming School, a French/ English school on 63rd Street between Madison and Park, where lessons were taught in both languages. As a child, I had studied in the French Lycee system, and we wanted Christophe to have the extra French. In fact, school had just started when my parents had their accident. It was not long after, that one day after school, Satoru walked over from the Seagram building on Park and 53rd to meet us so that we could all go to Central Park, for Christophe to enjoy the playground. We were sitting, talking, watching him play, when another Christophe, a classmate and his sister, Juliet, and their mother, Sally, came over to introduce themselves. The two Christophe's became good friends and we established a lasting friendship with Sally and her husband, Olivier. Many years later, she reminded me of how we looked when they walked into the park and saw us. She said we had an air of sadness and she instantly felt a deep tenderness for us. We also met another couple, friends of theirs,' with whom we made a small group with which we would socialize, exchanging dinners, picnics, excursions to the beach and concerts in the park. Sally was of English descent and her husband was French; Elisabeth was German and her husband, Dominique, was also French. The men both worked for French banks, Sally was a travel reporter, and Elisabeth was a painter and designer. We were a very nice, fun group and their company was a wonderful distraction from the sadness and pain that was never far away.

At that same time we met Henrietta and her son, Justin, and Jan and Jerry her husband, and their son, Stefan, on our walks to Soho's Thompson Street playground. Henrietta was Swiss and was working on creating a line of organic beauty products. Jan was a writer and her husband a painter. We spent many wonderful times with them; for Christophe it was ideal, as he had a very happy exchange with the boys. With these two groups, we managed to continue an outwardly normal life, encouraged and helped by all of them, in their warm, friendly way. Sally, Elisabeth and I came up with the idea of making and selling jet lag-friendly box meals for passengers flying around the world. We had many entertaining meetings designing the meals and the packaging. Part of the deal was to have limousines pick up the travelers and take them to the airport with their boxed meals. For some reason, we never got it off the ground, and an idea that was ahead of its time was wasted.

Jan and I separately came up with an enterprise we called the Chocolate Log Company. We produced a light-as-air Chocolate Soufflé Log cake with a recipe she had. At one dinner we had at their house, she served it for dessert, and I, who had been in the catering business, thought it was a great thing to sell to restaurants. So we went into production and actually made it happen, by going out to look for clients together. We kept it going for about a year but it did not produce enough of a living to warrant all the work, so we both decided that it was not really for us.

I had heard from Henrietta about a therapist she was going to that worked with Body-Centering-Therapy. She said it was helping her a lot and so I decided to try it myself. I went to him for about a year and found his methods to be very helpful. With not much talking, he made you listen to your body, that is, to get in touch with what your physical body was telling you. It was very interesting for me, as, with my training as a dancer, I had been taught to educate the body to move and to use discipline to obtain results. The daily training in dance class served to discipline and mold the muscles to do your bidding. With the Body-Centering-Therapy, it was the opposite, it worked very well for me and, slowly, I learned to listen to my physical being and get answers to my psychological problems. One day, after a session, I was riding in the elevator with two other ladies who were having a conversation. One of them was complaining about her mother and I don't know why, but I felt compelled to say to her, "You know it is best not to talk badly about your mother, as you don't know how long you will have her. Just love her. She brought you into the world." They both looked at me, like where in the hell did she come from?

I was finally reacting to my pain and started looking for challenges to get out of myself. The staring at walls had fulfilled its purpose and it was time to reach out to other forms of expression. I decided I would like to take acting classes, and found an acting teacher named Marcia Haupfrecht, who taught sensory acting technique. She was a wonderful woman whose classes I attended for several months in a rundown Eighth Avenue building on the second floor. I enjoyed them very much, even if, at times, I was a bit embarrassed, as I was quite a bit older than most of her students. The work was very helpful and some of the techniques would one day be applied in my future workshops.

After his experience designing and building our Japanese country house, Satoru was not very happy working at Phillip Johnson. So I suggested he leave and do what he really wanted to do. He had wanted to be an artist most of his life, but his family had insisted that architecture was more dignified -- and besides, all the men in the family were architects. Since I now had inherited some money, I suggested he leave Phillip Johnson and dedicate himself to what he felt passionate about. The first thing he did was create flower arrangements, making use of his Ikebana background, which he had learned from his father, the Ikebana master. He created the most beautiful works of art. He then went to shops hoping to interest them in using his designs for their window displays. Stueben Glass, on Fifth Avenue, became a client. Yoshi Yamamoto, the Japanese fashion designer, used Satoru's flower sculptures at his boutique on Madison Avenue. He also did some windows for Yves St. Laurent and Tahari, both also on Madison Avenue.

This, then, led to his deciding to transform common objects into sculptures. So, at week-ends, we would go looking for objects he could recycle into his works of art. The first things he bought were a series of wood columns that must have been holding up a house porch structure. He got them at an old antique shop somewhere on Long Island. We brought them home and he started to paint them with circular lines of color. He had bought eight and grouped them into two free-standing pieces of four columns in each. When he was finished, he named them The Angels. He placed them a distance apart in our loft and they were the first of a large body of sculptural works he made. We were so happy to be together on a full-time basis, each doing our thing in the same serene space. He transformed huge factory air-conditioning circular aluminum ducts by painting them, each differently. He had bought three; one more beautiful than the other. Slowly our loft became a fascinating gallery of works by Satoru and my father. (I had inherited half of my father's paintings and art, so we had also put up some of his paintings). We now lived in our space surrounded by their stunning art creations. To one of the ducts he hung part of a white wooden picket fence that, in the hole behind it, Satoru had painted clouds upside down on a hemp fabric that had been a bag for coffee grains. The title he gave the sculpture was "Unfulfilled Dreams."

I could see Satoru was in his element, happily producing his sculptures and doing his flower displays -- and I was getting on with my exploration into the psychology of the mind and the soul. I went back to Merce's to teach, as he had asked me to consider returning; I could set my own agenda, so I became the studio's student coordinator, and was in charge, with Merce, of student scholarships. I taught the advanced class when the company was away, and, alternated with him when they were in residence. I taught several repertory workshops and continued my rapport with him. I had always kept up my dialogue with Merce, as I saw him as my surrogate father, in a way. I probably, on hindsight, left the company prematurely. Merce had created such extraordinary roles for me and I feel it was unfair of me to have not stayed longer. He never mentioned it, but I am sorry I left too soon.

In the spring of 1988, we got a terrible call from Joke Ten Dam, my best friend from the years we lived in Rome. She now lived in Bristol, England with her Turkish husband, Tekin, and their three children, Gem, Tan and Alp. Alp had been in a freak accident on his way back from school. He had been skipping with friends on and off the sidewalk and accidentally missed a step. A car, coming behind him, not very fast, had caught his fall as his foot missed the pavement, hitting his head at a crucial point, and he had died. He was nine years old. My heart dropped to my stomach I was speechless!

I could not believe what she was telling me. The pain I heard in her voice was overwhelming. I immediately asked her if she wanted me to fly over to be at her side, but she had so many people there helping that she felt it would be better if I went over when there were no longer so many and she would need my presence more. As fate would have it, only a week before, they had all been watching a program on donating organs when someone was in an accident, and Alp had said that if he were ever in one, he would like to donate his organs. They had actually got the donor papers and he had signed them! So they donated Alp's eyes and heart to patients who desperately needed them. It was such an extraordinary coincidence, that, of course, it was all over the newspapers, and they were besieged by journalists trying to get the whole story. We arranged to go over to England that summer for six weeks to visit them and our friends Bishi and Marianne, who had bought a house in Dorset. We had never been there and decided it would be a good change for us.

Joke's shocking news was terrible. I could not imagine how one could go on after losing a child. One is supposed to die before one's child! My heart ached for her; I could not begin to fathom the terrible pain she must have been in. We somehow went on with this added sadness, trying to make peace with God over what I thought was his terrible cruelty. At the time, that was at least how I saw it. Satoru, being brought up in the Buddhist Shinto tradition, looked on death not as finality, but as a continuation of the soul's journey. How I wished I could accept that way of seeing things. It was beyond me, so I continued to look for ways to learn techniques that would teach me. I have spent, what seems to me, a lifetime, trying to come to terms with that idea. I still don't really understand it, even though I wish I did, as it would make death and dying less devastating.

These tragedies made me realize more and more, that there were no guarantees, that I should learn to live one day at a time that anything could happen to change everything in an instant. The challenge was to do the best I could each day and make use of the lessons I was acquiring. It seemed to me, the more I learned, the more I realized I had to learn. As I aged, I understood that knowledge was never enough, and it seemed that I was sure of less and less. So the quest went on and I learned to be thankful for all the small victories and the fact that every day offered me the opportunity to try anew.

Those first two years were filled with many events, which one can only call paranormal. I believed they occurred because, in some part of my being, I needed to hold on to Mama and Papa. The first time was when the bookcase doors opened at my parents' apartment, as I have related. The next happened when we returned to our loft after a week-end at their house in the country. As we entered the loft, there was the overwhelming scent of my mother's perfume called "Mitsuko" by Guerlain. Going up to the house was both a pleasure and a torture, as we had to drive by where they had the accident on the Taconic; and being in their house brought back so many memories of all the happy times we had spent there. All my fears would hit me in the stomach and, at such times, one or the other of them would send a sign to say I was not alone, that they were there. This time it was my mother with her perfume; other times, when I missed my father the most, a rainbow would appear, or a song would play on the radio with life-affirming words.

Papa's manifestations almost always happened when I was driving, as I had a fear of it, together with my constant preoccupation with whether they had done all they were meant to do. Those two years were fraught with huge ups and downs. Big things became small by their sheer magnitude and small things took on huge proportions. Nothing was in its right measure. It was as if this life that I was living had a mind of its own, and I was just running along beside it -- trying to keep up. It was just like when I was young, and I would run along beside my father trying to stay abreast of his large swift strides. I remember one such event that happened one night at dinner. I had cooked a cheese soufflé that we all really liked and baked potatoes. I was serving the soufflé and asked Satoru to please open Christophe's potato and put the butter inside each half. I watched him cut it and saw that he had cut it down the middle instead of lengthways. For some unknown reason this made me loose it and I said, "No. Don't you know I always cut it the other way?" and scooped up the offending object and threw it across the floor. Everything stopped dead, in total silence. Satoru got up and started to pick up all the pieces. As Christophe and I were watching him, mesmerized, I realized how absurd I had been and started laughing. After a few moments of hesitation, so did Satoru and Christophe. We always referred to that scene, fondly, as Adu's "Mad potato scene." Adu was the name Christophe had suddenly, one day, when he was about two years old, started to call me. He addresses me that way to this day.

Merce's Signals duet for Mel and me, Paris 1970.

Photo by James Klosty

A roller-skate solo I choreographed for our performance
at the Rowan Gallery in London, 1978.

Satoru 1977

Satoru in his Borsalino beret
Italy winter 1988

Satoru 1978

Satoru's piece for the Rowan Gallery performance in London, 1978.

One of Satoru's sculptures, "Cloudy Above". 1990.

Satoru and I, posing in front of one of the temples at Meiji
Jingu Mae on our Wedding Day. Tokyo, January 1976.

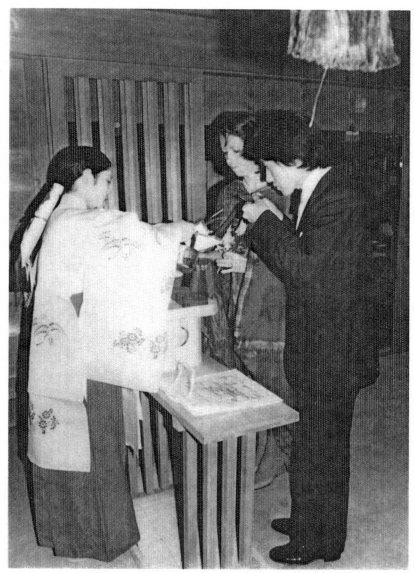

At our Wedding Ceremony drinking the ritual cup of Sake
to signify our marriage union. Tokyo, January 1976.

Satoru and I, posing with family and guests. Kisuke, Satoru's father,
to my left and Ryu, Satoru's mother, is to the right of Satoru.

My parents, my brother and I, just before departing on
our South American journey. Mexico City, 1955.

Mama. Mexico City, 1953.

Papa. Mexico City, 1953.

Satoru and I, when I was 8 months pregnant with Christophe, holding Tarokun, our Shetland sheepdog. New York, June 1980.

Satoru and I, with newborn Christophe. August 1980.

Little Onigiri cheeks, Christophe. New York, 1983.

Proud Satoru holding his precious son, Christophe
at 16 months. New York, 1981.

Christophe and I, while I was on Tour with the Theatre du Silence. Syria, 1982.

Satoru, Christophe and I, visiting my parents at their
country house in Upstate New York, 1985.

Satoru and Master Carpenters after lunch during the
construction of the house in Upstate New York, 1986.

Satoru with his Japanese House drawing, in the living
room of our newly constructed house. Spring 1987.

During a trip to visit Satoru's mother, Ryu. Tokyo, New Year's Eve 1986.

Satoru, Christophe, Maria and I, at the Rolls-Royce Enthusiasts' Club,
4th Annual Euro Rally. Veuve Clicquot Ponsardin, Reims. July, 1991.

The front gate of Fornacino di Gré.

The pool we proudly built

View of Fornacino from the back garden

Satoru and Christophe just after renovating the
Cantina at Fornacino. Tuscany, 1990.

One of Satoru's "Door Torso" sculptures in the central part of Fornacino. 1991.

Our red bomber

Our little village at the beginning of the dirt road
leading down to Fornacino. Chiusure, Italy.

At Satoru's sisters house with his nieces and sister, from left to right:
Asako, Kaoruko and his sister, Kimiko. Tokyo, December 1992.

At dinner with Satoru in Florence. February, 1993.

At a restaurant in Florence with Satoru's brother, Mitsuru. February, 1993.

With our Japanese family during our trip to Japan, to return Satoru's ashes to the family shrine. From left to right: Christophe, Me, Kotaro (Kimiko's son), and Mitsuru. Bottom from left to right: Kimiko and Ryu (Satoru's mother). Tokyo, 1995.

Satoru's family shrine in Tokyo. Tokyo, 1995.

Christophe on our vacation in Capri. Italy, 2004.

Christophe and I, at the Gala to raise funds for the Los
Angeles Philharmonic. Los Angeles, 2011.

During a Gala to raise funds for the Los Angeles Philharmonic. May 2012.

Photo by Pina Di Cola

Mama And Papa

Who were these two people I am talking about? Frederick and Patricia Hayman-Chaffey were two extraordinary souls born in Hastings, Sussex, in the south of England. Papa was born on January 28, 1920 and Mama on January 22, 1922. Papa's father was a tailor and managed a gentleman's clothes shop in Hastings. His wife, Violet, was his second wife -- as his first had died giving birth to their first daughter, who later moved to New Zealand and created a whole branch of our family over there. His father was a very strict disciplinarian and held a walking stick under the table to whack across the shins of his sons should they not behave. He had three sons, Don, the eldest, Frederick in the middle, and Kenneth, the youngest. Don would become a well-known film director, and my father, a painter and Renaissance artist. He designed costumes, lighting, wrote articles for a newspaper and a magazine, was a photographer, documentary film-maker, designer of furniture, inventor, and last, but not least, wrote a book called " *The Road Grew No Moss*" about his travels with his family. The youngest son, Kenneth, spoiled by both parents, was, in a sense, ruined, as he was never able to make much of his life and worked mostly as a hospital orderly.

Don and Frederick broke the mold of their simple beginnings and were to change their destinies through their means of creative expression. Both boys had their careers interrupted by the Second World War and Frederick later told me he had greatly resented those years being snatched away from him. During the war he was hospitalized, suffering from shell shock, and was one of the first patients to be given Penicillin, which was how he met Sir Alexander Fleming, the doctor that discovered it. Both boys married young during the war; Don's wife Edna was his life's companion until her death of cancer, a few years before my parents passed away. He remarried an actress and dancer named Paula Kelly some years later. Frederick was twenty when he married Patricia Stevens, a very attractive eighteen-year-old girl from Hastings. He enjoyed telling me that he had told her that she would have to pay her way, if she was to be married to him, and asked if she agreed, which is what she did till the day she died. It was something he also insisted I do. I have always been grateful for that lesson, as I, too, have never been supported by any man. I firmly believe that women should be self-sufficient, so as to maintain their economic independence and sense of self-worth.

It is hard to imagine how these four would expand all their boundaries and go out into the world and become the extraordinary people they became. Both Don and Papa left Hastings to go up to London to study their chosen art forms. Don went to the Film Institute and Papa to the Royal Academy of Art. I remember his telling me about one of his art teachers, who once told him that a painting he was very proud of was "A piece of rubbish." The lesson he learned from this, despite being very hurt, was that he should not be so confident as to lose his judgment or the rigorous assessment of the work. It was an example I was to take very seriously when I was ten and preparing to be a dancer. My father told me that he would do everything possible to help me if I promised to dedicate myself totally to my profession. I immediately told him that I would. I would learn that to achieve excellence it would come from a commitment to strive for something on a daily basis; to better oneself in order to have the best possible instrument; to be at the service of the chosen art form being pursued. I saw early on that through the acquisition of technique, it was possible to achieve the freedom necessary to free an artistic expression from being merely good, and allow it to go into the realm of the truly inspired. And one could become a vessel for something far greater than the sum total of oneself.

Frederick and Patricia bought Newbarn Farm at auction very cheaply. It was a lovely broken-down farmhouse in the middle of many sheep fields, which they had to cross to get to the house. It was just outside a pretty little hamlet on the Rother River called Newenden in Cranbrook, Kent, on the border of Sussex and Kent, about sixty miles from London. They lovingly restored the house and lived in it for about two years. I remember my father telling me that one time, when his mother went to visit them, she was so comfortable that she was overstaying her welcome. They were a young couple and understandably wanted their privacy. A week's stay was welcome, but they were getting worried she would never leave. So they decided to take desperate measures, and one night dragged chains across the floor in the attic above her bedroom. The next morning, she mentioned the noise, and asked if they knew what it could be. They told her the house was haunted and it was probably the resident ghost having a difficult time of it. That was enough to make her pack her bags and leave that very day. Poor grandma!

I was conceived there, and, close to my arrival date, Papa took his precious Astin Martin Lagonda car to the garage for a check-up to make sure there would be no problem when I made my debut. To get to the main road about a mile away, they would have to cross the various sheep fields all divided with gates. Papa had to get out at each gate to open it and, once passed, close it behind him. Well, the long-awaited day arrived. At around five in the morning, Mama went into labor, so they got ready and went out to the famous car. Papa put the key in the ignition, turned it, nothing happened. He tried several times to no avail; my poor mother was in pain dealing with the contractions, so Papa had no choice but to put her on his bicycle and push her across the fields. I can imagine what an ordeal that was for both of them, and I can just hear my father swearing all the way across. They finally arrived at the main road and at the home of their closest neighbors, the Bournes. They had to wake them up out of a deep sleep in order for John Bourne to drive them over to the nursing home. I kept in touch with them and, to this day, Muguette, his wife, who is still alive, reminds me of my near arrival in the sheep fields of Kent.

These two larger-than-life human beings were my foundation, and became my guardians, teachers, friends, work collaborators, accomplices and fellow travelers. I always called them Mama and Papa, but, truly, I looked on them as my Goddess and God. It was not until I got into my thirties that I was grudgingly willing to see their slight defects. The journey they undertook together, the challenges they met and overcame, were enormous life lessons for me, and informed and guided my every move in life. No school, no university, no one else could ever have taught me what I learned by watching them live their lives.

I was born at 9:00 p.m. on January 31, 1948, in a lovely nursing home called Kenchhill in Tenterden. It was there I took my first breath and embarked on this journey of life. I remember Papa telling me of when he and his father had snuck in to take a peek at me outside visiting hours, and how the matron caught them and sent them packing like two naughty school boys. Papa wrote a poem about me when I was born that he gave me when I was older. I cannot express how happy it made me to have tangible proof of my worth to my beloved Papa. It had been the force that has kept me going through the worst moments of my life. I feel that all any of us really need is to know that we are uniquely beloved by the two people, who, by their joining, have created us. It gave me the rock solid foundation upon which to go out and brave the world around me.

In 1948, when I was just nine months old, my parents decided to leave England and go to Spain, the first step in their travels around the world. They sold Newbarn Farm to the Curls, a family sent by their estate agents. They also bought all the furniture, and the beautiful Lagonda car. They now had enough money to fly the coup. In those days one was only allowed to take out of England 150 Pounds; they, of course, had much more as they were leaving for a long time. So I became the ideal receptacle for hiding the cash laying in my carry-cot. They stuffed it into my diapers and taped it to my body. At customs, when they were leaving, the officer asked them if they had anything to declare and Papa held me up and declared, "Yes my daughter." The officer was not very amused and waved them on, better to get them out of the way. They subsequently crossed many borders around the world in their travels and developed many strategies to fit different needs and situations.

SOUTH AMERICAN JOURNEY

Their first stop was Madrid, where they found a small apartment and Mama got a job at the British Embassy as a secretary to the Ambassador. Papa managed to arrange an exhibition of his paintings through the British Consulate and they concentrated on learning Spanish. They went to the cinema as much as possible to learn the language, figuring out by way of the images, what was being said. They picked it up quickly, being motivated to learn, as communicating was very important to them. Papa took care of me in the day mostly and when he had to go out, they got a maid to take over for him. Soon after they had got established, when I was about one, I got Typhoid fever from contaminated milk and became very sick. They had made friends with a doctor at an Embassy party and, mercifully, he became my savior. I had to be hospitalized and was quite ill for about a week, hanging on to life. I have often wondered what my poor parents went through, finding themselves in a foreign country away from family and friends, not really able to speak Spanish properly yet; but luckily, the doctor spoke English. Thinking back, I realize that probably my fear of death must have come from that traumatic experience. It was something that remained in the back of my mind, never far away.

They settled on the Island of Palma de Mallorca, in a small town called Fornalutx up in the hills, where they bought an old Moorish house for a song from the English writer Walter Starkey. I have wonderful memories of our time there, of my mother and me going into the beautiful garden full of fruit trees, and sitting under the trees eating all sorts of fruits. I would also walk down from the house to the little village a few meters away to the sweet shop, where I would be given treats by the owners. Since my first language was Spanish, they considered me one of them. In our travels I would also learn

French from my Lycee school days in Mexico, Portuguese from our two years in Brazil, and Italian from our time living in Italy. Our garden was the place where I would, at three, do my first dancing -- putting on long, full skirts and twirling and skipping around. Papa took several photos of me in my splendor. I loved dancing and whenever they played music I was off into my extravaganzas. I loved going on the bus with Mama and Papa to Palma on shopping trips. We would leave early in the morning, stop by the bakery and buy fresh bread and a tablet of bitter-sweet chocolate, which we ate with the bread -- a habit I have kept to this day, it is so delicious. There Papa prepared what would be his last exhibition in Europe at the Museum of Modern Art in Madrid. My brother, Charles, was born in Palma on October 8, 1951 when I was three and three quarters. I remember sitting outside Mama's bedroom waiting with Papa for him to be born. It was a sunny day, the walls were light blue and we were sitting on a wooden bench warmed by the sun.

Charles had little more than a glimpse of our Mediterranean home before it was sold to put money into the chest for the next stage of our parents' travels. They sailed steerage in a Spanish steamer with me nearly four and Charles just a baby. Intrepid, they knew no fear, always pushing on to the next adventure. They sailed across the Atlantic to the West Indies and on to Mexico. We arrived early in 1952, and, as was their habit, they immediately started to look for work. My mother again found work as personal secretary to the British Ambassador and Papa as night watchmen for the Embassy. My memories of Mexico are very vivid. I remember our maid making plaits with my hair, winding in colored ribbons; going horse back riding in the mornings and travelling out to see the magnificent pyramids; I remember the riot of colors everywhere you looked in the city and throughout the land; of visiting the floating flower market at Xochimilco while gliding on a boat. Those memories left a lasting impression on my soul that would inform the way I thought and the way I would subsequently look at life.

In 1955, a letter arrived in Mexico City offering my father a one-man exhibition of his paintings at the Hanover Gallery in London in the latter part of 1957. With this news Papa and Mama sat down to plan a journey home that would take us through every country in Central and South America, across the Atlantic to Africa, and, finally, to England. The greatest problem for them was going to be how to finance their journey. This was nothing new for them, but, nevertheless it had to be planned for. The result of that journey became Papa's book, *The Road Grew No Moss* published at the end of the exploration in 1959. On the jacket it was described as "This amazing true life story of a family who forgot to think about security, a book created out of life by an artist".

A part of the description of the journey as written on the dust jacket of the book reads:

> *"With his wife and two small children, the English writer and painter Hayman-Chaffey achieved what everyone said was impossible—the hazardous journey from Mexico to Brazil through every country in Central and South America using any form of transport available.*
>
> *Crossing the Andes became almost familiar; they had to traverse miles of salt-lakes in Bolivia with no roads to guide them; they had to contend with all the vicissitudes of the Pan American Highway—at times nothing more than a dangerous rocky track winding over snow covered mountains. On one occasion their Land Rover was rammed by a taxi and they narrowly escaped with their lives. This was to be the beginning of a comic opera plot in which they were sued and threatened with arrest.*
>
> *With a little money saved, they made the journey on what they could earn 'en route': exhibiting and selling paintings, doing all kinds of odd jobs. Each new country presented them with a new problem and they learnt to adapt themselves to all kinds of people and circumstances."*

That journey was an enormous challenge for them, which they met with grace, courage and creativity. From my point of view, it was an adventure filled with wonder, fear, uncertainty and a blind trust in my parents. I learned about how to tackle life on any terms it produced and found my way of coping. As Mama and Papa were preoccupied with earning the monies needed to move from one step to the next, it was my duty to help by taking care of my little brother. We were often, by necessity, left alone, safely ensconced in a hotel room or apartment, where I would be responsible for Charles's well-being. There have been times, as an adult, when I have lashed out at my brother in the heat of an argument, feeling that he should thank me for keeping him alive during those difficult years we were traveling in South America. I was seven and three-quarters when we left, and Charles was only just three. He was a handful, a lot of the time rebellious, resenting having to be left with me as his custodian. Our parents had no other choice and we never came to any harm, but I am sure that many of the problems Charles and I have had over the years stem from that time.

Probably my sense of sacrifice came from that period as well. I did not have a real childhood, like many children. It never occurred to me that I was sacrificing anything. It was only many years later, when I briefly went to a psychiatrist, that, on recounting my childhood, he observed that it must have been difficult and asked how I felt about it. I could not answer, tears coursing down my cheeks as I was choking with sobs of pain. I could not continue and had to leave. I never went back. I am sure I did not want to go to that place in myself that had probably suffered. I had blocked out all that was painful and only thought about the magic of all I had seen and done. To have had the privilege to live alongside my extraordinary parents was all that had mattered. They loved us! I felt that with every bone in my body, so nothing else was important.

When they were in Brazil, the last country they visited on the South American part of the journey, Papa and Mama were hesitating about whether they had enough time and money to go through Africa. So Frederick wrote to their good friend from Mexico, Nieves de Madariaga, who was now living in Italy, for her advice. Before they got her answer, they had decided that, morally they had to try to go through Africa and sail from Cairo back to England, even if it was cutting things very short, with only three hundred dollars to their name. On arriving in Cape Town, the purser brought them her letter saying, "No. Leave Africa until you have more breath and more financial help. Go straight back to London and give your exhibition." She ended by saying, "May great good luck and fortune await you on arrival in Cape Town." A little while later, as they were about to dock, the purser ran up with an orange envelope he had forgotten to give them. It was a cable, and at once Papa knew what it said. It came over him in a moment, a sickening realization that they had gambled with time and lost. I quote a paragraph from the book for his reaction.

The cable said:

Regret Father passed away peacefully December 10 letter follows, Mother.

Nieves had met my father when she went from Mexico to England, and like all who had met him, she had written to say: 'He is a saint and wants very much to see you again'. Perhaps a wire had gone to Rio to warn me, to bring me back in time to say good-bye, but I had already left. I remember hearing the wind as it whistled by the ship and Patricia's sobbing, and I thought of my mother's loss and of how my own great joy on returning was to have been in cheering my father with stories of this other world and in journeying with him in the thousands of photographs to the warmer lands he loved. Do we always tarry too long and hope for too much?

I looked up at my father as he was reading the telegram and it was the first time I ever saw him cry. I felt his terrible pain as my own tears filled my eyes. We spent Christmas in Cape Town and Charles and I were to see fake snow for the first time. All the houses had decorated their gardens with cotton wool snow and Christmas lights. It was very exciting for us and we exclaimed with joy when we first saw them. We quickly covered as much of South Africa as we could before our sailing back to England on January 17, 1958.

When the journey ended, Papa had taken thousands of feet of sixteen millimeter cine film. More than 10,000 black-and-white and 5,000 color photographs -- many of which he had developed and enlarged *en route*. He had painted enough for six one-man exhibitions held throughout South America, had travelled 10,000 miles by bus, car, train and airplane from Mexico to Venezuela, and, thereafter, driven 100,000 miles in a Land-Rover, sailed 4,000 miles from Brazil to Cape Town, driven 7,000 miles in the Union of South Africa and sailed 4,600 miles from the Cape to Southampton -- to stand once more on the shores of our native land.

We landed in England on my 10th birthday, January 31, 1958. These were the fundamental years of my upbringing, unique and unforgettable. It was an extraordinary experience of life and living like no other. We went straight to Hastings, where Papa's mother's house was. She lived with her mother, my father's grandmother. We also visited my mother's family, who also lived in Hastings. We spent a week at each house so that we could get to know our grandparents, and they us. It was so exciting for all of us to be together after my parents' long absence. I loved them all on sight and especially liked my great-grandmother, whom I called Nana Pomfrey, which was her maiden name. She was in her late eighties and was looking forward to living to a hundred to get a telegram from the Queen. Sadly, she died at ninety six, when I was in my twenties. I cried for two straight days. She loved her occasional cigarette, but her daughter did not approve, so she had to sneak one in the bathroom whenever she could. I caught her one day swinging the bathroom door madly back and forth and I asked her, "Nana, what are you doing?" to which she replied, "Shush. Don't say anything. I am trying to get the cigarette smoke out." She was a lady right up my alley and we became conspirators right away. Her daughter, though, I must say, was no slouch, as she, too, liked her whiskey at the end of the day and a good smoke! They were quite a pair and kept Charles and me most amused.

I also liked Mama's mother and father very much. Grandpa would take us into the back garden and play croquet with us. One day, I was up with my grandmother in her room watching her put on her make-up. I asked her, "How old are you, Grandma?" and she said, "You know, it is not how old you are, but how old you feel you are." So I asked her how old she felt she was and she answered, "Today, because you are all here, I feel like a young girl no more than maybe thirty." I liked that! To this day, I am only the age I feel I am.

After our visit in Hastings, we went up to London and stayed with my uncle Don and his wife, Edna and my cousin, Nicolette. My parents were deciding what their next move would be and we were arranging for me to start Ballet School. Beryl Grey and Oleg Briansky, friends of Mama's and Papa's, were on their South American tour when we were there. They asked Papa to do their lighting in Montevideo and Buenos Aires. They knew of my passion for ballet and suggested that when we got back to England, my parents enroll me in the Nesta Brooking Ballet School, a lovely boarding school near Primrose Hill. I passed the entrance exam and began my journey of becoming a dancer. Subsequently, I would pass all my Cecchetti Ballet exams with Honors.

My parents and Charles were moving to Rome, where Nieves was now living, working for F.A.O., the food and agriculture organization part of the United Nations. She suggested they move there as she could arrange for Mama to have a good job with F.A.O. Papa would continue writing his articles for the Brazilian Magazine, *O'Cruceiro* and paint and exhibit at the Bonino Gallery in Rome. I would stay in London and visit them in Rome three times a year, which I did for the first two years, until we found a school for me in Rome. I moved there to study with Grant Muradoff a famous dancer and teacher from the Diaghilev Ballet Russe De Monte Carlo. I would be reunited with my family, which I was very happy about.

RETRACING MY STEPS

In the beginning of August, we left for London to go and visit Joke and her family and Bishi and Marianne in Dorset. I had called my uncle Ken in Hastings to ask him to look for an economical car we could buy for our six-week stay. He found us a Rover that looked good and the price was affordable. It was black with red leather seats that we really enjoyed riding around in. Our first stop was Bristol, where Joke lived. We found a nice bed and breakfast, and a simple place to eat lunch, we did not want to have her worry about entertaining us; we just wished to be there for her in any way we could. I knew from my experience, that it was therapeutic to talk about what had happened. So when the greetings were over, I sat down quietly with Joke and asked her how the accident had happened. It was like a flood gate had been opened. She talked and talked and I listened. I remember saying to her that I felt her loss was much worse than mine, as one knows that, sooner or later, ones parents will pass away. Ones child dying was so unexpected.

I will never forget her answer. She said that I was wrong, that any death was painful and not one type or another was more or less intolerable. Even in the pain she was in, she could still think of mine. It was a true measure of our deep friendship. Occasionally, I would ask a pertinent question, and so the afternoon slipped by. We sat for many hours, and, towards evening, I suggested we take everybody out to dinner. The concentration I had needed to hear the terrible tragedy provoked a migraine, but I did not want to interrupt her and show that I had a problem. So I just tried to ignore my headache which was only getting worse.

They recommended a nice restaurant and we had a very pleasant dinner with everyone in good spirits. Her two boys and Christophe had played together the whole afternoon, so were buddies by now, and we did manage to laugh and have a nice time. After dinner, they returned home and we went back to our lodgings. By now my migraine had developed into a full blown agony, and I was feeling nauseous. As soon as we left them, I took my Anacin; by morning I was almost back to normal, thankful to be rid of the excruciating pain. We had arranged to meet Joke and her family to spend a day sightseeing around Bath, a World Heritage site. It is famous for its baths fed by three hot springs. The city was first documented as a Roman Spa shortly after the Romans invaded England in 43 A.D. It was also famous for its Georgian architecture and Satoru wanted to see the renowned Royal Crescent -- a group of town houses set in a huge semi circle. As an architect, he was always interested in the building traditions of other countries. We went to see the Pump Room, the shrine the Romans built around one of the hot springs. It is a very famous tourist attraction and, attached, is a fine restaurant where we had lunch. It was a wonderful day spent with close friends, healing and a welcome change for all of us.

We left Joke and her family at the end of the day and headed over to our other friends where we would be staying for two weeks. We had not wanted to stay too long with Joke, as I knew it was very tiring to have people around too much. On the way, we stopped to visit Stonehenge, a prehistoric, mysterious circle of upright stones built by Neolithic people around 2,100 years, B.C. The stones that form the monument dated back 4,000 years. As we stood there, we had the sensation of witnessing something other-worldly, charged with a very powerful energy. It was mind-blowing that something so simple could be so powerful. It made me realize how little I knew of my country and how much I had missed. This vacation was an exploration back into my heritage, the land where I was born.

We drove over to Marianne and Bishi's in Dorset to start our sojourn in this lovely part of the world. It was so nice to see them again, as we had not been together since our summer with them in Italy. They had bought their house when Bishi finished his work consulting on fisheries in Saudi Arabia. They were now going to settle in England. They took us all over the area and we had many a happy time. I was delighted to be exploring this part of England with them and Satoru and Christophe. It made it more precious and meaningful. One of the things we all noticed was how green the countryside was and how cool it was even though it was August. We had all only brought two sweaters each and I swear we spent the whole time we were there with one or the other on. Satoru was fascinated with the architecture, as now we were in the part of England where there are a lot of houses with thatched roofs. In some parts of Japan, notably in the historic village of Shirakawa-go, a World Heritage Site, they have the same type of roofs on the old country houses. They were very picturesque in charming little villages with funny names like Piddlehinton, Puddletown and others.

We stayed at their house for a week, and then we found a nice bed and breakfast nearby with their help. Our two weeks with them were a lot of fun and I also used the time to ask Bishi questions about his recollections of Frederick and Patricia. We had been children way back in Mexico when we were all living there. He was about ten years older than I and had some interesting observations. I was planning to write a book about my extraordinary parents, and was collecting friends' impressions of them. We would sit and I would ask him questions and he would recount memories he had of them. I never got down to writing the book, probably because it would be a very long and difficult process. England, of course, is famous for its pubs, and we would go at opening times for a pint and, sometimes, for a pub lunch -- Things I had not experienced living out of my country for so long. It was sad to say goodbye when we had to go on to Tenterden to visit the Curls who had bought my parents' house, and the Bournes who had driven them to the nursing home the night I was born.

I had written to Judy Curl and her husband to ask them permission to bury my parent's ashes in their garden. My brother and I had divided them, so that we could each do as we wished. I thought it would be nice to return them to their first house where I was conceived. We stayed with John and Muguette Bourne and called the Curls when we got there. They were charming and invited us straight away to go and have tea with them the next day, to choose the spot where the ashes could be buried. We drove over the fields, jumping out to open and close the gates of each field, and drove up to Newbarn Farm, my parents' former house. I was returning 40 years later, to the place where I had first seen the light of day and started on this life journey. I was moved with emotion at being back, this time with their ashes. Not the way I would have wanted it, but such is life! Judy showed us around the house. They had made a few changes to modernize it a bit, but, basically, it was the same as when they had bought it. The old Aga stove was still there and working well. We then went out into the garden to find the perfect spot for my dearly beloveds. There was a lovely patch of daffodils in full bloom that they told me bloomed every year, and we decided that it would be a nice resting place. We made a hole, placed the ashes in, and said a prayer. It comforts me to know that they are there. I am sure they would be happy to be back where their extraordinary voyage began.

John and Muguette were utterly charming and took us to see all the local sights: the church I was christened in, the nursing home where I was born, which was now a home for elderly people, and many lovely places that made me feel very proud of my little corner of the world. They had a beautiful Elizabethan house with a gorgeous garden behind and a grass tennis court. One afternoon, Christophe and Satoru were playing tennis and Christophe hit the ball through a small pane in one of their windows, much to our dismay. They were really sweet and told us not to worry, it would easily be replaced. I still remember Christophe's eyes open wide in surprise and guilt, wondering what was going to happen. We all laughed and complimented him on his shot, much to his relief.

Our last stop was London, to stay with Peter and Caroline ffrench-Hodges in Kensington. Peter was that rare human being who lives his life in a unique, surreal way. He expresses himself in a very interesting and unusual fashion; he keeps me on my toes when I am around him. My father had met him some years previously, when he had gone to the British Tourist Authority for help on an article he was writing for *O' Cruzeiro*. Peter was working there and they had become fast friends. Papa had introduced me, and I, too, became very friendly with him. Caroline, his third wife, was a beautiful perfect companion for him and I enjoyed her company very much. She was Dutch and part of the Shell Oil Company family. I will never forget the time when we were performing at the Sadler's Wells theatre in London with Merce, and he sent me a dozen Japanese lilies.

They were so fragrant that their perfume pervaded the hallways and went up to my dressing room. They were a gorgeous light pink and white and I took them with me when we left to go on to our next performance in Europe. He also wrote a very flattering review of my dancing for a London art magazine. He likened me to a Picasso painting. It was a very perceptive piece and I was very pleased with it. He and Caroline had stayed with my parents when they had visited New York a month before they passed away. He told me that when they were at the airport, when Peter hugged Papa and said goodbye, Papa had responded as if they would not be seeing each other again. Almost as if he already knew he did not have much time left. How sad, I felt, to know that maybe somewhere in his soul, Papa was already aware of his demise.

We found a car auction house where we could leave our car to be sold and Peter and Caroline took us to the airport. This sojourn in my country had come to an end. The memories it had awakened were gratefully accepted and much appreciated. It was a lovely walk down memory lane, refreshing with much food for thought. We would now be returning to New York with my birth place fresh in my mind, giving me a firm reminder of all that was special to me, about where I came into the world.

239 CENTRAL PARK WEST

When Charles and I put our parents' apartment up for sale, it was decided that Satoru, Christophe and I would move there to make it easier for me to sort through all of their documents and belongings. I had given away a lot of their clothes to the Salvation Army. My mother's huge collection of high heel designer shoes I gave to Natalie, Charles's ex girlfriend, as they were her size and she wore high heels. I also invited my mother's best friends to come over to choose something they would like as a memento of their friendship with her. Charles and I tossed a coin to divide Papa's paintings between us. I invited Toby, my father's ex-live-in girlfriend, to be present, even though they had broken up a year before he passed away. Papa had not given her any of his paintings and I felt that we should let her choose two for herself, as well an object of furniture he had designed. Charles was not very pleased with this, but I insisted and he had reluctantly agreed. We had also divided all the numerous books, and I kept Mama's jewellery and her fur coats. Charles kept the things he wanted of Papa's, so now all that was left were the documents, photos etc.

Right after our parents died, Charles had come up to me asking to have Papa's gold cufflinks that he always wore. I said no, that those should come back to me, as I had given them to him with the first money I made while working on Brazilian television in Rio de Janeiro in 1964. I had bought them because they looked very much like a part of his paintings from the 1960's. He loved them, and was never without them on his shirt cuffs. I had also bought Mama a beautiful gold ring like a sea sponge for her little finger. In fact I bought something gold for each of my grandparents, as well. Charles was very upset, but I was adamant about it, as I wanted to pass them on to Christophe when he was older. I gave him a gold bracelet of Mama's, as he had given her some of the gold coins on it, so it seemed to me I was acting properly. Some years later, I had a copy made of Papa's cufflinks by an Italian jeweller to give Charles for his 50th birthday. He was very moved by my gesture and I was pleased that I had thought of it. He had given me a beautiful Raymond Weil gold watch for my 50th.

After Papa broke up with Toby the summer before in 1986, I had been in Europe teaching with Christophe, and Mama joined us towards the end. We met her at Heathrow and went down to her house in Hastings for a few days, while she organized to have it sold. We then went for a little holiday together and Papa flew over to join us. Satoru was busy working and could not take off, so it was just us four. We went to Canterbury first and stayed in a lovely Elizabethan hotel. I remember when we parked the rental car in their garage there was a Mini Cooper parked next to ours and on the bumper it had a sticker that read, "When I grow up I want to be a Rolls Royce." We were so amused by that and it has remained in my mind ever since, I love the image so much!

I also remember that Papa was so attentive to Mama, maybe to make up for his past behavior. Mama loved champagne and everywhere we went for lunch or dinner he ordered it for her. I was very happy about this, as they were like young lovers again, after all my poor mother went through with him and his girlfriend. It was a great relief to be a witness to this time in their lives. I thank God for the mercy that this happened before they died, which helped me come to terms with their destiny. I had been given the chance to witness their return to love and it was very heartening for me to have that last memory of them.

Going through their documents was an arduous process. I had to read all their correspondence and paperwork, deciding what had to be kept and what could be discarded. Mama had managed to keep all the correspondence preparing the South American journey, the photographs, and the film, absolutely everything. I spent many a day in tears reading their letters to me and to each other. Now I am glad that I kept them all, as they are a tangible record of what our life was together. Their building was a large Central Park West co-op, with lots of porters and service people. One day, one of the elevator men told us that the cat of the family in the apartment below us had given birth to kittens. He suggested that it would be so nice for Christophe to have a kitty, thinking it would help him with his sadness over losing his grandparents. We already had Taro and the thought of another pet was not in our plans. The porter would not give up on us, and, finally, at Christophe's insistence, we relented and went down to have a look at them. Of course, they were really sweet, and we decided that when they were six-weeks old, Christophe could go down and choose one. He went one afternoon with Satoru. They recounted that they had been playing with four of the kittens, deciding which one to pick. Suddenly, out of the closet, a pretty black and white kitty ran straight into Christophe's lap. It was love at first sight! She became Kitty Hawk our precious kitty, who I later nicknamed *Chief Sitting Pretty Face*, the affectionate name Papa used to call Mama.

She flew everywhere with us, becoming very nonchalant about travel, taking it all in her stride. She was a character. When we took her back to the loft after selling the apartment, she was a bit lost in the enormous open space. The next day, we had to go out and leave her alone. When we returned, the first thing I did was look for her, calling her name, as she was nowhere to be seen. I went into a panic, looking for her all over the loft; we had not left anything open, so how could she just disappear? My over-active imagination invented all sorts of scenarios, none of them reassuring. Finally, after a good, long hour, running my hand over our bed, I felt a bump and looked under our eiderdown; there she was snuggled up quietly sleeping. She must have gone there for security, feeling lost in the strange space. Many were the times she would not show up when called; especially when we were up in the country for the week-end. At times I was reduced to tears of frustration, looking everywhere for her. She only came back when she was ready, no matter how desperate I got. We adored her. She was never ill, and had travelled back and forth from New York to Tuscany many times and from Tuscany to Mexico, where she finished her life a few years after we moved there at the ripe old age of eighteen.

Papa and Mama's apartment was very much an artists' living space, full of Papa's paintings and his Plexiglas furniture. He had designed his own couches, and a gorgeous Chinese red lacquer dining table that had to be brought up on the roof of the service elevator, because it was so big. We inherited it from them a few years before, when they had replaced it with another beautiful one. It was in two parts, white, with a subtle color design on part of each piece. The sections rested on two round cylinder aluminum steel bases. I inherited most of the furniture, except for their bed, which my brother wanted. All the bed frames and headboards were Papa's designs, as were all the side tables and night stands. He had a fantastic coffee table in the shape and color of a butterfly wing. For lighting, he had installed shiny aluminum poles on the ceilings from which to hang dramatic theatre spots on dimmers for the illumination. It was very serene, but, at the same time, dramatic.

I realized, as agents brought people around to see the apartment, that I would have to remove the lighting grid to tone things down a bit and paint the walls a beige color, as Papa had them a light grey. With the changes, we got a buyer and the apartment sold towards the end of November. The day we had the movers come to collect all the furniture and take it to our loft, it was raining, as it always seemed to do, when we had to move. It was a sad goodbye and the end of an era. We had lived many important moments there with Mama and Papa.

It was no surprise that Christmas that year was sad. We were alone and invited Shoichi and a few friends to come over. After Mama and Papa left us, it was the hardest season to get through. I would start to get anxious about it a few weeks before. The New Year brought with it the proceeds of the sale of the apartment and a decision had to be made about what to do with the money. Satoru had advertised teaching Tea Ceremony classes when we moved back to our loft, and his students came once a week, each Friday to study with him. He had three very dedicated students: George, who was a parole officer, Michael, his companion, an investment banker, and Kasu, a gentle soul of Japanese origin. Michael was working for Merrill Lynch and when I asked him about investing our money, he made an appointment with his boss to see what options I had. I went to meet with him and placed the money with Merrill Lynch, thinking that was the best solution. It did not take me long to figure out that it was not what I was comfortable with.

I had encouraged Satoru to design another house for the fifteen acres we still owned and he came up with a very beautiful concept for an underground house with glass skylights to illuminate the interior spaces. It had a central courtyard over which one of the skylights would be placed. It was completely different from the one we had recently sold and I envisioned it to be really spectacular. On the surface, it would probably look like a stone garden in a Kyoto Temple. So I suggested I invest my money in this new design. Satoru was not really very enthusiastic, as he was more concentrated on his sculptures. So I thought it would be best to invest in a house in Italy-- something we had thought about a lot each time we visited, but did not have the wherewithal to do. As money with me had a habit of disappearing quickly, I thought it would be best to call Beatrice, our friend in Tuscany who sold real estate, and had said she would help us when we were ready. I told her what we were looking for and what our budget was. It had to be partially habitable so that we could live in it while we were renovating. So it was decided, with her, that I would fly over to Tuscany and stay with her so that she could show me what she had found. Two weeks before Easter, I flew over to look for our future house.

FORNACINO DI GRE

The day arrived for me to leave and I kissed Satoru and Christophe goodbye at the airport -- promising to return with a new house for us in Tuscany. I picked up my rental car and drove up to Tuscany to Nieves' house, where I met Beatrice, who had several possibilities lined up for me to see. We had a nice lunch and talked about how we were managing and how Nieves' book was coming along. After lunch we saw three houses that were interesting but did not immediately grab me. It was late afternoon when we returned to her side (which meant the other side of the A1 highway), which was in the Province of Siena, leaving the Province of Arezzo. The next day was full, seeing many properties in the morning, none of which really appealed to me. We had lunch at a trattoria and Beatrice talked to me about an area I was not familiar with called Le Crete Senesi. She described it as a region made up of eroding clay hills dating back 3,000 years when they had been under the sea. They are interspersed with vineyards, olive groves, and wheat fields, and in July and August, some fields are covered in sunflowers. It is a spectacular area of Tuscany.

So, off we went after lunch, to see a house owned by three people: one, a German artist, her ex, and the other, her husband, a Russian nobleman descended from Catherine the Great. Well, I thought, it must be something, to come with such a pedigree. The house dated back to 1296 and originally belonged to the Abbott of the nearby Monte Olivetto Maggiore Abbey. It had been on the market for two years, which made me wonder what was wrong with it. To get there, we had to pass the small, charming, village of Chiusure and drive down a winding dirt road two kilometers to the house. The road was flanked on either side, part of the way, with sheer drops in the clay hills. The landscape was extraordinary -- I had never seen anything so spectacular! We wound down this incredible dirt lane and, rounding the last corner before arriving at the house, which was partially hidden amidst tall elegant Cyprus trees, was Fornacino Di Gre! As we drove up to the wrought iron front gate, I could see that it had been abandoned for some time. The garden was completely overgrown and the house itself needed lots of TLC. It had brown shutters on all the windows, which looked really ugly, especially as I disliked brown intensely.

Beatrice opened the padlock holding the gates together and drove into the courtyard. The house was on three levels: the ground level and the middle section and, to the right of it, the upper level. We walked up the front steps into the central section of the house. The inside was dusty and dark because the wooden shutters were closed. Beatrice went around opening them and light came flooding in. The house itself was in very good shape. This floor was divided into 4 bedrooms, a bathroom and a living room, through which one walked under an arch, up two steps into the master wing area with a second entrance and a bathroom. Then, up five steps into the master living room and up four more steps to the master bedroom, with an additional two windows looking out to the garden. The living room had a large fireplace and windows on both sides with built-in bookcases covering the wall around the fireplace. Here the ceiling was very high as it had the two levels for the living room and bedroom. The ceiling had the typical wood beams of old Tuscan houses and the floors were covered in the original cotto, the clay tiles of the area. This was very unusual that they had kept the original tiles. I immediately fell in love with this level; I envisioned it as our sanctuary away from the rest of the house.

We walked out the door of this part of the house and went down the front stairs to see the cantina. In these old houses, that part was where the animals were brought in at night or in inclement weather. It was full of things the owners had thrown in to get them out of the way. A large space the same size as the central part of the house upstairs was divided, one half by several small rooms and one large space where obviously the animals had originally been kept. Opposite this, on the other side of the courtyard, was a structure that housed three pig sties, a large garage on the left, and, on the right, the original bread oven dating back to 1296. It was in perfect shape! The entire house was surrounded by a 6,000 square meter garden with the most spectacular view of the surrounding clay hills and the Monte Olivetto Abbey. There was no question in my mind: this was our future house. I asked Beatrice to call the agent that represented it and to give him my offer. He called his clients in Germany who accepted it and I was on my way to being the proud owner of a piece of heaven in the Crete Senesi.

The next day we went to the Notary outside Montalcino to sign the preliminary contract of sale and to give him the deposit. I also needed to give Beatrice power of attorney, as she would be going to the closing on my behalf two weeks later. We then went to her bank where I opened an account to wire over the remaining money to complete the buying process. I gave Beatrice a huge hug and thanked her for her help. Apart from the agent fee she would collect, I gave her $ 1,000 more for doing the closing and arranging things for me. She would find a gardener to bring the garden back to shape and a few other things.

I was so excited and called Satoru to tell him we were now the owners of a historic Tuscan house dating back to 1296! He was really surprised that I had actually bought a house in two days! My business done in Tuscany, I called Ab and Tina Ten Dam, who were staying at Mehlika's house in Rome on holiday. They now lived in Holland and were visiting. I told them I had bought a house and was on my way back down to Rome. I arrived in the late afternoon and when I got there, their first words were, "Where did you buy the house?" I said, "You will never guess! Just outside a little village called Chiusure, in the Crete Senesi." Ab and Tina both burst out saying, "We were just there with some dear friends of ours who took us to visit the famous Monte Olivetto Abbey." They had had a cappuccino in the village and knew exactly where my new house was! Can you imagine -- Of all places, they were there a week before!

We decided to all go down to the Amalfi coast for the remaining days I had before going back to New York. I have always loved that area, and since it was spring, and the weather was so lovely, it was a perfect choice. We booked a charming, small hotel in Positano before leaving for the three-day week-end -- and off we went. Mehlika and I shared one room, with a wonderful terrace overlooking the village and the sea; Ab and Tina took the one next to us. We had a fabulous time visiting Amalfi, Ravello, and taking a boat over to the Island of Capri. I bought Christophe several big Easter eggs which were handcrafted and beautifully wrapped. I bought him four, each a different size. I bought Satoru a beautiful vase for his flower arranging made in the famous Amalfi coast clay pottery.

On Sunday night we returned to Rome, as Monday I had my flight back home to my two favorite boys. It never ceases to amaze me that there are times when everything aligns itself in such a way as to open all the doors for you. This was one of those magical times! At the end of May, when Christophe got out of school for the summer holidays, we would all be flying over to spend our first summer at the house. Satoru and Christophe were at the airport waiting for me, excited to hear all my news and to see the photos I had taken of the house. We returned to the loft in great excitement and I showed them the photos. They immediately liked what they saw and could not wait to see it in person. Beatrice had picked a rose for me to take back and I pressed it in my telephone book. I showed them the rose from our new garden. In just a month and a half we would be there!

I immediately went out to start buying sheets and towels to take over, as Beatrice had said they would be cheaper and of better quality. Plus wrinkle-free, as this, in Italy, would not be the case. They had beautiful sheets but they were mostly 100% cotton and had to be ironed. I continued my teaching at Merce's until it was time for us to leave. I found a cheap charter flight for us direct to Rome; the only hitch was that they did not allow pets on board and we now had Kitty Hawk. I decided we would have to smuggle her on, as she, like Taro, was a good traveler. Poor Taro, we had to put him to sleep that March as he had a brain tumor. He had never been ill and was twelve years old, running around like a puppy. All of a sudden, he had started turning in circles trying to catch his tail and collapsing. So we took him to the vet who told us to take him to the animal hospital on the East River. There they took an X-ray and found the brain tumor. It was in-operable; there was nothing to do and he had to be put down. It was the hardest decision either of us ever had to make and I was in mourning for over a year until Shoichi got angry with me and told me to snap out of it.

As soon as school finished, we were booked to leave. We put Kitty in my trusty leather carrying bag that I had used for Taro. The cab we had ordered came to pick us up to take us to the airport, as we had two cases and one carry-on each. We checked in and got our boarding passes. Up to there, all was well. The next hurdle was to get past the X-ray machines where we had to place our hand baggage. I was really worried, but put Kitty down on the conveyer belt and waited anxiously for her to get through. She made it, and just as she cleared the covered part of it, she moved and the policewomen standing checking everything noticed the movement, and asked me what it was. I quickly said, "Nothing. Just a vase I had that must have tipped over," whisked the bag off and almost ran to get as far away from her as possible. In the panic, I forgot my handbag with all my documents. Luckily, another passenger picked it up and ran over to give it to me. Whew! That was close!

Boarding was announced, much to my relief, and we all took our seats. While we were waiting for everyone to board, I heard that a Sky Marshall was on the plane and was sitting right next to me! I immediately got up and asked the hostess if she could move me, as I was allergic to cigarette smoke and needed to be in the No Smoking section further forward. The last thing I needed was for him to notice Kitty! She said she would try but the flight was full and it might not be possible. Bless her heart, she came back a few minutes later telling me the only seat left was right next to the toilet. I said that was fine and moved. Soon after the flight took off, the toilet got clogged and the smell was unbearable, but I was stuck there with Kitty and I would have to sit and bear it. Not only that, I spent the eight-hour flight leaning down, holding the bag up so that Kitty could breathe without it collapsing on her. Such fun and games!

I was very happy to land in Rome and put that horrible experience behind me. Customs was another concern, but, luckily in Italy in those days, they were not too fussy. They have a green section for nothing to declare and a red section for things to declare. Of course, I chose nothing to declare and walked through in a very determined manner. I had learned that if you walk with purpose and look straight ahead, you will rarely be stopped. Trusty Mehlika was at the airport to meet us in and took us to her house, where Christophe and I would wait for Satoru to go to Germany to his brother's who had arranged for him to buy a second-hand car. This was because we did not have Italian residency yet, and could not buy a car in Italy. In fact, that was the case for all of Europe. So Satoru would buy the car in his brother's name and drive it back to Italy.

TUSCANY SUMMER

Satoru was in Germany for a week and we got daily reports on his progress. Since we did not have too much money to spend, the choices were limited. Finally, he found a car that belonged to a university student, a Citroen 2CV that he said would be good for us. I liked the type of car and was happy he would buy it. He would leave after completing all the paperwork, and a day later he was on his way back to us. He returned late in the evening with a red 2 CV mini-van type of car (the type that, in France, they use for bread deliveries and such). He had a big satisfied grin on his face, waiting to hear what we thought of his acquisition. To say that I was surprised is an understatement; I could not believe my eyes. A mini-van! "My God," I said, "I spent two years going all through South America in a Land Rover and you buy us this camping van?" I was disappointed, and Satoru was absolutely crestfallen. He had been so pleased with his choice, and proud of his selection. I saw that it appealed to his sense of things that were out of the ordinary, but this, really? To add insult to injury, it was fire-engine red with a Crane decal running along each side of the van!

Mehlika could not help laughing and said it really was not so bad and complimented Satoru on his choice. I have to admit that, in time, I, too, got to appreciate the eccentricity of the thing. Anyway, the next day, we loaded our baggage into the van and off we went to our new house. I was so excited to show it to Satoru and Christophe and curious about their reaction to my choice. It was a two-and-a-half hour drive up from Rome. As we got to the surrounding area of the Crete Senesi, Satoru and Christophe exclaimed how incredible the countryside was. Approaching the outskirts of Chiusure, we were all getting more and more excited. We drove into the little dirt road that wound down to the house, which was two kilometers long, all the time both of them exclaiming, "Where is it?"

There was a part of the road that dipped down the hill quite steeply and then there was a big incline up. As we approached the steep upward part, the poor car did not have the power to make the climb. Satoru had to back down slowly and Christophe and I got off, so that, with less weight, he could get up some speed on the downhill part to get the necessary momentum to make it up the hill. I have to say it was really a very funny scene! Once up the incline, we walked up and got back in the car. We were all screaming with laughter. This was an occurrence that we had to repeat whenever the car was loaded down. Even without baggage, we had to go fast down the hill to make it up the other side. We became an instant hit with the villagers who saw us with the van. They had heard we were Americans and had expected us to drive up in a fancy car. When we didn't, and on top of it, the van was red, we were in their hearts. Tuscany always votes Communist, so the red was a big hit! As we rounded the last curve, I pointed to the clump of cypresses and the barely visible roof and said, "That is Fornacino di Gre." As we neared the house, more and more of it became visible until we drove up to the front gate. I got out and opened the padlock and we drove into our courtyard. Satoru and Christophe jumped out in a flash and ran around looking at everything all over the garden that now was more presentable, as Beatrice had sent a gardener to mow the lawns.

After the garden tour, we went up the steps to enter the main part of the house; again there was a mad dash to see everything. I could not wait to show Satoru our master wing! A look of marvel appeared on both their faces as they took it all in and I realized I had found the perfect house for all of us. We then went to see the cantina, the pig sties, the garage and the incredible bread oven. Oh, it was so exciting to see their pleasure and for me to see the house again! It was everything I remembered it to be. I had only seen it that one day in a rush, so it was great to realize that I had not made a mistake. We had arranged for Beatrice to come over to show us all the details, like where the electric panel was and so on. She arrived an hour later and when we were sitting out on our upstairs terrace having a drink together, she told us of her hair-raising experience at the closing of the house. Apparently the ex-husband was not happy with the price they had accepted and was ready to back out. Poor Beatrice was holding her breath while the other two partners tried to convince him to go ahead. She told us it was really a heart-stopping moment and almost thought she would have to call us to say the whole thing was off. Mercifully, the gods were on our side and the closing went ahead.

She also told us that she had met our neighbors, Mr. and Mrs. Borzi, who asked her who we were, and to take us down to meet them when we got there. They would become our saviors with many things, just like Mr. and Mrs. Rogers had been in Upstate New York. Mr. Borzi was the head of the Forestry department for the Province of Siena and a man with powerful connections, as we were to find out when we needed help. In fact, we would require his help right away, as we needed to have a telephone line installed so that we could call out and friends could reach us. In Italy, Beatrice told us that that could take months, so we had better ask Mr. Borzi if he could use his connections to get it hooked up quickly. He was an angel, as the telephone company showed up a few days later. They had to see where we were and how far the closest pole was to the house. It turned out they had to run a line all the way from the village, a costly affair. We were not complaining however, as to get this sorted out so quickly was nothing short of a miracle. Oh! To have the right connections! The Borzis also had many acres of olive trees and made their own organic extra-virgin olive oil, which they sold to us by the 5 Litre cans. The olives were pressed within 24 hours so they had '0' acidity. It tasted fabulous and all our guests over the summer raved about it. We used to serve it on toasted bread rubbed with garlic and smothered with the olive oil. A bit of heaven!

The house was, of course, empty, so Beatrice had kindly brought over two old mattresses and some pillows so that we would have something to sleep on. We went up to the Abbey where there was a lovely restaurant to have lunch, and then we would go to see about buying some furniture for the house. We found a nice, reasonable furniture showroom just outside Asciano, twenty minutes away. There we managed to buy the beds for all the bedrooms, a bunk-bed for Christophe, two couches, a dining table and chairs, night tables and lamps. They would deliver them the next day and we would be in business! It was so thrilling! Then we went to buy green paint to cover the brown of the wood shutters and doors, as all of us hated them. The next few days were spent transforming them and when we were finished the results were thrilling: the difference in the aspect of the house was like night and day! We were thrilled, I must say; every little thing we did was exciting for us, as the house was being transformed right in front of our eyes.

We had decided to invite several of our friends to stay and had given ourselves a month to get everything ready to receive them. We had invited all those that were going through difficult times. That meant three different sets of friends. The first to visit were Sally, Olivier, their Christophe and Juliet. Sally and Olivier were going through a difficult divorce. Olivier left after only a few days, but Sally and the children stayed on for another week. We wanted to take the children to visit Rome, which they were not too keen about, as we were having a heat-wave and it was uncomfortably hot. Sally and I came up with the idea of bribing them, by offering a half-day at the pool club. This solution was the magic necessary to get them to sit in the car for two-and-half hours. We got into Rome at six, as the air was cooling off. We parked the car at a garage above the Spanish Steps and walked down to the fountain at the bottom. The fountain and the steps were full of Romans and tourists, some dipping their feet into the water, others sitting on the steps passing the time of day. It is an impressive sight to see all that humanity and the classic sculpture in the middle of the water in the fountain down below. Rome's beauty will never cease to amaze me, it is so voluptuous and decadent.

Around the area of the Spanish Steps are the very elegant designer shops famous in Rome. Just beyond the first few streets is the Via Del Corso, where the more popular, less pricy stores were. Since the summer sales were in full swing, all the children and we grown-ups took advantage to buy a few beautiful things. As twilight was illuminating the Burnt Siena colors of the ancient buildings with magic, we made our way over to Trastevere to the Jewish Ghetto. I wanted to introduce everyone to Giggetto's, a famous Roman trattoria. One of their specialties is the crisply fried artichokes that, in my opinion, only they know how to make. They are brought out three on a plate looking like exquisite, crisp sunflowers, not the least bit oily, and absolutely delicious. It is a treat I never miss when I am in Rome. After dinner, we all piled into the car, tired, well-fed and happy. I, knowing the road best, drove while almost everyone else fell asleep. Just Sally and I talked quietly about the day. As we were approaching the Crete, we saw lines of fire in rows along the fields, where the farmers were burning the leftover grains after they had plowed the wheat fields. They do it to fertilize the soil, and, when you come upon it by chance at night, it is truly spectacular. We woke everyone up, so that they could see this amazing sight. A little further along, a porcupine was crossing the road in front of us with his family. Frightened by the car lights, they all spread their quills and it, too, was an incredible show: so ended our day with a performance by nature that was glorious to behold.

Since we had just bought the house, we did not have a pool yet and found a nice club nearby where we could buy a day ticket to go swimming. On one of our days, the two Christophe's were in the pool playing near the diving board, on which a well-endowed lady was preparing to dive. I was standing nearby and I heard Sally's Christophe say to mine under his breath, pointing upwards, "Look at her bosoms". They were both just nine years old and it was so funny to see them already acting like little men. All the fun was interspersed with clean-up work around the house. With Sally and family, we tackled the garage, which was full of junk that the previous owners had left behind. We were a sight for sore eyes, all decked out in our work clothes, filthy with straw hats tilted at rakish angles. We all had a lot of fun and the children saw it as a game, throwing things into piles that we would then load into our trusty red bomber and drive up to the village garbage containers. The time we all spent together in this way helped Sally and the children not to think so much about what was happening in their lives at that difficult moment. We were sad to see them go when their stay had come to an end. We hugged and cried and carried on shamelessly. We would be seeing them again when we returned to New York at the end of the summer.

Our next guests were Joke, Tekin, Gem, and Tan who had driven over from Bristol, England. They were managing to keep things going, but it was hard for all of them. The loss of their son and brother the previous year was still an open wound. We made sure to make their days interesting by showing them around our area -- the gorgeous Monte Olivetto Abbey, Siena, Pienza, and Montalcino. With them we also attacked more cleaning up, as they wanted to help us as well. So we cleared all the pig sties that were also stuffed to the gills with all manner of things. It was a lot of work and I was worried that it was too much. But I think the work helped them not to think, so I didn't protest. We tried to keep things jovial at meal times, and spent many pleasant times at the table. One afternoon, after the real heat of the day had passed, I showed everyone my water ritual. The one I had invented for our house video, "Premises," and had also performed at my parents' funeral service. I turned it into a game where everyone had to remember what they could of the order, and then each would do their interpretation of it. There was total silence, as they all sat on the ledge of our terrace, facing the house, looking at me do this ritual. It was to be an intense exercise to test each person's memory. Everyone got it just right, the timing of each was particular to them, but the sequence was almost perfect. We were all mesmerized by each version. No one refused, which I thought was wonderful, and Joke was the last to go and do hers. I was wondering what she would do, as I could see she was holding something in. She went all the way through, and, at the end, where one was to lift the vase with the water in it and pour it over one's head, she, instead, threw it in our direction and we all got a little wet. No one said anything and I got up and clapped my congratulations to everyone for their wonderful memories and execution. We all laughed and I gave Joke a big hug.

The days went mostly well for all of us except that Tekin was a bit brusque at times with his boys. One time, I felt I had to say something when he lashed out at Tan for something, telling him in a loud voice that he would plaster his head against the wall if he did that again. I have never agreed with verbal or physical abuse. I decided I had an obligation to intervene by quietly taking him aside, and asking him not to be so hard on the boys. His scene was offensive, I said, and that it was best not to deal with his anger in that way. It was a tense moment, but he listened to me and he calmed down. We were getting ready to go to the weekly open-air market in Buonconvento, a village nearby, when Joke came out all dressed and ready to go. Tekin took one look at her and told her to change her blouse, as it was too transparent. We all thought it was fine, but he made her change it anyway. Little things like that made us all aware of how difficult the tragic loss of their son was. For a man like Tekin, being Turkish, his tradition demanded he be manly, so he had no avenue to let off steam other than in those harsh ways of his. Their marriage eventually ended, as neither could express their terrible pain to each other; their traditions were too far apart for them to be able to handle the trial that destiny had dumped in their laps. It was painful to witness and we just tried to keep things light for the children. Their visit too, came to an end, and we saw them off with a heavy heart, as I knew it was not going to be easy for any of them.

Between each arrival, we had some time to ourselves to keep going with our improvements to the house. We had managed, with our friends' help, to get the garage and the pig sties cleaned. So now we attacked the room between the pig sties and the bread oven. This, too, was full of things and lots of trips were made up to the garbage. We were also deciding where we would build a pool the next summer, as we wanted to have a pool in the garden. Having to go somewhere else to swim was not very pleasant, so this project was important. Satoru felt the best place was behind the pig sties, away from the house, so the pool noise would not disturb whoever was resting in the house. I was a bit daunted by the fact that, behind there, the land had a steep incline from the back wall of the pig sties down to the rest of the garden. It was also completely overgrown with shrubs, prickly spines and masses of weeds. I, not being an architect, could not see what he saw, and was a bit in doubt as to whether that was, indeed, the best place. I thought the garden on the other side of the house, in front of the bedrooms and the living room, would be the best place, as it was fairly flat. Satoru was adamant and that was where, the next summer, we would build the pool.

ITALY AND NEW YORK

Our next project was the clearing of the cantina in the two week break we had before Mady and her son, Daniel, arrived from New York. Mady was the daughter of Irving Marantz, papas New York sculptor friend. It was not all work every day; we did stick our noses out to see that life was still in full swing beyond our confines. Morning excursions up to the restaurant La Torre, for fresh-baked pastries and cappuccinos were an occasional favorite. We also went up there some evenings, when we were too tired from the hard work to cook and felt like a treat. Melon and prosciutto crudo, pizza margueritas and fried artichokes we especially liked, followed by ice cream for Christophe and Panna Cotta with chocolate sauce for Satoru and me. Prosciutto crude has always been a favorite of mine; it is the smoked ham that they lay over the melon slices, or figs, when they are in season; the pizza marguerita is the one that just has tomato sauce and mozzarella with basil leaves on top. It is the simplest of all the pizzas, and we all loved it. Panna cotta is a dessert made with heavy cream and starch that is put in an individual mold and baked in the oven. It is only made in Italy and is a sinfully delicious dessert. La Torre became our stomping ground, where we took all our visitors and guests to eat at least once during their stay.

We had made friends with the family who ran La Torre for the Monte Olivetto Abbey, as the restaurant was on the Church's property. Paola greeted and seated the guests, her brother, Franco, was the cashier, and they both waited tables with a small staff; Franco's wife, Mirella, was the cook. The food was home-style Italian cooking at its best. We felt at home whenever we went up there, as they always made us feel welcome, and it was a pleasure returning every summer to be greeted by them. They made a great fuss over Christophe, so he loved going up there, as they always gave him something special they knew he liked. Monte Olivetto is a very famous Benedictine Abbey dating back to the Renaissance and is known for its beautiful book-binding. The Benedictines were also famous for their herbal remedies, which they sold in the Abbey gift shop. It is a huge Abbey but, sadly, there are only sixteen monks there in residence, as that particular order of Benedictines is dying out. It has many famous frescoes on its walls that enclose a beautiful courtyard. Inside it has a large nave and two small chapels on either side, with striking stained glass windows. It is painted light blue and white, which gives it a very serene air. We always took our varied guests to see it and on Sundays went to the mid-day mass to hear the monks sing Gregorian chants.

Their dining room is spectacular and we always knew how many were in residence by how many places had been set for lunch. Their food was cooked by La Torre and Paola told me once they insisted on only the very best ingredients. Many of the monks, I noticed, had come from South America. There was a magnificent olive press where they pressed all the olives that they had on their extensive property. They had their own large vegetable and herb gardens and a huge water reservoir. There was also a cemetery where all the deceased Abbots lay in a tranquil, shady corner of their large grounds. We loved taking people up there to visit; it was such a magical spot. Satoru found out that it was built on one of the nine power centers of the earth, a place where two rivers cross underground, forming a cross. It is believed that the energy in these centers creates a kind of vortex and all that live in its vicinity live longer and in better health, due to the positive energies. We noticed that there were several very old monks, and, in the village, we were told people lived longer there than in most other places.

The distance to the Abbey from our house was only four kilometers. In fact, from our garden, we could see it right across the way. If we could have flown, it would have been a stone's throw away. To get to the Abbey by car from our house we had to drive up two kilometers to Chiusure, our little village of 150 people, where there was a bar, a grocery store, a post office and an old peoples' home at the top of its hill. A friend of ours, Roberto, said he would go there when he was old, as it was such a fantastic spot. Up there you had a view of the whole valley below; it was like being up in the clouds. The Abbey was a farther two kilometers on the other side of the village. Our assigned doctor was the resident doctor for the home. When we needed him, we would drive up to see him there. In Italy, when you become a resident, you are entitled to the national health benefits and, as I was a EU citizen, had a right to be covered. Satoru and Christophe, being my family, also had the same rights. In that system you choose the doctor you want to be assigned to. The Borzi's had recommended Dr. Pizzichio and he was very helpful whenever we saw him.

Our neighbors also invited us over for lunch many times, which we really appreciated. Signora Borzi was a wonderful cook and enjoyed feeding us. They loved how Satoru would eat everything they put on his plate. He had no problem with his weight and never worried about getting fat, as his figure was always the same no matter how much he ate. I, on the other, hand, had to be careful, and missed out on a lot of delicious foods. They would have their daughters-in-law drop by with fresh vegetables, just picked from their garden. They had two sons and two daughters-in-law and one nephew. Soon after we arrived at the house for the first time, their nephew, Vincenzo, came riding up from their house on a beautiful mountain bike. He was about Christophe's age, which was almost nine at the time. When Christophe set eyes on the bike, he was on a campaign to have one as well. Christophe's tactic was to keep insisting until we bought him what he wanted. So, for his birthday that year on July 30th we bought him his own mountain bike. It was a very colorful affair and he had to pedal for like hell to get up those steep hills around us. He and Vincenzo used to race up and down on their bikes, and at the end of the day, Christophe would return exhausted.

It was time for me to go and pick up Mady and her son, Daniel, from the station at Chiusi, an hour away. They would be with us for ten days; we planned to drive them around to the beautiful hill towns nearby and to spend a day in Florence. They were not familiar with this part of Italy, so we would introduce them to its splendors. The day we went to Florence, we experienced, first-hand, the gypsies' stealing tactics. We were walking in the Piazza Della Signoria when, out of nowhere, we were surrounded by gypsy children, all with newspapers across their hands, asking if we would buy a newspaper.

In reality, what they were doing was using the newspaper to sneak their other hand underneath to pick-pocket. I caught one of their hands reaching for Satoru's pocket and quickly pushed him away; warning the others to make a scene to get them off us. It was a close call; Satoru almost lost his wallet and Mady her camera. This is an unfortunate reality of the big tourist cities of Italy, and leaves many a foreigner with a bad taste in his mouth.

For lunch, we went to a nice trattoria we knew, and as we walked in, the first people we saw were Luciano Pavarotti and his then secretary, Nicoletta. We were tempted to go up and ask for his autograph but we decided to leave them in peace. I remembered when I was with Merce, we were performing at the Spoleto Festival and were there for a week. One day, Mel Wong and I went to lunch at a restaurant just off the main road, and who should be sitting there, but Ezra Pound? That time, as we were performing there and people recognized us, we felt okay about going up to him when he smiled at us. It turned out he had seen one of our performances, when we had done *Signals*, where we had our duet, and had admired our dancing. He invited us to sit with him, and we shared a wonderful conversation while we all ate lunch together. What a privilege! But even then, neither of us had the gumption to ask for his autograph. If one goes up after a performance to ask an artist for their autograph, I think that is expected. But when they are out and about, I feel one should not invade their privacy, out of respect.

Our long day in Florence had been very eventful and we returned home satisfied and exhausted at the end of the day. Florence was a one and three quarter hour drive away, so it was not a journey we did often. Besides, I preferred, Siena as a city, as it is smaller and more intimate; less visited by tourists. Although I have noticed that it has recently become more of a tourist attraction. Mady's visit was also full of my listening and trying to give sensible advice. She was having trouble deciding to go ahead and divorce and wanted to come to some conclusion during this visit. I am good at helping people open up and am also a very good listener. However, it takes quite a bit out of one, and my summer had been full of listening and helping in any way I could.

The summer coming to an end meant getting the house closed for the year -- draining water out of the pipes, turning gas and electric off and closing all the shutters and doors. It was not our favorite task, as we were always sad to leave. Beatrice had suggested we hang clothes on the clothes line behind the house, so that anyone passing would think we were in residence. So up went underpants, T-shirts, trousers, socks and a dress. We would pile the baggage into our red bomber and make the trip back down to Rome, where we would leave the car in Mehlika's parking area. She would be in charge of starting the engine every now and then. She also had her own set of keys to the house and went up occasionally for week-ends.

Back in New York, the school year would start and Satoru and I would go back to our routines. Our ten year rental contract on our loft came to an end and the landlord sent us a notice of a rent increase and a new contract. He wanted to increase our rent from $ 750. 00 to $ 3,000 dollars a month, something that, not in a million years, would we be able to afford. He also did this with the other two tenants in the building. We immediately all got together, and found out that if we had lived in our spaces before the end of 1979, we had a right to be grandfathered in. That is to say, that the landlord would only be able to increase the rent by a small set amount. We wrote him a joint letter, to which he responded that he would start legal action to get us all out. Thus started a four-year legal battle, that added an enormous stress and a lot of worry to our already difficult existence.

On top of this, about a week after our return, I developed a torturous migraine that, try as I might, I could not get rid of. It raged on for a week, non-stop. Acupuncture, Papa's migraine medicine, massages and other remedies had no effect. In desperation, I went to see my doctor, who ran tests which came back without any signs of anything being wrong. He prescribed a strong medicine for depression, which, mercifully, stopped the pain, as it made me violently sick. The migraine went, and I had lost six pounds in the process, as eating had been almost impossible. I called him to tell him what happened. He mentioned that he thought the problem was probably due to the fact that I had taken on too much over the summer trying to help my friends. He diagnosed a severe depression and recommended I go to see a psychiatrist. He gave me the name of a woman whom he thought would be able to help me.

I made an appointment to see her, and went on the day we had arranged. I sat down where she suggested and started to tell her of the accident and the summer with my wounded friends, all the while crying non-stop. She said I was severely depressed, and that it would be best for me to come and see her once a week until I felt better. I asked her how much it would cost and she mentioned $ 200.00 dollars a session, I told her I could not afford that, so she suggested having one of her interns see me for half the cost. I said thank you, but I did not think an intern would be able to help me, and took my leave. I had an hour before going to pick up Christophe from school. I just sat in the car and cried and cried, wondering what I was going to do. I went into a coffee shop for a drink so that I could use the bathroom to clean my face, before presenting myself in front of Christophe. We drove home and Satoru asked how it had gone with the doctor and I told him what had happened.

The next morning, October 4, 1989, I awoke at 5:30, wide awake, and decided to sit down and write. It was the beginning of (what I call) my Prose Poetry books; this one I titled *Preoccupations with The Past*. It was a collection of seventeen poems, written over a period of eight days. I wrote about my past with my parents, and how I wished I had known more of their struggles. I liked that they were not tragic recollections, just beautiful memories of a life spent with them. As I was writing them, I felt a subtle thread emerging from my stomach. When I finished them all, the backaches that had plagued me since I had joined Merce disappeared. It was like all the pain and tension of my living experiences that I had hidden from the outside world down my spine were released, and floated out of me into the atmosphere. I never had a backache again, except when, in the process of moving and lifting heavy things it would get sore from the effort. I had begun to resolve the psychiatrist problem on my own and I became my own healer.

I include two of those prose poems here:

MAMA

I remember sitting in our
Garden
Together we ate oranges till
Sick
How close I felt to you
Mama
I remember your big
Earrings
Hanging next to your lovely
Cheeks
Big red ruby lips smiling at me
Exotic and fun, full of
Adventure
Riding on your horse flying
In the wind
How I loved you then, how I love
You now.

PAPA

Ever since I can remember
You were my God
Majestic and with a lions
Head and mane
Proud I was to be along
Side you
Running to keep up with
Your long strides.
Always running to keep
Up with you
Wanting to make you proud
Of me
You dreamed so much for me
I fulfilled your wish
You asked me at ten to promise
Complete devotion to dance
I promised not knowing
The magnitude of that promise
And ever since I have tried
With every
Fiber of my being to
Meet your wish
I remember the poem you
Wrote about me when I
Was born.

After that I wrote *Reflections on an East West Relationship* in October/November 1989. I would write seven, although I never published them. I wrote the last one in January of 1991. They became a means to an end, a way to confront on the paper my thoughts, and thereby release them onto the paper -- out of myself and the confines of my mind and body.

EXPLORATIONS

The first book had freed me of my backaches and, in some other way, gave me confidence. At any rate, I was more optimistic and was approaching our life with more calm. It was at this time that we met a lovely French lady called Delphine who was staying with a mutual friend of ours. Our friend had a luncheon for her, and her then partner Pierre, one Sunday at her apartment on the upper Eastside of Manhattan. As soon as we entered, we saw this charming, blonde, petite, very elegant lady. Flory, our host, came up to greet us and introduced us to Delphine. As destiny would have it, Delphine became a very important friend in our lives. We immediately had a connection -- she was sure that I was her father in another life and always referred to me as *mon pere* (my father) in French. She had the most beautiful, clear blue eyes and a wonderful, twinkly laugh. She would be very instrumental later in the development of my *Poetic Acts Workshops*.

Delphine was a soul in search of answers to the age-old questions of why we are here and what our mission is, the same search in which I was also involved, so we had a natural affinity. It turned out that she was a school teacher in a school for underprivileged children in a really rough neighborhood of Paris. She had a passion for teaching and loved the children she worked with. She, herself, had a daughter, who would become a doctor, and a son who became a lawyer. She was divorced from their father and her present companion was a French painter. He was very dapper and dressed in a very eccentric way, with flamboyant scarves around his neck, velvet waistcoat and handmade shoes. Her father was the curator of the Louvre Museum in Paris and she had a marvelous apartment just off the St. Honore a few blocks from the Louvre. Her family also owned a castle just outside Paris where they all gathered at week-ends. She had a little mini-Cooper to run around in Paris and a gorgeous Rolls Royce for special occasions. This, of course, we found out bit by bit, when we finally got over to Paris, after numerous invitations, a few years later. She would also help me try to get a gallery for Satoru's sculptures in Paris.

We invited Delphine and Pierre to our loft for lunch the following week to continue our conversation. We had a wonderful lunch, with brilliant conversation and laugher. Afterwards, we drove them down to see the World Trade Center and the Wall Street area, as they had not had time to go down there yet. We spent a very happy afternoon with them and exchanged telephone numbers and addresses. They left for Paris soon after and we would keep in touch with a prodigious correspondence until we eventually took her up on her invitation to join her on a Rolls Royce club rendezvous in Rheims, at the Veuve Clicoc Castle and winery, in July of 1990. We had many extraordinary times with her, and she is still my dearest friend to this day. I feel, as she does, that there is definitely something to be said for past lives spent together. She and I both felt very strongly a previous connection.

After they left, we continued our daily activities. One day, speaking with Henrietta while our boys were playing in the playground, she told me about a psychic healer whom Nadia, a friend of hers, had told her would be teaching a course called *Getting In Touch With Your Psychic Instrument.* The psychic teacher was called Demetrius Gregorian, who was Armenian. Well, the name alone gave me pause for thought. That was the name my mother had given a little toy lion Papa had bought her at Porta Portese, the Roman flea market, when we lived in Rome. She later wrote a children's book on the adventures of *Demetrius,* her lion. Shoichi was going to do the illustrations in his fabulous penmanship. Unfortunately, Mama never finished the book and Shoichi therefore did not do the illustrations, which makes me sad.

The course was starting at the beginning of December and we decided to enroll in it with her. In the meantime, she would arrange for us to each have a private reading with him. One sunny afternoon, he came to our loft for our readings. When I saw him for the first time that afternoon, I could not believe my eyes. He looked exactly like Mama's lion, Demetrius! He had a curly (what I thought was probably) a wig that looked just like the lion's mane. He had a lovely, generous face and a portly, short body. I wrote one of my prose poetry books on him and his course:

DEMETRIUS

That was the name
Of my mother's wooden
Lion on a plinth
Orange he was
A fluffy mane framing
His face
He had a mechanism
Underneath that when
Pressed by one thumb
Would make him
Collapse or tilt his head
To one side quizzically
He was my mother's
Favorite toy and he
Went everywhere she did
She wrote a children's
Book about him
And his adventures
So when one day
Nadia talked about
Someone she knew
Who had great powers
Of spirit and she
Mentioned his name
Demetrius I knew that
This was Mama's lion
In the flesh
I had arranged a
Reading with him
At a very low point
In my world

And one December
Afternoon he came
Bouncing up our stairs
I was standing at
The top and watched
Him ascend
He had the mane of
Mama's Lion curly jet black hair
And the smile too
I had been jokingly accused
By a dear friend that
I was falling for
Something less than serious
And that I should be
On my guard
So I was and my
First thought was
Oh! You've
Really done it this time
He was bubbly and
Full of cheer I
A little nervous
And ill at ease
We sat down and
He started talking
And the words that
Poured out were of
Things I deeply knew
And had felt
For two hours he talked
And joked and laughed
I cried and marveled
And laughed with him
That afternoon was the
Beginning of my communication
With all that was spiritual
And eternal and the

Start of my dialogue
With the world around
Me and those that entered
I felt he was a most
Precious gift from my mother.

That afternoon, he also had a session with Satoru, which, Satoru later told me, had also been very perceptive. We both signed up to take his course that would be held at Henrietta's friend Nadia's apartment on Central Park South. The course would start in January and we were looking forward to it, though Satoru a little less so. He was not totally convinced about it and took it with a little reluctance.

January arrived, the start of a new year, the beginning of a new adventure. We all gathered at Nadia's for the start of *Getting In Touch With Your Psychic Instrument,* to learn about ourselves and others, to be more aware, in touch with information from beyond. Demetrius was the person we went to learn from; we instinctively felt that he would guide us with wit and sincerity. He drew out the best in us and taught us, first by example, and then by making us each, in turn, try his techniques. We were fifteen altogether, each very different from the next and a revelation in the sense that the varieties of human spirit were incredible. Each was developing their psychic talent in a different way. All sorts of information came out, as well as the generosity and kindness of each of us. Demetrius was an able, funny, wonderful, teacher and guide. He would, at times, jump out of his chair and do a fandango, or slap his knee and stamp his foot to emphasize a point. He had lots of stories and anecdotes. We were kept on our toes and learned invaluable lessons. The course took place over a six-week period, meeting every Friday for two hours.

I have always been curious about all manner of things and this experience was food for my brain, which sent me off in many directions. It was one more piece of information that I would add to my body of knowledge. It would become a part of my slowly developing future, Poetic Acts Workshop. I was so impressed with the work, that, at the end, I asked Demetrius if he would be interested in giving the course at our house in Tuscany. The idea appealed to him and we worked out an arrangement whereby I would take care of publicizing the course and gathering the students to attend. I would also pay for his, and his companion, Rollodon's, air fares, and would give him all the proceeds of the students' fees. They would stay at our house with us and we would provide all the meals. He agreed to all the terms and I went ahead to plan for the course the following summer. Henrietta wrote to her sister in Switzerland telling her of the course and she and a Swiss Air pilot enrolled. My friend, Delphine, from Paris, would also attend and we managed to get three others. So, in all, we would be eight, as Satoru and I would take it again. I also wrote to the director of the College of Psychic Studies in London asking if they could put up the course flyer I had made, hoping to attract more students to come over to Italy for this unique opportunity.

I got the most extraordinary letter back from the director, which I quote here:

Dear Susana Hayman-Chaffey   *23.7.90*

We have put the notice on our board and hope it may attract some participants—though I do not expect that many of the people who look at our board would be able to take off for Italy.

I am writing because of your name. It is such an unusual one, that I think it must have been your parents whom I knew when I and my husband were living in Brazil in the 1950's. I expect you were then one of the family travelling around the world with them?

Or maybe you are the Mrs. Hayman-Chaffey we knew at that time? (My memory won't dredge up Christian names at the moment—they will probably come back in the middle of the night.)

This is just by way of a greeting from the past.

With all good wishes,
Yours sincerely,
Signed by her,
Mrs. Brenda Marshall, President

I sat spellbound when I read her letter, realizing that everything we do always has a consequence. My instinct to help others, through

Demetrius, brought me a precious gift that I would not have received, had I not set in motion his course. It would be the beginning of a long correspondence between us, which was to be my saving grace so many times, when I was suffering the pains of abandonment. I include a few excerpts from my response to her letter.

Dear Brenda Marshall,   *September 18, 1990*

I regret that this letter will reach you so long after your extraordinary letter of July. As soon as I received it I called the College and was told you were away and would return on Tuesday. I tried then but you were out and I stupidly did not leave a message for you, to at least thank-you for your letter. Then the course started and there was not a moment. However when it ended I tried again but the college must have been closed for the summer holidays as no one answered.

I am back in New York and finally able to sit down and write to you, to tell you how much your letter touched me. It was my parents whom you met; I was nine years old at the time.

I then went on to tell her of their accident and my reactions, my career, and about Satoru and our son, Christophe.

The day your letter arrived I was a bit depressed worried that I would not have the required number of people to attend the course. It later turned out I did, and all went very well. I saw your letter as a sign of encouragement and when you wrote the last line "This is just by way of a greeting from the past" I sat and cried. It seemed to me my parents were reaching me through you, as it were.

At any rate I was most grateful to you and your fateful wonderful letter. I would love to know anything you can tell me about your meeting with them. I am thirsty about anything I can discover about them. I am very curious to know if you were already involved with the Psychic Studies when you met them. And if so, did you talk about this with them?

*Thank-you again for your fateful and timely letter and please
excuse the long lapse of time in my answer.*

With best wishes, Susana

We had an incredible correspondence that lasted many years; her
letters always seemed to arrive at a moment when I was down and
depressed. Her words always helped me recover and gave me hope.
Satoru and I finally met her on one of our trips to London, when she
graciously invited us to tea. It was a wonderful meeting, with lots of
memories and stories of her life and meeting us in South America.

DEMETRIUS IN TUSCANY

The beginning of 1990 had started with the course we took with Demetrius. At the same time the lawsuit about the loft began for us and our downstairs neighbor, Steve. The upstairs tenants were relatively new and they had nothing to do with the case. The proceedings took place in the city building code offices near Wall Street. We were recommended to a group of lawyers who were supposed to be very good at defending loft tenants. We hired them to represent us, and Steve, not being able to afford a lawyer, represented himself. I was well-prepared, as I had kept every receipt for all the work we had done on the loft. They went as far back as 1979 in order to prove that we had lived there since then, to qualify to be grandfathered in, so our rent could only be increased by a few percents. This whole endeavor would take three years at a cost of $ 60,000 dollars. It would turn out to be an incredible added stress that caused us a lot of tension and almost took us to the point of bankruptcy.

The thing I remember most about the events was the first day when we all met at the Department of Housing offices: the landlord's lawyer, our lawyer, Satoru, Steve and I. As we were waiting for the presiding officer to arrive, the landlord's lawyer made a speech about the fact that he could not adequately represent his client. Our side had too much evidence and it was useless to start the process. We all looked at each other and wondered what this actually meant. It turned out to be a grandstand method for him to put us into confusion. The building officer arrived and we all filed into the office where the case would be heard. The landlord's lawyer, again, made his speech and the hearing officer ruled that we had to go ahead and present the case. That was the first day; we were sure, after the lawyer's speech, that we had probably won the case by default. This proved to be an illusion and we were interrogated exhaustively over the next three-years.

I approached my part in the proceedings with an aggressive stance, as I remembered all the details of our work on the loft and our daily living there. Satoru never answered a question directly; he went with the tactic that he could not recall. He was the only one who drove the opposing lawyer into fits of frustration.… a fact that made me very happy. But he infuriated me at the same time, as he was not supporting my version in any way. Steve was a bit nebulous in his recollections. So I came out looking like I was fabricating my answers. At any rate, the whole process kept us on our toes, angry, frustrated and outraged. At one point, there was the question of where we lived when I was pregnant with Christophe. So the opposing lawyer reached my gynecologist, and managed to get hold my records to see the address we had used as our residence. That my doctor gave him my medical records was outrageous and illegal, but there was nothing we could do short of taking legal action against him as well. He had died in the meantime, so all that was out of the question. Since we also had the apartment address in the West Village at the same time as the loft address, he contended that we were actually living there and not at the loft. The 1979 issue of the two addresses, and where we officially lived, was crucial to both sides.

To return to the beginning of 1990, we finished the course with Demetrius, and I continued to write my little Prose Poetry books. In January, I wrote "Wonderings About a Fragile Bond", which concerned the relationship with my brother. In March/April, I wrote "Taking a Leap Into Thin Air," about the building of the Japanese country house. From May to July, I wrote "Remembering the Business of Living," which dealt with many different experiences I had in living my life. Satoru continued with his flower arranging and sculpting and Christophe was happy with school. At week-ends, we would drive out of the city to Long Island or up to our neighbors. On one of our trips to Long Island we saw a beautiful wicker couch with big fluffy pillows covered in a lush cotton fabric with a subtle flower design, imported from Indonesia. We immediately thought it would be really great for our house in Italy. We went into the store and saw that they had two, with two armchairs and two ottomans.

We asked if they would give us a bigger discount if we bought the whole set and they took another 10% off, so we bought them and arranged for everything to be delivered at the loft.

That spring we had decided to send a container of furniture and some of our possessions to our house in Tuscany. Having taken residence in Italy, we had eighteen months to send over our household belongings without having to pay the 25% duty, otherwise required. In May, when the shipping company brought the container for us to load, our landlord, having been notified by someone who had seen us loading, called to ask if we had decided to move out after all. I very coldly answered no, that we were just shipping some things to Italy. In retrospect, I wish we had moved out then. It would have saved us so much heartache and money. I firmly believe things would have turned out very differently had we moved to Italy at that time. Unfortunately, we thought that it was important for Satoru's new career to be in New York, and Christophe had also just started at a new school in Brooklyn Heights for gifted children called Saint Ann's, where he was doing very well. Having lived twenty-five years in New York, I felt it was the center of the world, and the thought of leaving was beyond me. In fact, it took us until 1993 to finally leave. When we did pull ourselves out and had moved to Tuscany, we wondered why it had taken us so long. It made me realize how much the choices we make can have lasting effects on future events.

School over, the container on its way, it was time to head over to our house for the summer. Our things would be arriving, Demetrius' course would be taking place, and we would be renovating the cantina. We had a full schedule planned and there was no time to waste. We arrived with great pleasure to our Italian home and breathed the fragrant air of the hills deep into our lungs and gave thanks for the privilege of having this gorgeous house in one of the most beautiful landscapes we had ever seen. We had noticed that the first week we were there, our ears would have a low buzzing sound and I realized that, due to the extreme silence surrounding us, we were hearing the sound of our blood coursing through our bodies. I had remembered that John Cage, curious about whether total silence was possible, had gone into a soundless chamber at NASA. There he discovered that he could hear a buzzing sound. On exiting, he asked the engineers what that sound was. They told him it was the sound of his blood coursing through his veins. We would be aware of it for the first week, until our ears became accustomed to the silence. We did not realize how living in a city like Manhattan, the noise that we were constantly absorbing, was affecting our ears.

The month we set aside before anyone arrived was dedicated to renovating the cantina, receiving the container, and placing the furniture that was arriving from New York. The day the container was scheduled to arrive, we were wondering how it would make it down our steep winding dirt road. We were amazed when the driver, having called ahead and inspected the road, said that he could negotiate it, no problem. We had hired a few village men to help unload it and to put our things in the different areas we had chosen to put them. We also needed the extra space for Demetrius' course, as we would use the cantina space for his workshop. We found Elio, who lived down our road, to help us with the renovation, as he was a plasterer and builder. Since he was retired and did not have a company, he would be much cheaper than using a regular building enterprise. It would turn out that he was the one who we used for all the work that we eventually did at the house.

Elio became our boss, in a way, we served as his assistants whenever we did any renovating. So we took on the cantina, and worked solidly for a month with him to get it finished. Christophe was also pressed into helping, although he did not do too much. We had our Geometra (the person who supervises the designs for the Commune) make up the plans for opening the space, as all modifications in Italy have to have a permit and be approved. We took out all the dividing walls where there were rooms, and made beautiful arches with bricks, to open the spaces up. Once we had done that, we had a man come to sandblast all the brick work. That left a huge pile of sand that we used in the garden to make a sand pit for Christophe to play in, and the rest went on top of the small mountain we made in the back of the house for the debris from knocking out the separating walls. We covered the dirt floor with white ceramic tiles, to give more light, and we ended up with a really gorgeous, open space. Satoru used an old iron furnace we found there for a sculpture he later called "Hiroshima mon Amour," which he gave me. He also made three sculptures from three old wood doors we also found in the cantina. He painted them and we hung one in our wing, another in the entrance of the central part of the house and the third in the cantina. They were his beautiful signatures on the different walls.

We were now ready to receive Demetrius and the students that would be arriving for his course. Everyone would be put up at the house, as we had the room, and it was more convenient. Satoru went down to Rome to pick up Demetrius and Rollodon, his companion, arriving from New York, and Delphine, who would be flying in from Paris. He greeted them in with our red bomber, much to their delight. As there was only a driver's and a passenger seat in the front, Rollodon and Delphine would have to sit on top of the luggage. Satoru had taken a single mattress to put on top of the cases for them to sit on. Demetrius, ever the entertainer, had brought with him his trusty cassette on which he played his collection of operas. They had a fantastic time singing and laughing, and drinking the wine Satoru had brought with him as a greeting for them. They showed up at the house slightly inebriated, laughing and carrying on. Demetrius and Delphine were opera lovers and they had played their favorite operas full blast on the way up. Of course, to get up our impossible hill, they all had to get out and that, too, caused a lot of laughter.

Demetrius would also be doing private readings with everyone, which would give him extra income and provide the students with deeper insights. Since Delphine was the first to arrive, and would be there alone for two days before the rest, she had her reading first. We had worked out a system where Satoru was in charge of breakfast, with me assisting, and I would be in charge of the other two meals. The whole plan got slightly out of hand when the students arrived, as we had not set a meal schedule. So breakfast slid into lunch and everything got backed up. That summer we learned that definite times had to be set for meals, and who did not make them, went without. As it seemed we were always in the kitchen making and serving food.

A few days later, everyone arrived and was installed in their rooms and the course began. It was a wild success, and I have to say we were all very happy with the results. We had found time to also show everyone around the countryside, visiting famous towns and churches. We had some fabulous meals out and about and I remember that time with great, fond memories. One evening, we took everyone to the hot Springs at Bagno Vignoni. We went at night after dinner to a spring just outside the town where the hot springs would cascade down into a pool at the bottom of the hill. It formed a natural fair-sized lake and the water was warm. It was best to go late at night under the light of the moon, as it was cooler and getting into the hot water was a pleasure. We all scooped up the white mineral silt off the bottom and spread it on our skin. It was a natural purifier that left our skin soft as silk. It was such a privilege to be out under the stars in that beautiful, surreal, setting, partaking of the bounty nature was offering us. It was absolutely free, as it was not part of the spa up the hill. The last night, we arranged to go up to the Abbey restaurant for the final meal. They set up a long table for us all and Christophe went from one to the other, getting a sip of wine and ended up tipsy, making everyone laugh with his antics. For us, it was a very welcome event that had gone well and we felt very satisfied having pulled it off. Demetrius was fantastic and I cried when he and Rollodon went back to New York.

When everyone left, we were once again alone and a little bit lonely as we had to re-adjust to being just us three. The summer went quickly as it always did, since we were so busy improving the house and visiting towns and villages we loved. We bought some fruit trees and roses to add to the ones already around the house. When we bought the house, it had three pomegranate trees, two peach trees, two rose bushes, a gorgeous mimosa tree, a huge rosemary bush and six cypresses. In the front garden, we added three plum trees, two cherry tress and several rose bushes. Over the years, by adding more roses, we ended up with forty varieties of gorgeous rose bushes. We also planted twenty lavender bushes, which perfumed the air when they were in bloom. We made a vegetable and herb garden and all summer we ate the succulent tomatoes, cucumbers, string beans, lettuces, onions and carrots we had planted. We also had the bounty of the fruit, which was such a treat. We bought all of the trees at the famous Siena market, which took place every Wednesday, in a square just outside the ancient city walls. It was a very popular market, to which people from all over the region used to gather to go shopping.

They had everything from clothes to pottery to plants to food to house wares. In fact, we bought a set of the famous Deruta blue and white plates there.

Our next project, for the following summer, was going to be the construction of a pool, which we were very anxious to get built. So, again, it was time to return to New York and our life there. We packed up our things, closed the house, and with Kitty in tow, returned. Another summer had flown by, full of great accomplishments and new experiences. We had met new people, worked hard and communicated with each other in a serene and wonderful way. When I think back at those times, I realize that Satoru and I hardly ever exchanged a harsh word. I was more temperamental than Satoru and had my moments of explosion, for one thing or another. He, however, rarely reacted badly to my explosions; he just let me at it and stood by bemused and calm. Only once did he respond by pushing me when I was backing him into a wall with a problem he was not responding to. So we actually never had any serious disagreements and our life together as a couple was, as a result, very calm, due to his complete serenity. It was a great example for Christophe growing up, to see this rapport between his parents.

POETIC ACTS

When we got back to New York, I started to put together my "Poetic Acts Workshop" in order to start teaching it. The idea for it had grown out of a desire to put to use all the various methods of healing I had explored and learned in my search to understand and enrich myself. The workshop was based on the principles of complete concentration and awareness, the re-integration of the mind and body, and revitalization of the spirit. I offered techniques for relaxation, breathing, meditation, and yoga to help bring students to a place where they could explore the depths of themselves in a secure environment. They were simple exercises anyone could do which gave me clues as to where they were in their search. There was a constant question and answer system throughout the sessions for the students to keep in touch with the process as it happened. I used writing, simple movements and the making of visual images with whatever was at hand -- to further explore their human potential. At the end of the six-day workshop, the students would have a better understanding of themselves with the tools to continue their exploration into the possibilities open to them. I called the workshop "Poetic Acts" as the object was to live "Poetically," completely concentrated, present in time and space. Now, many years later, I call them "Inner-Being Retreats."

My first students were Satoru and Maria Luisa, who was my brother's girlfriend visiting from Rome. She and I were good friends and always got together when she was in town. I told her about my six-day workshop and she was very interested to do it. So we started one Monday, and it was a revelation to them, as well as to me. The course was structured so that I began by having them lie down. I gave them verbal instructions to relax then guided them into breathing techniques, after which I led them into a ten-minute meditation. At the end of each section, I would ask them what they had felt. This part was very important, as it gave me an opportunity to see where they had a problem, and how to help them resolve it. We then went into simple Yoga exercises and, after that, I gave them a white sheet of paper on which they were instructed to write down what came to them spontaneously.

The sequences were always the same, except that one day they would end with writing, another with movement, and, thirdly, with the making of visual images. These they had to make from the things they found in the space we were in. Satoru chose to fill a bowl with water, and then he took a blank sheet of paper, rolled it up and lit it with a match, then dropped it into the water when he could no longer hold it. It was not only a visually stunning image, but the burning paper dropping into the water made an amazing hissing sound. I will never forget it, it was so dramatic! Maria Luisa, who worked with flower arranging, chose some dried flowers we had and re-arranged them to her liking. They were both so different and very much represented their characters. The end result on the conclusion of the course was for Maria Luisa a total revelation. She said that she had achieved in six days more than she had done in twelve years of psychotherapy. Satoru was also fascinated and learned something about himself that he later used in his sculptural work.

Jan. 31, 1992. Susana, Birthday. From Satoru Oishi.

Memory,

I met almost 16 years ago.
We started roughly and lovingly probably
big wave sometimes.
But somehow from somewhere from someone
united us very tight together,sometimes we
couldn't breathe even but this invisible man
brought us into LIFE together,loving laugh
and cry, scratch each other.
But I still feel the day we met 16 years ago.
About 11^{1}/2 years ago. You given birth to our
dearest son Christophe.
Chritophe is a proudest son. He is a very kind
and generous like his mother. And he is a pure
child at same time. And also he is a richer
than me. But he buys us present. Sometimes I feel
like facing my father.
The other day,you brought me down to a child
part of me through your course,WHICH I amazed me
and appreciate me. Because I know sometimes I am
like a BIG STONE myself.
I am very happy that you brought us child and
pure essence of lives together.
ARIGATO-NI Susana-San.

A VERY HAPPY BIRTHDAY   From Satoru-San.

For me, it was a complete eye-opener; to see that what I had so painstakingly put together from all my research actually had a very positive effect. It helped! I had managed to invent a system that produced results. I then started to do it regularly with Satoru and Christophe. Christophe liked it so much that occasionally, when he came back from school, he would, on his own accord, ask me to lead him and Satoru in the work. I was very excited about Christophe's reaction, as I felt that to be able to reach and help a young life was a most important achievement for me.

It was at this time that I asked Christophe if he would like to write a little prose poetry book of his own so that we could do readings at the loft for an audience. He was interested, and, with a little help from me, got started. He completed his book, over a period of two months; it was a very charming collection of pieces for which he also made drawings. I had decided to do the public readings to share with others our thoughts, using the words as a means of communicating ideas and events that might be helpful to them. Just before Christmas, we gave our first public reading. When I was putting on my make-up, Christophe asked me if he, too, could put make-up on. I said of course, if he liked. He decided to paint a green line on his forehead, another down both cheeks and one across his chin. He was dressed in his best white linen suit and looked really spiffy. At one point, as he was looking at me putting on my make-up, he asked me, " Adu, why are you so perfect?" and I had to laugh, saying to him, that it was only in his imagination; that I, like all of us, had my defects, as he well knew. He was not convinced, and I loved him so much for his utter innocence. We were a great success; twenty-five people had come to our event and, afterwards, complemented us on our readings. Their comments on particular poems indicated to me that they had really become involved. We did about five readings that year before we left in the summer for Tuscany. For Christophe, it was a wonderful boost to his self-esteem, and I promised him I would try to see if we could get his little book published.

That fall, our trusty Citroen DS21 gave out and we had to sell it to a junk yard. We bought a Honda Civic with a car loan and loved the car and how it ran. It was my first Japanese car and I realized that it was with good reason that they had the reputation they did around the world. It was a superb piece of machinery and never gave us a moment's worry. It was the first car I ever bought brand new and we were very excited to have it. The loft problem continued with excursions down to the hearing offices. It was a seemingly endless process costing us a lot of money with few tangible results, except lots of wasted time.

As the New Year came around in 1991, we were beginning to think about arranging, long distance, for the design of the pool we wanted to build. In Tuscany, we lived in the Crete Senesi (the eroding clay hills), the province which did not allow the building of pools. Our neighbors had built one illegally and told us it was the only way we would be able to do it. This meant that we would not be able to contract a pool builder and would have to build it ourselves, with the help of people whom we would have to find. I contacted a friend of Beatrice's who designed pools and called him from New York to tell him of our problem. I asked if he could design a pool that did not look like a pool. He came up with a wonderful design which looked like a water hole for thirsty horses. It had a gradual sloping descent into the larger body of water and really looked very beautiful. However, when I asked him how much it might cost, the total was way beyond our means. So he came up with a simple rectangle, 5 meters by 7 meters, and 1 and a half meters deep. The way he designed the structure, he told us a freight train could run over it and it would not budge. The meter and a-half depth was the European law for pools that did not require a lifeguard on duty. Our neighbors had told us that when there was a government pardon, we could then apply for it. This was a system for the government to raise money when they needed it and a way for those, like us, to have something be legalized. This did happen a few years after we built it, and our pool became legal.

My relationship with Charles was still very difficult, and I was very upset by that state of affairs. I felt strongly that Mama and Papa would be so disappointed, but try as I might, there was no solution in sight. Our estate lawyer, a wonderful man, whom we both liked very much, kept encouraging us to write to each other, to try and solve our differences, but it was to no avail. Satoru was a witness to how much this situation weighed on me and the effect it had on my emotional state. But there was precious little he could do, either. I continued to heal from the loss of my parents, as time was a great helper, but, of course, it was not something that could ever be erased. At best, it would be kept at bay, buried somewhere inside, then raise its head occasionally -- and I would plunge into the depths of misery.

I wrote to Delphine in Paris about my "Poetic Acts Workshop" and her response was immediately positive. She was part of an association called R.Y.E., which stood for Recherche du Yoga dans L'education (Research of Yoga in Education). Their function was to find techniques that could be used to help teachers in the French Educational System. They held large retreats for teachers twice a year, where they invited specialists in different well-being therapies to come to teach them their methods. The teachers could then apply them to teach their students. Delphine had attended many courses over the years with this organization, and was a great believer in the effect the various techniques had on her teaching English to her students. She wanted me to meet with the founder, Micheline Flak, and suggested I fly to Paris to talk with her about my workshop. I saw this as a wonderful opportunity to start teaching my work, especially since it would benefit teachers and their students.

I got to work on arranging some Merce technique classes at the American Center, so that it would pay for my flying over and my basic needs while there. Delphine set up an appointment for me, so I flew over in early March for ten days. My times with Delphine were always an adventure, as she was a curious, inquisitive soul like me and so we were always pushing each other on. I loved being with her and learned a lot. She picked me up at the airport and we went to her charming apartment where I would be staying. The next day was the meeting with Micheline Flak and we talked about my work and how well it would fit with R.Y.E.'s programs. I had a wonderful connection of minds with her and she wanted to see if I could teach my workshop at their next retreat in late August in Evian. It is a beautiful town on the French side of Lake Leman and opposite Geneva. The famous Evian water comes from there. I was very excited to be invited and called Satoru right after to tell him the good news. Visiting Delphine was a whirlwind of activities: performances and exhibitions to see, lectures to hear, and passionate, interesting discussions to have on things that interested both of us. At the end of the ten days, I returned to New York with my mind full of ideas and images that I had seen. That time she also introduced me to her dear friend, Maria a stunning, statuesque Parisian beauty with two equally stunning whippet dogs that went everywhere with her. We spent many a fascinating time with her and her companion, a very charming dentist. I would become very good friends with Maria and had many memorable conversations with her.

Delphine also introduced me to a gallery owner and his beautiful wife with whom I got on very well. I had brought over slides of Satoru's work so that I could show them to possible contacts. I met with quite a few people and galleries but on that trip I was not able to get any commitments, which was disappointing. It is not easy when one is just starting out and it takes time and patience to find the right fit for ones work.

Satoru had asked me to buy him some more of his favorite French workers' jackets that he always wore. They were a fabulous cobalt blue, made of thick cotton, with buttons down the front and two large pockets on either side. He had first seen the jacket on a worker sweeping the streets in 1976 and had gone up to ask him where he could buy one like it. He told us we could find them at La Samaritaine, a big department store not far from where we were. We found it and overalls to go with it. They became Satoru's proudest acquisitions and whenever I was in Paris it was my duty to replenish his wardrobe. His other clothing fixture was his Borsalino beret, which he saw in Rome the first time we were there together. It was dark blue cashmere with a visor in front and looked absolutely stunning on Satoru. He loved the hat and only changed for his other Borsalino white panama hat for the summer. He was truly elegant and very striking in his hats. Women in Rome would surreptitiously hand him their visiting cards in hopes of his eventually contacting them. I was very flattered with this sort of attention to my husband. But I was secure in the knowledge that his rule of not fooling around -- which he made me agree to as a condition of my accepting his marriage proposal -- was unbreakable. We were both committed, and, as Satoru had said, it took a lot of the worry and pressure off our relationship. It made our love strong, as we were able to concentrate on it 100%, with no outside wasted energy.

I returned to New York and soon after, Satoru went to Tokyo to visit his family, as he had not been back to see them for a few years. He was also going back to take one of his Jasper Johns color Target prints to Japan. He had been given it by Jasper as a thank-you gift for his work with Simca Prints, the company with which he had worked printing Jasper's work. He had asked his brother to see if he could locate a buyer for it and Mitsuru had managed to find someone who was interested, but wanted to see it in person. We really did not want to sell, but our financial situation was deteriorating, as my inheritance had been used up buying the house, making the improvements, the loft law suit and just our everyday living expenses. So off he went and we stayed behind, anxious to see what would happen. The buyer liked the Target and so agreed to buy it. When we had gone to Sotheby's to have it appraised we could not believe our ears. We had thought it might be worth a few thousand dollars. Instead, they quoted a huge figure we could not have imagined, which was why we decided to sell it then. The Japanese buyer offered a bit less but the sale was in cash, so Satoru had agreed to sell it to him.

On that same trip, his sister had wanted to introduce him to her new religion called Sukyo Mahikari, meaning "True Light" founded in 1959 when Yoshikasu Okada, a former officer in the Japanese Imperial Army, received "God's revelations." It worked with light given through the hands and was a kind of religion that was taking hold in Japan at the time. His sister had become very involved with it as they claimed to be able to heal people. At the time she got involved, her husband had been diagnosed with stomach cancer. It actually turned out not to be cancer later on, when more tests were made. Nevertheless, she was a firm believer in Mahikari's healing powers and claimed to have cured him with it. So when Satoru was in Japan, she insisted on taking him to one of their meetings and persuaded him to become a member. When I heard about it, I was a bit suspicious, as organized religions that profess to save you are not my cup of tea. His mother and brother had refused, as had all her children and her husband. Satoru, being the kind, gentle soul that he was, did not want to hurt her feelings. She insisted he had to find the branch in Queens where he could continue the practices. His stay in Tokyo over, he was to return home.

A POOL IN FORNACINO

Satoru's homecoming was a relief, as we could now breathe a little easier with the money from the sale of Jasper's print. It was sad to have to sell such a precious work, given to him by Jasper Johns, which was earned with the fruit of Satoru's labors. It truly was a stunning piece. I know it hurt him very much and I felt terrible. The school year by now was nearly over, and we would soon be heading over to Tuscany and our house for the summer of 1991. We had the pool project to accomplish in our free month, before guests started arriving. We sublet our loft for the summer to the son of a friend, and packed our things and Kitty and headed out to the airport. Only once did we have to smuggle Kitty over, when we took the charter flight. All the other times we bought a ticket for her to travel in the cabin with us. Once in Rome, Mehlika our great friend, picked us up and took us to her house, where we stayed overnight and picked up our red bomber to go up to the country.

Driving up was always exciting, and arriving at the house was an adventure, wondering how it looked after our long absence. We always found it intact with the laundry still hanging on the line as we had left it. We called our pool expert Alan Wrightsman, to set up an appointment for him to go over the design and discuss how we would proceed. The poor man had broken his ankle just before we had contacted him, and had to be driven by his wife to inspect the site. In fact, he was not sure, given his cast, that he would even be able to do the work for us. He made a great effort and now we would be meeting him in person for the first time. He had just had the cast removed and was a little unsteady on his feet. We had Elio, our builder, come down to be there when Alan came, so that he could give him the directions of how to build the pool. Elio had never built one before and was a bit nervous about taking on the project. It took a bit of convincing, but he liked us and wanted to try and help.

Alan's instructions were very clear and Elio understood what we would have to do and what to order in terms of materials. We would need steel rods for the cage that would be constructed all around the perimeter, cement blocks, sand and gravel. We had a positive meeting and, all set with his instructions would be able to start as soon as we had cleared the space for the pool. Because the ground was on a sloping incline from the back of the garage and pig sties, and was full of overgrown weeds, thistles and spines, we had to hire a man with his backhoe to clear and level it. To one side of the area there was a beautiful peach tree that I desperately wanted to save. Elio recommended an excavation man named Pieri, who came the next day to see the area he would need to clear. Pieri saw the space and in his inimitable Italian way, started throwing his arms all over the place as he contemplated all the difficulties he would have in doing the job. This we were used to, as every project started with all the problems, but they were always resolved and the work would proceed.

The first challenge was how he would get his huge backhoe into the space, as there was a wire fence in front of the area that he would need to clear. We would have to make an opening and a road to pass into the space. The next problem concerned my precious peach tree, which Pieri doubted he would be able to save, as it would make his maneuvering very tight. However, he said he would see what he could do. We set the start day two days later, as he had to finish another job first. He showed up with Elio at eight a.m. sharp, ready to begin. It was truly incredible to see that piece of machinery work and how adept he was at handling it. The big arm that he commanded to reach out and scoop up the vegetation and the earth was like his extended hand, so delicate and precise. I used to stand there mesmerized watching him as he slowly, but methodically, cleared the space and created a big terrace out of it, as if by magic. As for my peach tree, he wound a rope around the trunk to pull it as much out of his way as possible, so he could work. He wanted me to know that he was doing this super human effort for my peach tree, because, he said, "Lei e bella e la voglio bene," meaning, you are beautiful and I like you very much. He was sort of in love with me, and, as a result, was ready to move heaven and earth. He was very sweet and would show up in jeans and a skimpy tank top to show off his muscles, and would strut around like the proud Italian he was. I always asked him how his wife was, to tease him.

Once the space was leveled, and we now had a large open terrace, Pieri measured the pool size and started the excavation, making the hole where we would then build the pool. This work took a few days, during which time we would all be around to help, if needed, and I would go to make lunch for us. We would go to our terrace in front of the central part of the house, and have some kind of spaghetti, meat and salad. This is what they liked, so I was ready to oblige. We had many fun lunches and drank our glasses of red homemade wine. Elio had vines on his property, just up the road from us, and always made his own wine. He made a very tasty, simple wine which we all enjoyed. By the end of the day, we were all exhausted, Christophe as well, as he ran around helping when he could, in this great adventure of building a pool for the very first time.

The excavating finished, we bid Pieri goodbye, and thanked him profusely for his good work and paid him. I also gave him a big kiss, which made him blush. Now it was our turn to work hard. First the sand was delivered, which we had to shovel into the bottom of the pool area, then it had to be watered, after which a layer of gravel had to be spread over the sand. The steel rods had to be placed in a criss-cross pattern; and then, the cement truck arrived, to pour in the cement. This, then, had to dry, while we sprayed water on it occasionally, so that it did not dry too fast and make cracks. After that phase was over, we had to make the steel cage all around the sides of the pool, so that the structure would be solid. Then the walls had to be made with the cement blocks and steel rods, which were placed in each hollow cement block, and would then be filled with cement by the cement truck. All this was back-breaking work, which we all took on with determination, hell bent on getting this thing accomplished at all costs. Elio said he had never worked so hard or so doggedly. Satoru and I were possessed and Elio had no choice but to go along with us. We even worked in the rain; nothing, but nothing, was going to stop us.

It took us two weeks to build the pool and then it had to be painted. We wanted to save the added expense of tiles, so decided to paint the cement with the proper waterproof pool paint. We did not want the usual Hollywood blue, and found a white paint that we really liked. It would create a light-green blue, sparkly pool that looked gorgeous. I cannot tell you how proud we all were of our incredible accomplishment. After all, we were not pool builders, but we had made a beautiful pool! For years afterwards, every time we took a dive into it, we would say to each other, "I can't believe we actually built this," making swims worth so much more. Satoru had also made it the perfect size, not too big and not too small, not a square and not a rectangle. It sat majestically on this new terrace that had been created.

Our first guest that summer was the son of a French student of mine called Julien, whom we would meet in at Florence airport. He was going to stay with us for two weeks and his mother, Marseline, would join him at the end of his stay. With the new pool, entertaining was a breeze; we did not have to pile in the car to go to a pool club -- Yay! All we had to do was walk to the back of the house and plunge in. The boys had a great time all day, jumping in and out at will. Satoru's insistence on placing it there was brilliant, as those of us in the house could not hear the noise from the pool. That summer, as we had fewer guests, we were able to start meeting more of the permanent residents.

Beatrice invited us to a party at her house where we met a charming English painter called Hardress Waller, with whom we made friends. He makes me laugh, as he always describes his first meeting with me by recounting my telling him, within the first five minutes, about losing my parents in the car accident. Very dramatic, and it was true. I remember that for the longest time, I had to tell anyone I met about the accident. It was as if I needed to tell them that I was damaged and, therefore, they should take care, or some such thing. Crazy, really, but it seemed important. Now I wait longer before I mention that, and I use it as a way to get into deeper waters with people I am talking to. It works very well, as having mentioned something tragic like that helps them open up, too, and we get to first base very quickly. Everyone has something difficult to recount and will tell you about it if they feel comfortable. I have met and connected with people all over the world in this simple, effective way.

We saw a lot of Carlo and Anna La Corte, and their daughter, Benedetta. We had met them the first summer when we were at the supermarket shopping. They had heard about us from Beatrice and came up to introduce themselves. Carlo was Sicilian and Anna was from Bologna; their daughter was Christophe's age and they had a mutual attraction to each other. We became very good friends and saw a lot of them. They had a lovely house in Asciano, the town closest to us, twenty minutes away. Anna was a wonderful cook and we really enjoyed going over to their house for lunches and dinners. We also invited them to visit us, as they were curious to see what new thing we had done, since we were continually working on one renovation project or another. Christophe and Benedetta were always finding ways to get us all together, so that they could see each other. They were both ten at the time, and it was so sweet to see them enjoying each others' company. Since Satoru did not speak Italian, I was his interpreter and translated back and forth for Carlo and him. Carlo was very fascinated with Satoru, as everybody always was, and had lots of questions about Japan and Japanese history.

Marceline came to pick up her son after two weeks and stayed on with us for a few days. We had enjoyed having Julian and Christophe had liked having his very own guest to play with. Then we had two of my students from Merce drop by, as they were traveling through Europe. It was nice to see them under different circumstances and we really had a great time in their company. For everyone that came, it meant taking them sightseeing. Our favorite places were, of course, Siena and, next, Pienza -- a stunning town at the top of a hill, which you approach from the valley, driving up a winding road planted with Cyprus trees all along the route up. It was the town Pope Pius X had discovered and went to for his summer holidays. It is also famous for its Pecorino cheese made from sheep's milk. It is a delicious cheese which comes in various versions. Fresh, semi-seasoned and fully-seasoned. The taste gets stronger the longer it is seasoned. Pienza is a very picturesque town and very popular with tourists in the know. Of course, midnight swimming in the hot springs at Bagno Vignoni was also a must.

So the summers flew by and the house took on a new, improved appearance, thanks to the work we did. It was a labor of love; it gave us all a chance to work closely together and to share our house with dear friends, who came to play with us and enjoy a little bit of our heaven on earth. We lived intensely and passionately, always more in love, more in wonder at our communication with each other. Christophe and Satoru had some really special times in Tuscany, away from school, and alone together, playing. Whenever Satoru worked, he would involve Christophe, who would work alongside him making his own creations. I did that with him, mostly in New York, and Satoru, mostly in Tuscany.

We all had the feeling of having spent other lives together before and many astrologers we had seen had told us that we had. It was a feeling hard to describe, but we were all very aware of it. We felt so familiar, not at all like father, mother and child. More like very old friends, sharing this time on earth again.

MAHIKARI

We returned to New York at the beginning of September, as usual, hoping that the loft case would soon be settled. It kept dragging on and was a constant expense due to the cost of maintaining our lawyers to defend us. We hated that expenditure but there was nothing we could do to speed the case along. Satoru continued his sculpture work and flower arranging and was also trying to find a gallery to represent him. It was not easy and I felt for him, every time he went out to a gallery appointment and came back with a negative answer. He was happy doing his work, though, and had already produced a large body of sculptures. I loved them and our loft became more of a gallery every day. I continued teaching at Merce's and writing; Christophe and I gave more of our readings for invited audiences, which we liked doing. I had decided that he and I should share a glimpse of our thoughts as we had written them, and make a kind of performance art.

I continued the meditating and Satoru and I would take our walks as before to our favorite café in little Italy. The time we spent on our walks was a great way for us to be aware of our thoughts and to continue our dialogue with each other. We kept in touch with our friends, which was very rewarding, since we were all of similar sensibilities and had many lively, interesting conversations about what life meant and how one could best live it. Satoru's sister, Kimiko, came to New York for a conference on global warming and to meet with the Mahikari group Satoru had found in Queens. She wanted Satoru to go there every day to practice their giving God's light through the hands. I was not very convinced about the work, nor did I appreciate any organized religion where you are kept a slave to their dogmas. I don't like the idea of a religion telling you whether you are a good person or not, setting up proscribed rules of conduct. Knowing more about it now, I am sorry I did not insist that Satoru not become involved, as it seems, from all I have read, to be a cult sect, really. At the time, I did not have a computer, or know how to navigate the internet, and since neither Satoru nor Kimiko really explained what it was all about, I was not aware of all the negative things associated with it.

I like the Buddhist idea that we are all Buddhas in our own right, and, therefore, are personally responsible for our behavior. I like the concept of accepting life as a journey that understands that suffering and joy are part of living. There are no outside conditions, no punishments, only those that you, yourself, inflict. It is not easy to do, as we carry with us fears and anxieties that make total acceptance difficult, but I take that responsibility with the knowledge that it has to be worked at every day. I fall woefully short many times, as it is within our nature to trip ourselves up with the conditioning that is all around. It is all well and good to practice it on a mountain top, in a beautiful place, away from the daily struggles of living. I try and continue to learn to accept the challenges calmly and with grace. So I was reluctant to get involved. Kimiko wanted Christophe and me to become members. My family was atheist and the only time I ever went to mass, was when I was at boarding school in London. We all went to a Protestant church near school to the service every Sunday, as were boarders. Actually, I quite liked the service and it was nice to go in the company of my classmates. I think maybe Satoru was a little bit disappointed that I did not join the Mahikari, but never insisted or made any comment about my resistance. His sister was not too happy.

They went almost every day, and Satoru became more immersed in the rituals. Their theory was that one could bring light through the hands to others, thereby helping with whatever was ailing them, physically or emotionally. That, in itself, was not the problem for me; in fact, I thought that was a good thing. I did not like the other ideas they spread. Kimiko stayed with us for two weeks. It disturbed me slightly that Satoru was becoming a bit enslaved by the whole thing but I did not want to say anything about what he was doing or insist that he stop. Kimiko left and life went on as usual. We were talking more of moving out of New York and going to live at our house in Tuscany.

The loft case was finally coming to an end. We had the last meetings with the hearing officer and I was beginning to realize that our lawyers were not really helping us win our case. A crucial piece of testimony by a lawyer from Washington D.C., who had rented our apartment on West Fourth Street, was deemed by them not to be relevant and I stupidly did not insist. In retrospect, I realized they had already been bought off by our landlord as that very crucial piece of information would have lost the landlord his case. We were beginning to have financial difficulties keeping up with all our expenses, and were having trouble meeting all the bills. That, and being bought off, caused them to drop us flat. It dawned on me that it was a waste of time spending money on lawyers, as they were heartless mercenaries out to get our money, and when we could no longer afford their exorbitant charges, be damned with us. So they sold us out, which we learned that summer, when Steve, our downstairs neighbor, called to tell us we had both lost our cases against the landlord. We had spent $ 60,000 on it to get nowhere. How much better it would have been to have moved over to our house in Tuscany, rather than to hang on in New York, spending all the money that it cost to do that. We were not mentally able to realize that New York was not the center of the world, as we seemed to think, and Satoru could have worked just as well in Italy. Our destiny was to learn the lessons that we did, but how I wish that we had had the guts to leave at the end of our ten-year lease, when our landlord offered us $10,000 to move out. We thought it was a pittance, as we had spent much more on renovating it. He had not budged and so we had embarked on the three-year ordeal to nowhere.

Back to Italy and our house, the pleasure we always felt driving down our dirt road was exceptional, waiting to see what shape the house was in and looking forward to our first plunge into our fabulous pool. When we had unpacked, we would drive down to our neighbors, the Borzis, to give them the presents we always brought for them and to say hello. They invited us to lunch, which we very much liked. That summer we were really able to enjoy the house as we had no more renovation work planned due to scarce financial resources. We had Kathy Kerr (a former colleague dancer in Merce's Company) and her husband, Josh, visiting with two English friends of theirs they had been visiting in England. At the same time, we had Maria and her husband, Piere, who had driven over in their silver Alpha Romeo from Paris, with their two beautiful Whippet dogs. I had met Maria through Delphine. They had a wonderful country house in Normandy, to which she invited me for a week-end when I was visiting Paris in the spring. It was there, walking on the beach with the dogs, talking with her one morning, that I had one of those rare moments. When everything in nature is in perfect harmony, and, out of the blue, I sensed that I was part of something magical, and tears of joy and gratitude flowed freely down my cheeks. When I left Paris she gave me a fabulous pair of high-heeled Yves Saint Laurent grey and white patent shoes with which to make a solo someday

We were with a remarkable group of fascinating friends with whom to go around exploring our rich historical area. They spent a week with us, and every day was an adventure. Christophe loved walking with the dogs and seeing everyone's reaction to them. Josh was a researcher in the behavior of hyenas in Africa, and would spend some months a year there for his research projects. He had intriguing stories to tell us of his work, and we were fascinated. Christophe was spellbound with the tales and had lots of questions. Our conversations were incredible and I remember we laughed a lot. During their visit in August, John Cage passed away. The Cunningham studio had my telephone number in Italy and Alice, the studio's student coordinator, and a good friend of mine, had called to tell me. We were devastated, as we all loved John. He had been like a father to us all in the Company and we would miss him terribly.

SIGNS OF TROUBLE

Soon after this news, Kathy, Josh and their two friends, and Maria and Pierre, with their two dogs, went back to England and Paris, and we went on with our lives, as usual. About a week after they left, Satoru's eyes started to look a bit yellow and he was feeling itchy. Being August in Italy, most everyone was away on holiday at the sea or the mountains and, of course, our doctor was one of them. So we had to go to Siena to see Dr. Rugani, the husband of Gianni Nicole's daughter, who lived in Italy. We had met them previously when Nicole suggested we look them up when we were in Italy. He had a clinic in Siena with his sister. So we called her up to ask if we could make an appointment with her husband to check on Satoru. He was actually an anesthetist but had a doctor's degree as well. He gave us an appointment and we drove into Siena, a half-hour drive from our house, to meet him. His diagnosis was that maybe he had yellow jaundice, but he was not completely sure. Tests would have to be done; in the meantime, he suggested that Satoru stay a few days at his clinic, so that he could give him some stabilizing drip solution to help his condition. Since Satoru was never ill, we were not unduly worried, sure that it would be something treatable and that would be that. We decided to take his suggestion and checked Satoru in, and I returned home with Christophe to get Satoru's pajamas and things he might need for the days he would be in the clinic.

While he was there, we decided that it would be best for Satoru to fly to Tokyo for an in-depth diagnosis, and to be near his family. We had rented out the upstairs part of our house to an American couple, as we were short of money, for two weeks. We stayed in the cantina, which was cool, and poor Satoru, on returning from the clinic, laid in bed, weak and feeling terrible. Christophe and I were both anxious and I made arrangements to buy a ticket for Satoru to fly to Japan. All this was going on while our tenants were in residence. I did not tell them anything and they went about their holiday. I had to stay until they left, so could not fly with Satoru, which, of course, I was desperate to do, but we had no choice. So I took him down to Rome to get his flight. Mehlika, hearing about this, managed, through her contacts, to get Satoru upgraded to business class where he would be able to stretch out. She met us at the airport to make sure everything went according to plan. His brother, Mitsuru, would meet him at the other end. I had asked Mitsuru to call us when Satoru arrived to let us know how he was. It was decided that he had to be hospitalized to have tests done and they would let me know what the results were. I called almost every day, as I was very worried about Satoru's condition. Mitsuru never gave me any definitive answer and was very vague about Satoru's diagnosis. It was extremely frustrating and I could not wait to get on an airplane to Tokyo.

A week later, our renters left and Christophe and I closed the house and flew to Japan. It was a twenty-eight hour ordeal, not helped by my state of mind over what we would find when we got there. Mitsuru picked us up at the airport in the late afternoon and I asked to be taken directly to the hospital. As soon as we got there, we were introduced to the attending physician, and I immediately asked him about Satoru's health. The doctor answered very directly that Satoru had cancer of the liver and that it had spread to fifty percent of it, as well as to the bile duct. He said that there was nothing more they could do and that Satoru probably only had two months to live. I almost fainted from the shock, but held on, as I did not want Christophe to know what was happening. The doctor advised me that they had not told Satoru what he had, so it would be up to me whether or not to tell him.

I had left Christophe in the waiting room with Kimiko, and when I walked out of the doctor's office, the first thing he asked me was, "Is papa going to die?" I answered "It is in God's hands." Paddy was the name Christophe called his father. I said we must think positively and send Paddy lots of strength to get over his illness. We were then taken to see Satoru, who was in a ward with two other patients. He looked weak but was so happy to see us. He smiled in that beautiful way he had and it was all I could do not to burst out crying. I had not decided about telling him or not about the cancer, so I had to look positive for his and Christophe's sakes. By now we had been up for 36 hours my eyes were burning and I was concerned about getting Christophe to bed. It was late and past visiting hours so we were not allowed to stay too long. We kissed Satoru good night and left him, my heart breaking with the terrible news.

The prognosis was the absolute worst nightmare; I felt as though my dearly beloved would leave us to face life on our own! My beautiful soul-mate would be abandoning me, something I had always asked him not to do. I wanted to go before him, as I could not stand the pain of living without him. I, of course, did not fully accept what the doctor said; I was positive we could beat this thing and immediately started to look for alternative therapies. The doctor had said there was nothing further traditional medicine could do, so that was our only choice. Once back at Satoru's family's home, we ate something and I put Christophe to bed and read him a story to help him fall asleep. I then went to bed but never closed my eyes with the realization that Satoru was so ill. I went over all the possible scenarios to cure him and struggled with the decision I would have to make about revealing his diagnosis. The doctor had only told him that they did not know exactly what he had and would have to wait and see how he reacted to the medications they were giving him. In Japan they don't tell a patient he is dying, so it was up to me. The worst thing was that I could not call my parents to ask their advice, as they were gone six years now. So I was alone, and torn between being honest or not, when Satoru asked me what the doctors had said to me.

The next morning, we had breakfast and immediately after went to the hospital to visit Satoru. We were all happy to be together and he got up and put on his dressing gown and took us down to the guests' visiting lounge. He liked the hospital, as it was more like a hotel than a hospital, which was nice for him and for us. We could pretend he was on holiday there. We sat and talked and caught up on our time away from each other and how he was feeling. I had, after much soul-searching, decided I would tell him the truth. I could not live with myself if I lied. I felt I had to give him the choice of deciding how to proceed with his illness in terms of alternate therapies. Mitsuru had found a Chinese herbal remedy that had to be boiled and drunk every day and suggested Satoru take that, which he did. I looked up what a cancer cell was and saw that it is a cell that has been starved of oxygen and so it was important to introduce oxygen-giving foods to help the regeneration of the cells. That meant a macrobiotic diet with lots of oxygen-giving seaweed, green leafy vegetables and no meat, dairy or sweet things.

I gave Christophe some money to play on one of the game machines in the lounge and told Satoru that I had to be honest with him out of respect, so I had to tell him what his doctor had told me. I did not tell him how long he had to live, as that, I felt, was beyond anyone, even a doctor, to say definitively. Just that he had cancer and we needed to decide what approach to take to beat this thing. He sat there listening to me and I could see his heart sink. I think it was a shock, but somewhere in his soul, he probably already knew. To this day, I ask myself if I did the right thing. It is such a heartbreaking decision to have to make with someone who is more than life itself to you. I would have rather been in his place instead. He asked me if I had told Christophe and I told him that Christophe had asked right away if his Paddy was going to die. I told him I had answered that it was in God's hands. He was happy about that, as he was worried about how Christophe was going to deal with his illness. Christophe came back when the money ran out and we bought some snacks and a drink for him. We tried to go on as if nothing had changed and Satoru was just undergoing a cure for his illness. It would be the beginning of many days travelling back and forth to the hospital.

When I was looking through my files for this memoir, I came upon a letter that Satoru had written to his tea students. It made clear to me that Satoru had already intuited his diagnosis, even before I had told him:

When I started sick mid August I knew something serious, if I spent forty four years of my life, I must know subconsciously good or bad. Gradually I've gone for worse and worse. So, Susana suggested to go to hospital in Siena, Italy. I have stayed four days for tests and injection and left for home. A week later I have called my mother in Japan and asked about kidney stone in the family or yellow jaundice and my mother said, "No one in my family". And next day Susana called about one of the prescription pill were finished and I should continue or not and told the doctor no one in my family had kidney stone or yellow jaundice. Immediately doctor told to Susana to come to hospital. Susana come back immediately and told me that I might be a quite serious. Go to hospital in Siena or go back to Japan. So I decided go back to Japan. Three days later I was at plane on the way to Japan. Luckily Mehlika had a friend at airport same company I was going to Japan. So I could sit wheel chair at airport. Christophe and Susana could come in at gate. I have to have many many thanks to Mehlika and also her friend. Brought me to upper grade seat. But my condition was so bad to take sixteen hours ride. By the time when I arrived in Tokyo, I was really exhausted. I sat wheel chair again and no strength.

When I came out from the gate, my brother and my sister there waiting for me. When I called to my brother, my tears came out I couldn't stop. After long drive home my mother were there. She seems very healthy compare to myself. My brother gone to pick up my insurance card from Prefecture office, after came back, my sister and mother chosen good hospital not far from home. My sister and my mother had taken me to the hospital and they taken my blood and question. They couldn't find a room for me, they introduced another hospital. Doctor called ambulance. I've gone with my mother with ambulance to this hospital. My sister gone to bus trip to Takayama. Now I stayed there three weeks and a few days at this hospital. How many times I've tested, finally they said they found tumor outside liver area but they cannot operate. It's too dangerous. So they recommended another hospital to seek cure for my tumor. Even I knew what I have. When doctor told me about my condition I sensed like a dream. Also same time I sensed real. At same night, my tears came out. Couldn't stop. Little while I felt sorry to my dearest family. Now I am looking forward to face my illness and recover.

After started ill and slowly couldn't walk long, I started think, what's wrong with me? I need to be walking without thinking my health or body. How I have been lucky. When I had pain in my right side of stomach a few months ago. I didn't think a major problem. So I missed a warning signal from my body. I was out of touch from my foundation. I have to apologize to my art body, and also to whom given my body and spirit and also my dearest family. But soon I am going to walk on the ground, with my loveliest family. Wait for me dears!

There was a visitors' room on every floor with a television and snack machines. We spent a lot of time there with Satoru. During Satoru's stay at the hospital, the Sumo wrestling championships were on every day and we watched the wrestlers moving ahead in the competitions. They are extraordinary athletes and the ceremonial aspects of the competition were very intriguing. Everything in Japan is about ceremony; it is an important aspect of their tradition, as formality is the foundation of daily life. We existed in this unreal situation, watching the Sumo wrestlers and witnessing Satoru's treatments at the hospital. The only other thing they could possibly do was to operate to insert a tube to drain the bile out of his body. The medical team had refused to do this, as they felt it was useless. Satoru and I pleaded with his doctor to do this procedure and, thankfully, he agreed. It was an important step to give us courage and to get the poisonous bile to drain out of his system. They kept him a long time and, in some way, it was a comfort to him, he later told me. To be in the same reality as his roommates, who were also ill, like him, made him feel normal in those circumstances.

We had decided on the Chinese herb remedy Mitsuru had found; we also continued with the macrobiotic diet. This meant that I would be cooking all his meals and taking them to the hospital. We found out from his doctor that the only other therapy he could do, but was not a real solution, was to undergo a cold thermal type of treatment, which would have unpleasant side effects. Satoru was leaning towards doing that but it made me very worried about the risks he would be taking with very little chance of positive results. So we decided not to undergo the therapy and to continue with the path we had chosen. This, too, later proved to be a point I worried about. What if Satoru had done that therapy? Would the outcome have been different? Questions and more questions plagued me day after day. We don't want to accept the reality, so we invent all manner of things trying to play God with life. We don't want to acknowledge our total impotence when facing the questions of life and death. There is nothing in our Western training to prepare us for the acceptance of death. Not as it is with the Eastern philosophies that accept death as a natural evolution in the process of living. Life continues on another plane and the journey goes on. The body is just the house where the soul resides for a given number of years and then dies. Even after all I had had to learn about death and letting go, I still was not able to grasp that philosophy. I was holding on to life and was simply not willing to accept that Satoru's body was on its way to extinguishing itself. He was sad, I could tell, but was putting a good front on it all, being charming with the nurses and his doctor and all who came to visit him. He was the talk of the ward, everyone being so impressed with how he was handling himself and of his unfailing good spirits with everyone.

We had found a game parlor two doors down from the hospital where Christophe liked to go to play with the machines. We would give him some money and off he would go. We did not want him sitting all the time in the hospital, as it was depressing and boring for him. Tokyo was, and still is, a very safe capitol city, so there was no worry about letting him go down to the arcade. It was a good distraction for him as we were at the hospital all day to be with Satoru for those weeks he was there. We had very little money and had been able to buy our three air tickets with my credit card, thank goodness. I had to ask Kimiko for a loan, which she gave me, to buy the food for Satoru's diet and have a little money for our day-to-day needs. I would get up early every morning, cook Satoru's food for the day, and then take the subway to the hospital.

They were very difficult times, worrying about what would happen to Satoru and how to proceed with the reality we had been saddled with. The money issue was also very unsettling, as we had bills that had to be paid, a loft and a house to maintain and the only income we had was from the royalties of the patent agreement. The first four years of those, we never saw anything because the money was being spent by Charles running the company, with, it seemed, no positive cash flow. When we started receiving our share of the royalties, it was a modest amount that did not cover all our expenses, even with the renting of our house and part of our loft. Tokyo has always been an expensive city, so it was really difficult to survive. But survive we did. I lost ten pounds in the process, but was healthy otherwise. Christophe was doing well under the difficult conditions, so I could not complain. We had our health and were able to keep going.

The family thought we should stay in Tokyo and find a school for Christophe, but that was an unrealistic option and one that I could not handle financially. Kimiko went to give light to Satoru every day and insisted we become part of the Mahikari group to be able to help Satoru. So she took us to their headquarters in Tokyo to take the introductory course to become members. Satoru also wanted us to do this. So, for his sake, we did. It was important for him and gave me the training to be able to give him light when we were no longer in Tokyo. I knew Christophe and I would not be able to stay and explained this to Satoru. I told him we would understand if he did not want to leave. It was a very heart-wrenching decision on my part, but I really could not abandon everything and just move to Tokyo. We would stay until his condition was stable and the doctors said he could leave, if that was what he wanted. We stayed until the middle of November and, by then, Satoru had decided he wanted us to be together. He would return with us to close the loft in New York and then we would all move to our house in Tuscany. That was where he wanted to be, so we would go ahead with that plan.

Looking back, I realize Satoru had always been preoccupied with a fear of cancer. I remember he had gone to play tennis with his friend, Kasu, and the next day he felt stiffness in a muscle in his arm and wanted to see our doctor, in case it was something serious, thinking it could be cancer. Another time he saw that his urine was a slight purple color and, again, he went to the doctor to give him a sample to have tested, only to be asked by his doctor what he had eaten the day before. When Satoru told him that beets were one of the things, the doctor explained that it was the beets that had stained his urine. I suppose since his father had died of cancer, his fears became exacerbated. I kept telling him not to think like that, as it would not help things in that regard.

TOKYO

Satoru stayed at the hospital for about three weeks, and our routine was the same every day. It was interrupted for Christophe and me to attend Mahikari meetings with Kimiko. We were there for the whole of the Sumo championship, and made friends with all the nurses and Satoru's doctor. He was a very decent man who wanted the best for Satoru, and, of course, for us as a family. It was not often they got a mixed-marriage couple in their midst and we were treated especially well. The day finally arrived when Satoru was allowed to return home. Mitsuru came to pick us up to take us to their mother's house. Satoru was really very fragile after being in bed for three weeks, and it would take a while for him to get the strength back in his legs. He could not sleep on the traditional futon bed on the floor, as the permanent bile-draining tube had to be off the ground for the bile to flow down and out of his body. We decided that the only place he could sleep was on the living room sofa, which was a traditional western couch.

His mother, Ryu, allowed this for a few days and then said that he could not sleep there anymore; he had to use the futon. In 1983, Satoru's father, Kitsuke had died suddenly of cancer on the operating table when he had gone in for surgery on his stomach. They had found his body was riddled with cancer and he passed away. No one could believe that he had never complained of pain, or anything, until the stomach problem. Satoru's mother had been alone for almost ten years. She was different without Kisuke; I know that his father would not have insisted that Satoru sleep on the floor. At that point I got upset, as the tube would not be able to drain. I called Kimiko to ask her if we might move to her house and arrange a regular bed for Satoru. She agreed, and, as luck would have it, I found, on my walk around the house, a western couch that someone had thrown out. Christophe and I brought it to the house, cleaned it and set it up as Satoru's bed. Her house, being traditionally Japanese, only had futons to sleep on. This turned out to be a much better solution, as I was having serious troubles trying to get along with Satoru's mother, who did not speak English. I fear she was not very happy with me. I could communicate with Kimiko, as she spoke English and it was easier for me to talk with her. She had a lovely house full of sunlight and was very pleasant for Satoru. She was also there to give him the light treatments in the morning and then left for rest of the day to go to the Mahikari Center. I would take Satoru there, also, most days, as he felt it was helpful. He would be given the light by whoever was there that day and he, in turn, would give light to them and others. Christophe and I did the same, as we were part of the group. He was more involved with the Mahikari after his diagnosis, believing that it would save him. I hoped it would; anything would have been fine, as all I desperately wanted was for Satoru to miraculously recover from this terrible illness.

Satoru wanted us to go to visit the Mahikari temple a few hours outside of Tokyo, up in the Japanese Alps, for a special yearly ceremony they were having. We took a taxi to the bus that would take us to the Temple. It was a beautiful, sunny, day and the drive up in the hills was lovely. The Temple was huge and very impressive, set in luxuriant grounds with a sparkling lake nearby. It was a whole day event and, in the early evening, we returned to Tokyo. Satoru was so happy about the day and it was a pleasure to see him cheerful. Our days were spent going to Mahikari and taking short walks out in the sunshine. Satoru's nieces and nephew would come to visit, which pleased him.

When it was time to return to New York, I bought the tickets with our credit card, thankful that we still had credit to be able to do that. I was happy that Satoru wanted to stay with us, as we were a family, and in such difficult times, it seemed right that we should stick together. I knew, though, that he would also have been happy to stay with his Japanese family, but I would not be able to manage that financially. I was worried about being away from the security of the Japanese hospital, and at the mercy of the American health system.

We had to give up our health insurance just the year before Satoru got ill because we couldn't afford the premiums, so we had no coverage, which was really frightening. I knew we would not be long in New York, but, nevertheless, anything could happen in the meantime and that would have been a disaster. I prayed for our protection and that nothing further would go wrong with Satoru. With my heart in suspense, we left Tokyo for New York. We had said goodbye to all the family and Mitsuru took us to the airport. I was sorry for Satoru's mother, as it must have been hard for her to see him leave. I knew, though, that she was not as devastated by his condition as I was, since death was not so final for her with her Eastern way of thinking. It was difficult for me, though, to know that it would probably be the last time his family would see him alive. I had no other choice, so, with a heavy heart, we left.

Saying Goodbye to New York

Charles picked us up at the airport, and drove us back to our loft where we put Satoru to bed, as the journey had been exhausting for him. I immediately set about organizing the throwing away of fourteen years of living in the loft, and packing what we would ship to Italy. We arranged for a 40-foot container to ship our things. I asked the shipping company if we would have to pay taxes on them, as it was the second shipment and they said that, no, we would not, as it was of our personal things. The container would be delivered in front of the loft on the 2nd of January, 1993, and I had to have everything ready by then. We would be flying out on the 3rd and would stay the last night at my brother's apartment. My dear friend, Rina Yerushalmi, a theatre director who had been our collaborator in The Center, came to help me throw away the things I really did not need. We were constantly taking garbage bags to dumpsters. I was grateful for her expertise, as I would not have had the guts to throw out all we did without her invaluable help. Satoru's students came to do the Tea Ceremony with him several times, and invited us out to dinner before we left for Italy. It was so nice to see his relationship with them and how they respected him. All our friends invited us to their houses and extended their kindness and concern for us. It was very heartwarming. We went up to visit the Rogers, as they wanted to see Satoru. I had written to them telling them of his illness and they were very worried for us.

The minute we got back, the Honda finance company was after us, as I had not had the money for our payments for a few months. We had left the car up in the country at my brother's house, so it was not in New York. The repossession men called and rang our bell at all hours, but I did not answer. They were frustrated, as they could not find the car and did not know it was in Upstate New York. At the same time, I had to appear on my own behalf to finish the loft case, and arrange the final paperwork for the return of the loft to the landlord. Since our lawyers had abandoned us, it was up to me to deal with the final procedures to close the case. On the appointed day, I presented myself at the court and when it was my turn, I appeared before the judge. He was a particularly cantankerous man and wanted to know why I was representing myself. I told him our lawyers had deserted us, due to our difficult financial situation. He was very unpleasant. It was an awful morning and I left there crying. It was the end of an era for us and we were heading into an uncertain future. Satoru was slowly going to be leaving us, and our life, as we had known it, was coming to a close. Twenty-eight years of my life in New York was also coming to an end, and in such a dramatic and awful way. I had lived through so much and still life was testing my endurance. I felt so alone and vulnerable, with all the weight of these experiences crushing my spirit. I was in survival mode, trying to tie up all the loose ends and leave before anything major happened to Satoru. I was scared every day that something dramatic would happen to him. Christophe was not in school as we would be leaving on the 3rd of January. I had to keep an optimistic front for Satoru and Christophe, as I did not want them to worry about all the details.

Our friends were wonderful and helped in any way they could; inviting us to dinners and asking Christophe to play dates with his friends. We spent our last Christmas in New York with Charles at his loft. It was a nice reunion, as we were on good terms, which was the one positive thing about that awful ending. I had arrived in New York on September 15, 1965, seventeen years old, full of hope for the future. Innocent, ready to meet life head-on, never imagining that I would have to face so much in my twenty-eight years in that most extraordinary city. New York was where I had made my career, met my husband, had my son, faced my parents' deaths and was looking at Satoru's eventual passing away. It felt like a lifetime, yet we were both only forty-four. They say you are never given more than you can handle, but I must say, there were times when I just felt I could not take any more. I went one last time to the Cunningham studio to say goodbye to Merce and all my friends there. It was a tearful leave-taking; I had spent so many happy years there. Merce had been like a second father to me. He gave me a big hug and kisses and told me to have strength for the days ahead and not to lose faith. I had told him about Satoru; he had lost John Cage that summer, so he knew what I was going through.

A day before the container arrived, we realized we had forgotten to bring back from the Rogers' house, the wooden box the Japanese carpenters had left us. It had all their instruments inside, but I was busy trying to get everything packed and ready so could not go to pick it up. But Satoru wanted the box and decided he would go. There was snow on the ground and I did not want him to drive. However, he insisted and we rented a car for him to pick up the box. I spent a scary five hours waiting for him to do the round trip. In retrospect, I realize it was a crazy thing for him to have done. He managed to go and return without mishap, much to my relief, and he was happy the box would be going to Italy. That journey was an absolute measure of Satoru's strength of purpose; he would find the strength needed to achieve what he wanted.

The next day, I had hired two men to help load the container which took us five hours. It was filled to the brim; not another thing could fit. It was taken away that evening to the port in New Jersey, ready for its journey to Livorno, Italy. It would arrive three weeks later, all being well. That evening, after broom-cleaning the loft, we closed the door and walked out of fourteen years of life in that beautiful space. We spent the last night at my brother's apartment, and the next morning, I returned to the loft to meet the landlord's son to hand over the keys as ordered by the court. The son proved to be really obnoxious and was insisting that I had taken some lights, which, of course, I had not. I had even left the huge wall of mirrors for them. It was a bitter ending. I also had picked up the Honda from Upstate and drove it to the Honda showroom as arranged, when I called to tell them I was returning the car. So I had closed all our obligations, and we were now ready to leave the next evening for Italy. We had said a tearful farewell to all our friends and were off to an uncertain future. Charles drove us to the airport and we bid him goodbye. An important chapter in our lives had come to an end.

FRIENDS INDEED

When I had been in Tokyo, I wrote or called all our friends to tell them of Satoru's illness. It was as if I needed to get the news out of my system to be able to grapple with all that I would have to deal with as a result. The responsive letters and telephone calls were overwhelming and so much appreciated by all of us. To know that they were all rooting for Satoru, sending their positive energies and prayers for his recovery, and encouraging us to be strong. We had the great fortune to have made so many wonderful friends, who, in our greatest moment of need, were there in mind and spirit.

My brother also wrote and I include excerpts of his letter here:

20 September, 1992

My dear Satoru:

I write to you at a moment which for you I suspect must be among other things a painful, frustrating and seemingly helpless moment in time.

My heart and mind and thoughts of best wishes, positive thinking and kindest and sincerest feelings of love and brotherhood reach out to you and I can only hope that in some remote way you are receiving some of their effects.

What I am sure of Satoru is that your inner strength and inner peace at this time can only help you and you must bring it to the forefront to do battle with this madness, this challenge that destiny has asked you to confront. This mountain that you are being asked to climb in order to reach the next plateau. That you are up to the challenge goes without saying, you must at all costs bring all your mental strength to bear down on this issue and to overcome it as I know you are capable of doing!! I know only too well that it is all easier said than done, but destiny in it's own very particular way presents each and everyone of us with our own individual challenges to confront and overcome. That this one has been presented to you is both unfair and unkind and yet you must remain convinced as I and indeed all of us are that you are up to the challenge and that you will overcome it!!

I am most sorry that I cannot be in Tokyo with you at this very moment, but believe me when I tell you that my thoughts every moment of everyday and I spend a half hour in the morning and the evening doing everything in my power to transmit all of the positive energy that I can towards you. I only hope that it can be of some small help in this trying moment for you. My thoughts are with you.

Here's to a quick recovery!! All the very best, Charles

Excerpts from Shoichi's letter September 22, 1992

My dear Satoru-san,

It has been a long time since the Stouffer's dinner where we had last broken bread together. So long ago, that I am beginning to forget how the chicken (was it?) tasted. Nothing quite like a free meal, and it is becoming scarcer due to the closing of Café Oishi where I was a longtime habitué, alas. But enough of that. How are you? And why am I writing you in Japan? Really, Satoru-san, you mustn't break our heart by getting sick like this. Please hurry and get well.

Were your days in Italy productive? I often imagine you eyeing this and that object for possible use in your sculpture in the little villages of Tuscany. I imagine you could be hoarding a slew of instruments for future use as I write. If you are, my advice would be: don't get caught! (Personally, I find it more discreet and pleasurable to concentrate on the figurative aspect of art. Any cute nurse? Satoru-san? Any nurse, to be exact?) But on a more serious note, if you are establishing your residence in Siena after the convalescence, I look forward to that day and to our traditional schmooze-n-snooze sessions. You and Susana-san and Christophe and kitty and me that would be sublime. So rest well and concentrate on getting out of the body shop a.s.a.p. And we'll make sure you are well tuned up from that day forth. Until then, I shall just have to correspond by writing, but please do not reciprocate by writing back. Just read and rest, that's all you should do right now, Well, Do take care of yourself,

Shoichi-san

Shoichi was always so exceptional in his communications with us and we had such a close and loving friendship with him. He was also such a support for Christophe as his godfather. I include a letter he wrote to him when we were in Tokyo.

September 29, 1992

My dearest Christophe,

Excuse me for typing this letter but you must agree that its neatness makes my words look and sound more intelligent, more literary, even. You'll learn all these tricks in good time, God willing. How are you, my dearest one? How's you Japanipponese? No one expected you all to be in Tokyo at this time but what can you do? That's life, isn't it? Although Papa isn't well, the important thing is that you are together. Both Papa and Shushi need you more than you may realize and for that reason I am very glad that you did not stay in Italy. And I hear that you are behaving exceptionally well, like a thoughtful man, which makes me very proud. Remember, Christophe, until Papa recovers, and I have no doubt he will, you are the man of the family. But you are allowed a time-out now and then and to be a child, too. So find what entertainment you can and try to make the most out of your stay in Japan. And let's look forward to Christmas which is just around the corner. Okay?

Love you as always, and where's Kitty? Will write again soon. Love to Shushi

Our friends, Jan and Jerry, and their son, Stefan, whom we saw a lot of in New York, sent us many letters of support, but I include only two here; we appreciated them so much as we felt their love was such a Godsend.

Darling of our hearts, Satoru, how we miss you and Susana and Christophe. "I left My Heart in San Francisco" sounds boring to us unless it is sung into a glass. Forget Sinatra and Bennett--- their accent is wrong--- they have a band. The very best, the only way I hear it now, is your way. And I feel the warmth of the circle that we make around you when you sing. I keep those moments in my heart because of the generosity of the grace and freedom you create them with. You have given us many gifts Satoru--- the poems about love, the songs and the drawings through the years, are what we keep in our Satoru Box. What we want to give you now is our love and friendship, long distance, which is hardly any fun at all. You must recover quickly because there are many who depend on the purity of your soul, and on your laugh. We wish that we could be with the three of you to help your strength come back, and the easier times to come quickly. But from a distance we are sending you all we can, which is our love and prayers.

Love, Jan, Jerry, and Stefan

October 1, 1992

Dear Satoru, Susana has telephoned to say that you were ill and in Tokyo. When I told Jan she cried. I remember Susana cried for me when I was hit by that car. We imagined you were still in Italy in that beautiful house making art from strange things. But being in Tokyo, sick, that's much more colorful! You know this will make you a better artist.

When I was recovering, I thought about a painting which I eventually made and called 'Car Crasher'. The secret is to take the pain and pass it onto something that gives you strength. I always felt that in your work, you took things that came into your life and transformed them. You make them beautiful.

*We need for you to be well and making us smile, Jan Stefan
and I send our energy and our love that you will soon be well and
back in New York.*

Love, Jerry

Steven Kolpan our dear friend, whom we had first met at the Dupuy
Canal House when we were building our Japanese House in Upstate
New York, and with whom we did our video collaboration on the
building of the house called 'Premises,' sent Satoru this letter:

13 October 1992

Dear Satoru–

*I just spoke with Susana, I want to send you all the healing energy
in my being, all the healing energy in the world. As I am writing
to you I can see you so clearly in the tatami room of the beautiful
house you created. You are conducting the Tea Ceremony—you are
totally focused and powerful. Your energy surrounds the house, but
it is centered in Cha-No-Yu. As I write, I am reliving this perfect
moment, a moment that you, Susana and Christophe created to
share with me, the energy runs wild.*

*Satoru now is the time for you to center your energy and focus
your power again. The ceremony is different, yet it is the same in so
many ways. Just like Cha-No-Yu, you must totally involve yourself
in the ritual that is life that is work that is art.*

*Your name is Satoru. <u>Sato</u> means strong one, a man of strength
(right?) Now you must collect that strength and radiate the energy,
even if you must fight to do it. Because you <u>are</u> Sato you cannot
lose, you must not lose.*

*It is time to do your best thinking, your best work, Satoru,
you have always held back so much of your talent, out of modesty
and generosity of spirit. In the past you have approached your
art in pieces---Architecture, Cha-No-Yu, Ikebana, sculpture, and
video. Now is the time to forget about the individual disciplines
and art forms, and let the pure energy emerge to create something*

magnificent. And you know you can do it, because the world is waiting, we need you to create.

I love you,
Steven

⸻

I am so grateful for my inability to throw anything away and to have created files for all the letters and communications we have had from our friends, families and each other. We have moved from one side of the world and back, almost constantly, and yet I somehow managed to bring them along. I am thankful to myself for my utter dedication to all that is friendship and valuable in our lives. We have learned so much from so many and there will never be an adequate way to thank them all for their love and caring.

Lastly, is our dearest Sally, who wrote us lots of wonderful letters over the years. Out of all, I include this reflection she had on Satoru and my relationship.

October 13, 1992

Dearest Satoru, We're all thinking of all of you with our loving prayers and thoughts. I spoke with Susana yesterday and she certainly gets around. She can't wait to see you. Your bond is perhaps the strongest I have ever seen. This is something many couples NEVER have. Not even a minute part of your closeness. This is a gift that you have both worked very hard on and so fortunate for Christophe to know.

We all wish we could be with you during this difficult time. Your kindness to others is RARE, and also your humor! It'd be fun to sit with you and have our laughs together which we so often did in New York.

We think of you at each moment and pray that you are comfortable and know you are well surrounded. Susana and Christophe make a good student-teacher team and so much better than being in school right now. Please tell Susana she's not to write me as she's so busy and I know that our friendship is forever. You'll always be my guardian angels. We love you,

Sally and the family.

DESTINATION TUSCANY

We arrived in Italy on January 4, 1993, and Mehlika was at the airport to meet us in. She took us to her house where we talked about what our next plans were. I could see that she was worried for us and was very kind. She prepared a lovely lunch and then we headed up to our house. We were very curious to see how the landscape looked in the winter. We had not been there in that season, and I was thinking it might be very grey, but instead there were many trees that were green, and the scenery was much more colorful than we had imagined. The sun was shining but the air was very cold. When we got to the house and went inside, we found the floors flooded with water. It had been so cold that the pipes had burst in the bathroom. All the water had seeped into the rest of the house and gone downstairs as well. I realized that, in my hurry to leave, I had forgotten to drain the water out of the pipes and turn the water off. It was freezing, so I immediately called our plumber to come and fix the pipe. We also had to have him install heaters in all the rooms, as we had not had to do that before, not living there in the winter. It was a shock to see this after a long flight and with Satoru in his condition.

I called Carlo and Anna and told them of our predicament and asked if we could rent their little guest apartment while the work was being done at the house. They did not hesitate a moment and told us to go right down, as they would prepare the little apartment for us. As soon as we arrived there, I suggested that Satoru go to bed and have a rest, as he was looking very tired. Carlo and Anna were charming and very concerned for us. I went back up to the house to see about what type of radiators to install and how to run the gas lines to them. We decided the simplest way was running the gas lines in copper round the outside and into each room. The copper did not show too much on the bricks, so that was the cheapest and simplest solution. I then went to the supermarket in Asciano to buy food for us and took it to our new temporary abode. Christophe was playing with Benedetta, which was a relief, as I did not want him to worry too much about Satoru. On my return, I found Satoru sleeping comfortably and I put away the shopping. I then went upstairs to the main house to talk with Carlo and Anna. I asked them about the school in Asciano where Benedetta went because we had decided that Christophe should go there, too, as it was the same little public school for our small town of Chiusure. The next day I would have to go to the *Commune* (Town Hall) to see about getting residence for Christophe, so that he could attend the public school. Satoru and I had both taken residence in 1989 so that we could get our *Permesso di Soggiorno* (The Italian resident permit to stay in Italy) that is required of all foreigners within two weeks of arrival in Italy.

That took a few days and while we were waiting, we went to the school to see about enrolling him as soon as possible. Christophe spoke very little Italian, as we had never been in Italy long enough for him to really learn it. He was very sweet about it and did not seem overly worried. With that wonderful child innocence, he trusted us and never complained. As Benedetta went to the same school, he had a friend and all would be fine. The next day, we went up to the house to see the progress the plumber was making with the heaters. I had mopped up all the water off the floors and, by now, the floors were dry. The only sign of the water damage was downstairs in the cantina, where the water running down the walls had left a mark. This I would paint when the walls had properly dried. The work was going well and in a few more days we would be able to move back home. We took a look outside to see the garden and the amazing view. They were really stunning, even in winter.

We then went up to Chiusure and the old people's home where our doctor was that morning. I had called his office to make an appointment with him, as he was our chosen doctor for the Italian medical coverage. I, being a European citizen, had a right to the Italian health service and Satoru, as my husband, was also included. This was a great weight off my shoulders, as now anything that might happen, would be covered by the Italian National Health and we would not have crippling medical expenses to deal with. Our doctor, Dr. Pizzichio, would be assisting Satoru throughout his illness at home. He was a very intelligent man, not trying to play God, but always advising and doing what was within his means. I had asked him about finding a homeopathic doctor so that Satoru would have the homeopathic remedies to go along with the Chinese herbal medicine that Mitsuru had gotten for him. He gave us the name of a famous German doctor called Gertrude Schaffel, who had an office in Siena. We went to Siena to see what she could do for Satoru. He had a very good session with her, as she was optimistic and set a course of homeopathic remedies for him to take. As she was a private practitioner, we would pay her per session.

Satoru and I felt comfortable with Dr. Schaffel and had faith in the treatment that she recommended. At one point, she scheduled an appointment for Satoru at her office in Tavernelle, to measure the energy in his body with a special machine she had. It would tell her how his body was fighting the cancer and help her adjust her remedies. We were doing all we could do medically and the only thing we still had to do was go to the Mahikari Center in Florence to introduce ourselves, and for Satoru to get light from the members there. Kimiko had gotten their information from the head office in Tokyo for Satoru. He felt he needed this, so we went to meet them. They had a very nice chapel and were all very kind. We went there whenever we could, as Satoru really felt better afterward. It was an hour and three quarters away, but worth the trip. We tried to go at least three times a week. We would go in the early morning, after we left Christophe off at Chiusure to wait for the school bus, and be back in time to pick him up when it was over. School in Italy is from 7:30 a.m. to 1:00 p.m. so that the children can return home for lunch. Then there are afternoon sessions for languages and sports. I would drive Christophe to the top of our dirt road just outside our village of Chiusure, where the little school bus passed to pick up the children.

Christophe was enjoying school, as he was the only foreigner there. All his classmates wanted to sit next to him, and took turns doing so. He became the class *beniamino* (the favorite student) and was immediately invited by the boys in his class to join their basketball team, which he accepted, delighted to play with them. He had not been on a basketball team at school in New York as there was none. He was a natural and ran like a gazelle across the basketball court. The boys were very happy to see they had a very good player in their midst, and he got on famously with everyone. We were off to basketball games all over the countryside, all of us parents following each other in our cars from one game to the next. Satoru came most times, but, occasionally, he was too weak to come. I used to yell myself hoarse rooting for our team. It was great fun and they won many games.

We discovered a magical countryside every morning when the mist would be hugging the valleys and hills. One day we could barely see the abbey above the mist, and another time, just the tip of a hill. It was a constantly changing scenario, one which, every morning, as we drove up to wait for the bus, presented us with a brand new panorama. We never ceased to be amazed and thankful for the extraordinary landscape that was our gift everyday. Satoru was stunned by this beauty and I was so happy that we were there to witness this miracle. I am sure that, in his heart of hearts, he probably would have been more comfortable in Japan, his own country, with his own language, but he had wanted to stay with us and I gratefully acknowledged his sacrifice. It made me happy for him, that he was in this beautiful place, and near Siena, his favorite city for its wonderful architecture. The Piazza Del Campo, Siena's main square, is an architectural gem and many was the time that Satoru would ask me to drive him there to see it. On our way back, he would sing Charlie Chaplin's song from *Limelight (1952)*, "Smile," which he sang in that beautiful way of his. I felt he was trying to maintain his courage in the face of the sentence he had been given. The words are heart-wrenching, yet encouraging at the same time. How I wished that he had not got this terrible illness. I could not understand why such a beautiful human being had to be struck with that devastating blow. Why him? Why not someone else less worthy of life? There were so many miserable people running around committing awful acts and yet were totally alive and thriving. It seemed unjust to me, and something I could not come to terms with.

I lived with the specter of death on a daily basis. It was debilitating, exhausting, demoralizing. We tried to keep our spirits up and I never fully accepted that he would die. I felt we could beat this thing and he would get well. Our life would go on and all would be as before. So we faced every day with hope. I admired beyond measure Satoru's courage and good cheer. He did everything in his power not to worry us; he was a wonderful, caring soul. My dearly beloved was hanging on for us. Since his diagnosis, Satoru had stopped his sculpting work and took up drawing with charcoal pencils on beautiful parchment paper. He did a gorgeous series of hearts that were done on two pieces of paper that, when joined, made the whole heart. He used bright colors: reds, yellows and black. He gave one to Christophe and one to me on my birthday, the 31st of January. There was a series of rivers, which, I think, represented his bloodstream, and they were very dramatic, covering the whole page. Only the heart series had the two sides to each piece. I had read in my research into cancer that it was helpful for the patient to try to draw his feelings about the illness. We had bought all the tapes by Bernie Siegel and followed his advice about listening to classical music, especially Bach and Beethoven.

I also tried to get him to talk about his childhood, hoping to help him get out anything that might be the cause for this manifestation of the cancer. My feeling was that no one really understands why cancer suddenly surfaces. We know that it lies dormant in each of us and that at some point, for unknown reasons, the cells are starved of oxygen and start attacking healthy cells. This is a simplistic way of putting it as I am not a doctor; it is in layman's terms of what I understood from all the research I did about the disease. We would sit out on sunny days and Satoru would talk about his childhood. He remembered many things that upset him; I was wishing for a miracle and tried everything to entice one into being. Dr. Siegel had written that fifteen percent of cancer patients can recover miraculously, just like turning a light switch on and off. I read of the many cases he had witnessed and was hoping with all my heart that we would be able to find that mysterious something that would help Satoru turn the switch off.

Satoru was a willing participant and tried all he could, as I had read to him Dr. Siegel's case studies. One example that struck me was of a woman who had a few days left, who, when asked what her dying wish was, had answered that she wanted to be taken to a favorite lake. On being at the lake, something in her turned that switch off and her cancer just started to disappear, and she subsequently recovered. I was searching for something similar, not understanding that we all have a destiny, all have lessons that we are to learn in this life. I would come to see that Satoru's illness was a part of that destiny, and, as a consequence, also Christophe's and mine. We had to learn the lessons that Satoru's cancer would force us to face, like it or not. For we who remained, the journey would prove to be a long one with many ramifications that would manifest themselves for the rest of our lives. The absolute finality of an illness like cancer, and the impotence one feels, in some measure, condition the choices one makes, as Christophe and I were to find out.

EMERGENCY

The heating was working well and we were nice and warm in the house. When it was sunny we were able to sit outside and many days we ate lunch on our terrace. Kitty was enjoying her freedom going out every day and a beautiful marmalade cat came to make friends with us. We called him Tigre for his stripes, and he got on well with Kitty. One day he came with his new kittens to introduce them to us. They were very cute but a bit frightened, as they were born in the wild and not used to people. We found them up on our terrace as we walked out and they all scampered off, except one who literally flew off the terrace with his four feet spread-eagled in flight. It was the most amazing thing. He landed without mishap and ran away.

A few weeks after we moved back, we got a phone call from the shipping company saying that our container had arrived. The agent had bad news for us, though. The year and-a-half we had to import our personal belongings had passed and we would now have to pay the 25% tax on the $ 250,000 value we had declared for insurance purposes. It was a sum completely beyond our means, and I explained that I had precisely asked about that in New York when we contracted the company to ship our things over. He apologized for the bad news and would see what he could do. He knew someone in the import office and would see if taking him out to dinner and explaining our situation would do the trick. He would get back to us; in the meantime, we should not worry, as he would do everything possible.

That same evening, as Satoru got up to go to the bathroom in the middle of the night, he accidentally stepped on the bile-draining tube and had ripped it out. At three in the morning, we woke Christophe up and drove to the emergency room at the hospital in Siena. Luckily, it was fairly quiet when we got there and we did not have to wait long for Satoru to be seen. A very nice young doctor checked Satoru and had him admitted for the tube to be re-inserted. He also told us of a very special cancer center in Ravenna that specialized in Satoru's type of cancer. He gave us the address and telephone number and suggested that when the tube was put back in, we should see if they could admit Satoru there. Despite the fear we felt with this mishap, we now had something to look forward to. We had always been told there was nothing to do and now it seemed like there was some hope. Satoru was taken to a room with two others; I settled him in and told him I would go back to get some of his things for the few days he would be there. So, at dawn, we drove back home, shaken up with the night's unexpected events. I made breakfast for Christophe and told him not to worry, that everything would be all right; that we had to be positive and pray for Paddy with all our strength. After breakfast, I drove him up to get the school bus and then returned home to prepare the things to take for Satoru and to cook his food.

I drove over those hills like my life depended on it; I wanted to get to Satoru as fast as I could. I was worried about him being in a place where he did not know or speak the language. As soon as I got there, the head doctor on the floor was making his rounds and I was able to speak with him and find out how they were going to proceed with Satoru's tube. He said he would schedule an operation to re-insert the tube for later that day. When I asked him how long Satoru would have to stay, he told me about three days, depending on how things went. I was able to stay with Satoru all day, as I had arranged for Christophe to go with Benedetta to Carlo and Anna's house. I would pick him up from there after I had given Satoru his dinner. In Italy, one brings one's own plates and glasses and cleans them at each meal. I was cooking Satoru's macrobiotic diet so he did not eat the hospital food. It was difficult journeying back and forth, as our house was forty-five minutes away, but I wanted to stay with him as much as I could. Christophe was in good hands and it was better that he was not at the hospital. The Japanese hospital experience had not been great, so I was anxious to keep him away from anything similar as much as possible.

At the hospital, we had time to talk about things and how Satoru was feeling about everything. He gave me that beautiful, crooked smile and, in his angelic way, told me he was accepting the destiny he had been given and would fight to stay alive. We talked about the center in Ravenna and if he wanted to try and go there to see what they could do for him. He was enthusiastic about it and so we decided that I would contact them and see when we might go there for a consultation with the specialist. They operated on Satoru that day to put the tube back in while I nervously waited in his room for them to bring him back. I lost a lot of weight from the time we found out about his cancer, due to all the stress, as I was so nervous and upset I had absolutely no appetite. I ate the little I did to keep up my strength and that was all. I was thoroughly fed up with hospitals and all they signified; they were depressing places to spend any time in. Satoru was always charming with everyone and was very much appreciated by one and all.

This is the letter Satoru wrote to Michael, his Tea Ceremony student in New York. I insert it here to show in his words the events so profoundly affecting his life.

March 17, 1993

I haven't written you little while, I am sorry. How are you? Everything is normal? For me about four weeks ago I had a little accident. I stepped my plastic tube on the way back from the bathroom. Whole tube came out. So I had to go to Siena Hospital for emergency, stayed two days and doctor recommended to see specialist in Ravenna (three hours from the house) So we decided go to Ravenna for special check up and treatment. This specialist in Ravenna recommended to do chemotherapy to put directly into my liver and few other areas. (This only affect for cancer cells not other cells) and they did operation for me. It was a success. I spent altogether two weeks in Ravenna. Doctor in Ravenna recommended doctor in Siena. I have to continue treatment every three weeks until my health improve. At this moment I started treatment three days ago, so I have two more days to do treatment. This is very mild treatment. But my legs are bit weak, so it is not easy to walk around. But my spirit is up. So I feel good and relaxed. But I must tell you that Susana is working so hard, I feel bad about I cannot help. And also Christophe. Send love to George and deepest sympathy to Kasu, Love Satoru

---

Each time I read Satoru's writing, I can't get over how childlike it is, almost as if his command of English is not very good. Instead, he spoke very well in his special way and we all understood him. His words were few, yet so clearly did they express what he meant.

Finally, the day arrived when Satoru could return home and I packed his few belongings and we drove back to our beautiful corner of paradise. Christophe was overjoyed to see his Paddy back and looking good. He, too, had lost a lot of weight so was a bit weak and sat down as much as possible. He did not want to be in bed, so tried to sit in the sun on our terrace when the weather was nice, which was almost every day, as we had a sunny winter that year. We would take little walks around the garden, but not too much. I had called the hospital in Ravenna and made an appointment for three days later to give Satoru a chance to settle down at home a few days before having to face the four-hour drive up to Ravenna. We only had our red bomber, which was not so comfortable for Satoru, so Marianne and Bishi, knowing our plans, offered to lend us their Volvo, as they would be away for two weeks in England. They were staying for a few months with Nieves in Cortona while Bishi was waiting for a new assignment in Saudi Arabia.

The day we had the appointment in Ravenna, we arranged for Christophe to spend the night with Carlo and Anna in case we had to stay. The day we drove up was sunny, and we were full of hope for what we would find there. We arrived on time and met the specialist. He was a charming man and explained what they did at the hospital and how they could help Satoru. They had to perform all their exams, and after that, they would tell us what they could do. Satoru was admitted so they could begin the tests. When the results came back, it was clear that the cancer was very far along and it would be more of a challenge, but they were hopeful that with their special treatment, they could help his situation considerably. They said that had we found them sooner, the results could have been much more positive. They would do the best they could, and we were not to worry, as he was in good hands. We spent the day there. So it was up to us to consider whether Satoru wanted to go ahead and we decided that it was worth trying.

We thanked the doctor and drove back home, stopping for dinner at a nice restaurant in Ravenna the doctor had recommended. I called Anna to tell her we would drop by to pick up Christophe around 10:00 p.m. I spoke with Christophe to tell him we were very happy because the doctor was going to operate on Satoru and make him a lot better. He sounded happy and was anxious to see us again. We picked Christophe up and drove home, all of us exhausted but hopeful. I would be taking Satoru to be admitted in two days and I had to make arrangements for Christophe and prepare Satoru's things. We drove up in the early morning after seeing Christophe off on the bus to school. We arrived at the hospital at noon and he was admitted and taken to the room he would share with four others. They then came to prepare him and give him the medicine he needed before the operation. They would operate the next day and I would stay overnight on the chair next to his bed, as I wanted to be there for the operation. I would return home to be with Christophe the next day.

The operation went well and the doctor was happy. Now Satoru would have to stay a few extra days to make sure everything was proceeding as it should. Satoru was groggy and tired but seemed happy to have done the operation. It gave us something to hope for even though it had not been an easy operation for Satoru. The doctor told me he had been very courageous and everyone admired Satoru's fortitude and good cheer. I could not stay the night, as I had Christophe to take care of, as well, so I went up every other day until it was time to take Satoru home.

I drove back home in the late afternoon after seeing that Satoru was stable, as we did not want to leave Christophe too long without one of us near him. So, in the late afternoon, I drove back, exhausted and worried, to pick up Christophe. I read him a story until he fell asleep and then gratefully went to bed myself. The next morning, the shipping company called to say they had tried everything but there was nothing further they could do. They suggested I go myself and meet with the customs officer to see if I, in person, could persuade him to find a way to resolve the problem. Satoru was going to be in

Ravenna for two weeks. I had arranged to go to Livorno on a day I did not go to Ravenna and we made the appointment with the customs officer. Off I went on the arranged day, and after a three-hour drive down there, exhausted and looking grey, I presented myself.

He had been told of our desperate situation and, I guess, on seeing me looking so tired, he took pity. We started talking about the problem and I was asking him if there was any way we could find a solution. He leaned over to pick up an enormous book of laws to see if there was something we could use to avoid the customs cost. As he was leafing through the book, I kept talking, hoping that some information I was giving him would help. As I was telling him that we had just got Christophe's residence, I asked if we could not import the things under his name. Wouldn't he have the same rights we had when we took residence? His face lit up and he said, "How old is your son?" I said he was twelve years old. He said, "Let me see if there is anything in the law that mentions an age limit for importing." He started reading and found no mention of age, so with a bright smile, he said, "Signora we have the solution. We can import the things under your son's name but he will have to sign all the documents. Can he do that?" "Of course," I said. So he told me I had to send the copy of Christophe's residence document and a letter signed by Christophe stating that the possessions were his personal belongings. I gave the officer a big hug and invited him to have a drink with me. He thanked me but said he could not, as he was on duty. He then suggested I send a fax with all the documents to the port storage company to see if they would wave the storage fees. They were considerable, as our container had languished in port for over two weeks. He said he would call them and explain the situation and he thought they might waive the charges, which is exactly what they did. This was another example of the great humanity of the Italian people. I left there, thrilled I had overcome that enormous obstacle and thankful for my dear Christophe, who would be affixing his signature to all the documents.

This accomplished, the container could now clear customs and be delivered to our house in Tuscany, a four-hour drive from the port of Livorno. Four days later, I picked Satoru up from the hospital and drove him home, much to his relief. Being in an Italian-speaking country, not understanding very much of the language, was stressful for Satoru. So we were very happy he would be back in familiar surroundings. The agent called the day after our return to say the container would be leaving Livorno and arriving at our house the next day. I went up to Elio, to get his help finding three other men to unload the container with him. Bishi and Marianne were back from England and she offered to come over to help by cooking for everyone and do anything else that was needed. I had arranged as much as I could to receive the container and hoped that it would go smoothly. I did not want all the commotion to disturb Satoru.

The Journey up the Mountain

We had had continuous sunny days but, wouldn't you know it, the day the container was due to arrive it was raining. Just like the time we had to move from my parents' co-op after we sold it. It seemed our moves were always to be done in the rain. The driver of the shipment called when he got to Chiusure and I drove up to meet him and guide him down to the house. He saw immediately that he would not be able to get back up with the empty container, as he would not have enough traction without the weight to drive it up the hills. So what was I going to do now? Everyone was at the house waiting to unload and we could not get the container down and out. We had to find a solution. We all put our heads together and decided that I would have to call a moving company in Siena. Would one have a van available that day to come and transfer our things from the container to the van and make the necessary trips to get everything off? We called a few companies to no avail, then the last one we tried could do it, but it would have to be after their lunch break. So the men I had hired returned to their homes and would go to Chiusure at 3:00 p.m. when the movers would be there.

It was still raining hard outside with no sign of letting up, but we would have to do the best we could, with all the traipsing in and out unloading our possessions. Marianne was a godsend, always cheerful and looking in on Satoru and cooking his meal which he ate in his room. I was busy coordinating and went in to be with him as often as I could. Marianne cooked us three a delicious lunch which we ate in the kitchen. The moving people called at three and we all met up in Chiusure to start the transfer. I returned with the first load and then waited at the house to direct the men where to put the things. The previous summer we had made two rooms on the main floor into one by creating an arch of bricks between both rooms. That way we could have a big living room instead of the small living room and Christophe's small bedroom. His room would be a big guest room opposite our other bedroom that Satoru and I were using now, as it was smaller and warmer than our wing that was too big to heat adequately.

I also needed that big space along with the cantina to store all the furniture and boxes that were arriving. The men worked hard in the rain and were getting wet despite their raincoats, as they could not use umbrellas. Each time they came with a load I would direct them where to take it. Their muddy shoes were dirtying all the floors, but there was nothing to do but keep going. Little by little, the cantina was filled with boxes and furniture and our wing was also completely full. There was no room to move by the time they finished. I had managed to get most of the living room furniture where it belonged, as I wanted Satoru to at least be able to have a nice living room to sit in if he wanted to. It took several hours to get everything in and when the men were finished Marianne offered them coffee and a delicious cake she had baked. Everyone was happy for the treat and to get the job done. I don't know how we would have done it without everyone's good cheer and willingness to work in the rain.

I was hoping all the traffic had not disturbed Satoru too much; it was so difficult to manage all that had to be done while poor Satoru was lying in bed recovering. He never complained, but I have to say, I wish we had not had to do all that while he was so ill but, unfortunately, circumstances were such that we could not do it any other way. It was a lot for all of us to handle, but we had managed it and were getting on with life. There were times when I was so exhausted and worried, I was not sure I could keep going. After the delivery of our belongings, I would spend part of the day, when Satoru was resting, trying to unpack some of the boxes. It was difficult, though, as I could hardly get into the cantina or our wing, they were so full of things. I finally gave up and dedicated myself to Satoru's well-being. Part of his cure was going to the day hospital in Siena for his chemo treatments. We met the doctor in charge, a very nice man who told us what the procedure would be. The sessions were usually in the mornings, so we would drive in and I would wait for

Satoru, walking around Siena or sitting in the waiting room until he was finished. One day I got my courage up to ask the doctor how long he thought Satoru had to live. He told me that, unfortunately, he did not think he would last until the spring. I was shocked and did not want to believe him, so I put it out of my mind and prayed and prayed for God to have mercy on us and allow Satoru to live.

I took Satoru to all the sessions that had been scheduled, but things were not getting better. We even stopped going to the Mahikari center in Florence, as Satoru was getting weaker by the day. He just did not have the energy necessary to make the trip. Bishi called one day to ask if he could come and see Satoru and I said of course, so he came that afternoon. He wanted to be alone with Satoru, so I left them together. When Bishi came out he said to me, "Susana, Satoru is dying. You have to let him go, he is so tired." Up until that moment, I had refused to see what was happening and finally had to accept the reality that Bishi was pointing out to me. It was terribly painful to have to realize that I could not play God.

I thanked Bishi for making me aware and sat and talked with him for a little longer while I served him tea. After he left, I went in to Satoru. He recounted a dream he had had the night before where he was walking up a mountain in a beautiful landscape, and there were people dressed in lovely costumes offering him food and presents. At the top of the hill was a gate and there was a bright light there. They were inviting him to go in. I said, "How beautiful. Would you like to go?" He said he was not sure. The next evening he had the same dream, so I said to him that if he wanted to go he should not hesitate. Christophe and I would be all right; we would miss him always, but he should go there if that was what he felt to do. The next day was Easter and I had been worried about making it a happy experience for Christophe, so I had invited our dear friends, Roberta and Roberto, from Rome. They arrived the day before Easter. I had organized an Easter egg hunt for Christophe and Benedetta, whom I also invited with Carlo and Anna. We had a nice day eating lunch on the terrace outside, as the sun was out and the weather was warm. Satoru even came for a walk with us, as he seemed to have regained some of his energy. The next day, however, he woke up not feeling well and asked me to call the hospital and his doctor, to send an ambulance to pick him up. The ambulance arrived and I followed it to Siena while Roberta and Roberto took care of Christophe. The doctor met us when we got to the hospital, ready to examine Satoru while I anxiously, sat outside in his waiting room. He called me in after and said that Satoru would have to be admitted to the hospital as he was very ill. I asked him if he could do more for him in the hospital than I could do at home. He said that, no, there was nothing, as all they could do was administer morphine for the pain to keep him comfortable. I asked him if our doctor could do that and he said yes. I felt it was better for him to be at home with us, and not in an impersonal hospital in a foreign country. Satoru also asked me to call the Mahikari center to see if they could come to the house the next day. I called the director and he said he would come with two others in the late morning.

Roberta and Roberto had to return to Rome for work and so we were left alone. Satoru asked me to send Christophe to his room as he wanted to talk to him. Christophe was with him for a half-hour and then came out. I did not ask what his Paddy had said to him. Christophe just told me that his Paddy had asked him to take care of me, and other things that he never revealed, and I never asked him about. I realized Satoru would not be with us long. The time had come and I must be strong for both of us. I called Dr. Pizzichio and asked him to speak with the doctor in Siena to coordinate what he would have to do to make Satoru comfortable. He arrived in the early afternoon and administered the morphine for the pain and said he would be on call anytime that Satoru needed him. We went to bed early as usual that evening and Satoru kept wanting to get up to go to the bathroom. The cancer had spread rapidly when Satoru had decided he did not want to take the Chinese herbs anymore. He wanted to have a cappuccino and croissant and eat whatever he wanted. I felt I had no right to stop him, and let him do as he wished. The Chinese herbs had kept the cancer from progressing, but once he stopped, it spread quickly, which was why we were at this stage now. It took all my resolve not to insist, for selfish reasons, that he continue with the herbs.

I would get up and have him lean on my back for support and walk him slowly to the bathroom right next to our room. He was so thin and weak, I later realized that his poor body had become like one of the victims of the concentration camps. He was skin and bones, but it was as if I had blinkers on; I only saw my beautiful Satoru as he was in his full splendor. My eyes and my mind had not looked at the reality, and it was only later that I would allow myself to remember the terrible truth. We made the trip to the bathroom several times; I was beginning to feel more and more desperate for him. After a while he stopped wanting to get up and I could hear him struggling for breath. The doctor had given him the morphine that would keep the pain at bay till the next day. So there was nothing I could do. I was feeling more and more panicky hearing his breath becoming more and more labored. I was desperate, then, suddenly, as if a cloud had lifted, something came over me and I became calm. I placed Satoru's head on my arm and lay down with him and started singing in a soft voice about all the beautiful things we had all done together. Gradually, his breath slowed down and finally stopped completely. He had left serenely and in peace. I looked at my watch, it was close to three in the morning. I continued singing softly till the early light and softly rested his head on the pillow and got up to get dressed.

I had held on for Satoru, but now I just sat down and cried and cried. The loss of my precious soul-mate was the very worst thing I could imagine. I had been abandoned by the three most important people in my life. Christophe and I were totally alone now, to face the world and our uncertain future. How would we manage? How was I going to tell Christophe? I waited for him to wake up on his own, as he was on Easter holiday, and I wanted to put off as long as possible telling him the sad news. He had known this was going to happen, probably from the day he asked me, point blank, if his Paddy was going to die. Now, I told him quietly in his room, he looked at me with his eyes wide and slowly started to weep as I hugged him. We sat on his bed crying together until we had no more tears left.

I called Dr. Pizzichio, who came immediately and upon examining him, pronounced Satoru dead. He had to call the doctor from the Commune in Asciano to come and examine him, to ascertain the cause of death, in order to write the death certificate. Satoru passed away at 3:00 a.m. on April 13, 1993. Satoru was forty-five years old, now in Peace with his father and two year-old brother and my parents. I felt he was in good company and sent them all my love and asked them to take care of my precious soul-mate. The times of facing death every day were over. They had been debilitating and desperate, but this was much worse. I wanted the world to stop turning so that I could get off.

The Mahikari director and the nice couple we had made friends with at the center arrived mid-morning, I had completely forgotten that I had arranged for them to come the day before. I had to tell them of Satoru's passing and they were so sorry to hear the news. However they would be able to give him the light, through their collective hands, to send him on his way. I know Satoru would have been so happy for this. It was fateful that he had asked me to call them to come, and that they were able to be there and send him on. I know Satoru's sister would have been happy about this, too, as she was a very strong believer in the effectiveness of the doctrine. They told me his face was a light color which was a significant fact for the journey he was undertaking. Had his skin been a dark color, it would not have been a good omen. I was grateful for that! It meant he was at Peace.

After they left, slowly the people from the village started coming and asked to sit with Satoru. I knew nothing of their customs, but they told me that that was what they did in Italy. So I went to get chairs for them and they would take turns coming and sitting. Very solemn and respectful, they came with their rosaries and prayed for Satoru. I was very touched. It was like a scene out of *Zorba the Greek*, very moving and pagan in a way. For a long time after his passing, they would discretely leave food they had cooked for Christophe and me on the terrace. We were so thankful for their great kindness. We could not have been in a better place for Satoru's passing, as the human warmth of the people was supreme; we felt loved and cared for. All Christophe's school-mates and their families came to pay their respects, as well as his teachers. Everyone was overwhelmingly kind and offered to help anytime we needed.

Time stands still for no one, and so, we would go on, hurt and crippled by the pain. Yes, time, I knew from experience, would heal us outwardly, but not the pain that would always lurk just below the surface. The only thing that consoled me, and I recounted to Christophe, was Satoru's dream. He knew where he was going and had decided to go there happy, knowing the welcome he would receive.

It was a small mercy that gave us some peace. I felt overwhelmingly sorry for our precious son who, had, at the age of seven, lost his adored grandparents and now, at the tender age of twelve, his beloved father. I could not possibly imagine the magnitude of his pain. I had been lucky to have my parents until I was thirty-nine. It would be a constant thought at the back of my mind bringing up Christophe.

SONGS IN THE NIGHT

I called Satoru's brother and sister in Tokyo, and his brother in Germany and my brother in New York. I then called Carlo to ask for his help arranging the funeral. I just could not deal with that in my emotional state. Next I rang Nieves, in Montalcino, where Bishi and Marianne were staying, who, in turn, told Beatrice and Cuth, our Australian psychiatrist friend. Carlo called a funeral home in Siena and asked them to come and take care of preparing Satoru. I got Satoru's clothes ready and it would be Carlo who dressed him. He would be cremated and the Commune in Asciano gave me the information for the Cremation Society of Siena. They sent a very kind gentleman to come and talk with me about their procedure and a date was set for Satoru's cremation. We had to wait for our families to arrive from Japan, Germany and New York. We drove down to Rome to pick up my brother and then Mitsuru and Kimiko. It was an emotional meeting with all of them after which we drove home. Hiroshi was driving down from Germany with Kirsten and arrived in the afternoon with an enormous bouquet of white flowers. My cousin, Nicolette, and her husband, Jeff, and Shoichi all asked, when I called them, if I wanted them to come for the funeral or after it, and I chose the latter.

I made room to accommodate everyone, and Satoru's sister's first request was to see Satoru. But the coffin was in Siena and had been closed already. I had not known she would want to see him. She was upset about this, but I told her the Mahikari people had seen him and given him light. They would tell her how they had found him. She wanted to know about his skin color. She called them and spoke with the director who told her how he had looked and what they had done, which seemed to please her. They arranged to come and pick her up the day after the cremation in Siena, to go to the Center in Florence where she would spend the day. They would very kindly drive her back in the evening. The next day we would all be going to Siena for Satoru's cremation. It was in a beautiful place overlooking Siena; the kind gentleman from the Cremation Society had come to be with us of his own accord. I was very moved by his generous gesture. Nieves, Marianne, Bishi, Beatrice and Cuth came separately. We all gathered around Satoru's coffin and read or said our farewells. Cuth read a beautiful piece she wrote which she gave me afterwards and I include here.

Satoru

We are saying goodbye to the form Satoru made for himself in this life, here with us. We will miss his beautiful body, his harmonious movements, above all the authority of his very quiet voice. But the difference will be less than with many people, because Satoru in his physical presence could achieve with a touch, with a half word, what it takes most of us many sentences, gesticulations and heaving's to do less well.

He exerted with infinite gentleness a force that could be as effectual as the tide when it turns invisibly in the sea. His energy, joined to Susana's more sweeping impulse, formed a team that was irresistible.

Satoru—light, in both senses of the word, and so aware of the exact beauty of line and color—while visibly with us, achieved, silently, and with accomplished perfection, anything from washing a plate to composing a room or a new kind of picture. And he could express even contrary emotions in a single smile. I have seen him do it when the occasion demanded.

So it should not be too difficult for us who loved his visible presence to realize that he is with us now, as ever. We can let him go on the journey his soul had undertaken, as he dreamed it, up among the beautiful, happy beings, on the grassy slope towards the temple, and know that at the same moment he is here with us. We will hear his so quiet voice—I can hear it now—whenever we wish, over our left shoulder; it will be heard very especially by the two people he loved so dearly, Susana and Christophe.

I feel strongly that he will answer any question Christophe may turn to ask him—important or not—perhaps more clearly than he could have through the intermediary of words. And that Susana will sense, within her now, his understanding and his force even more closely joined to hers, carrying her forwards, into the life they shaped together. She will express him in visible achievements here, while he, from just over the way, with the slightest of gestures, moves with—and moves—her tide.

I had not written anything down as I wanted my words to come out as I felt them. I talked of our life together and Satoru's great humanity and how I would miss him. I am now sorry, these many years later, that I have no concrete record of what I said. I held Christophe's hand throughout and admired his absolute grace. He was living up to his heritage, with fortitude and strength. He shed a few tears when our relatives and friends went up to him, but I kept holding his hand for support. We were always very close and this would not change over time. It would be us facing our futures, heads held high.

After the ceremony, we all went into Siena to a restaurant overlooking Piazza Del Campo, Satoru's favorite square, for a farewell drink to him. Then to the house, where we would lay out all we had made, and others contributed, for lunch. It was a sunny day and we ate out on the terrace. It was a bittersweet moment, where we all had some memory of Satoru, sometimes funny, sometimes sweet and always with great respect. I remember saying I was going to write a book about our life together. Slowly our friends took their leave and we were left with our small family. My brother, Charles, Mitsuru and Kimiko, Hiroshi and Kirsten as well as Christophe and I, all retired early, exhausted. The next day, Hiroshi and Kirsten, left to return to their house in Germany and, two days later, Christophe and I would drive Charles, Mitsuru and Kimiko to Rome for their flights back to New York and Japan.

I drove back with Christophe to our empty house and had dinner, after which I read him a story. He had asked if he could sleep in my bed with me, and I had thought it was a good idea. We continued this until he felt secure enough to return to his own bedroom some weeks later. The flowers Hiroshi had brought us stayed alive for two whole weeks, as vibrant and beautiful as the day he brought them. We were stunned, yet not surprised, as Satoru had loved working with flowers and we felt this was his way of showing us his continued presence. It was comforting and reassuring. When I had expressed to my brother that I was worried about living in our house on my own, just with Christophe, he had said to me, "You are going to have to get used to it." And so that was what I did.

For several months after, Satoru would make his presence felt by reproducing the smell that came from his body during the last months of his cancer. It would materialize when I was down and feeling desperate. It was strange, just as suddenly as I became aware of it, it disappeared when I was able to let him go. It took me much less time to let him fly away into his new life than I was able to do with my parents. Maybe I had learned to understand that it was important to be strong as quickly as possible. I had no support now, and had to be a source of strength for Christophe. However this did not stop me from seeing Christophe off to school, then immediately crawling back into bed to sleep until it was time to get ready to greet him back from school. I was completely exhausted from the strain of living with death on a daily basis, and all that had to be taken care of at the same time. I did not want him to see me in this way, and was grateful for the hours of his absence. It took me two years to just physically get over Satoru's passing, and the same amount of time to be able to drive the road I had so many times travelled on to take Satoru to Siena.

I called or wrote to all our dear friends about Satoru's passing and we got so many phone calls and letters, which I eventually answered, though it took me a while. All the letters we got were so moving, but I will only include a few here as it is a way of my sharing the words.

From Jan and Jerry

New York City April 22, 1993

I have tried so many times this week to write. We have all thought of Satoru and of the three of you together there in Italy, imagining you walking in your beautiful hills, singing. For us, he is there with you now, we think of all the nights we spent together, of all the special times we have shared with you, and I know those special times will go on, because he is in our hearts, because he is by our side. Jerry says, "Bless his heart." And we do. We bless his heart and we bless the beauty of Satoru and of his sweet and gentle life. We love him for all that he was and is. I think of him disappearing at Christmas and coming back with a poem, a drawing, pulled that moment from his heart, so much more than any gift he could have bought. Satoru could always surprise us. Satoru could always make us laugh. We have a white rose in the vase that Satoru used to sing into. It is our memory of him; it is our way of helping him through this passage in his life. For Jerry he is still strong and healthy like he was the last time they were together. For Stefan and me, we also know the Satoru of his illness, and the grace with which he bore it. He was all about beauty. It was in his manner, it was in his eye. We will miss him, we will always miss him. He comes into our thoughts at odd times, for unexplainable reasons and we bless his soul as well as his heart. He left this world with much love.

Our love to you both, Jan and Jerry and Stefan.

Merce Cunningham sent me this beautiful letter also:

June 12, 1993

Dear Susana,

Your sad news arrived today. I am so sorry to hear of Satoru's death. Although he died peacefully, it must be no less difficult for you. I hope Christophe and you both will heal, thankful too you are where you are. It is a terrible ache, but it does go away, although life is different.

I send you all my love, Take care.

As ever, Merce.

From Marianne and Bishi

July 25, 1993

I have been thinking about you a lot, and had such a strong feeling about Satoru—driving along an avenue of beech trees on my way to work—with the dappled sun coming through the branches. Somehow the white of the ancient trunks and the filigreed lightness of the pale green leaves evoked Satoru—his strength, purity, and transparent fineness.

I'm sure we who loved him often failed to allow enough silence for his insights to sink in—But underneath he had such tolerance and understanding of us all! And we were blessed and continue to be blessed by what he shared with us. I hope that friends and family have been around and that the special peace and beauty of your home have given you respite.

A big abraco to you and Christophe, Love, Marianne and Bishi

This last one is an excerpt from a letter sent by Meg Harper, a beautiful dancer who danced with me in Merce's company, it seems so long ago.

I have been thinking of you, praying for you and Christophe, since hearing of the death of Satoru. I have tried to write to you before but I couldn't find the words. I still have not found them but need to tell you how deeply you are in my heart and how greatly I respect your strength. I find it a mystery why one person is asked to undergo so much tragedy in such a short time, even in any time. Losing the three people who have undoubtedly meant most to you is something I cannot understand, and is so painful to consider happening...... I think for myself I could not bear it. That is not much help to give you, and is why all my efforts to write to you have been unsuccessful.

But this morning I wanted to try again. I was looking at 'Signals' on the video a few days ago and felt this deep hole of missing you, missing your beautiful way of dancing, that no one can come close to, and that leaves

Signals vacant, when others try to dance it. And there are all the other dances you gave an authenticity to, you held the stage with your rock-like presence and riveted the eye with your clarity. In all my work recreating old pieces of Merce's, your presence stands out, watching you on the screen, I forget what I am supposed to be doing, and just sit there in awe, and in respect.

If there is anything I can do, ever, but especially now, to help you in any way, I would be honored to have that chance. It would mean a great deal to me to stay in some kind of touch with you, as I feel we were a kind of family, having spent those years dancing together.

For now though I send you all my love and a prayer for your peace,

Meg

So there I was in our Tuscany, in the middle of those magical hills, fortunate to be surrounded by genuine, loving, caring people. I had my beautiful son close to me, constant testament to the best of Satoru, and in some strange way, also of my parents. Could I ask for more? No! I had shared an extraordinary seventeen years with Satoru; he had taught me so much. He had left me more aware, more sensitive to those around us, and to the way I would live my life on a daily basis. We had loved each other profoundly, we had shared pain so strong it took our breath away, we had fought together to understand, to learn. We were given all the emotions and feelings that two human beings could possibly go through, we were given our incredible son Christophe, who, in his turn, showed us by his being, things we could not have known without him. He was only twelve years old, but, as Satoru had said when he saw him in his bassinette in the hospital with all the other babies just born, "He looks like a little wise old man." Indeed, many times I felt I was the child and he the parent. So our life will go on and we shall do honor to the three people who have left us, for their teachings, their extraordinary love, for all that we can express for them, in moving forward, living our lives. For as long as I can remember, I had been afraid of death. Now that I have lost the three most important people in my life, I am no longer afraid. Christophe and I will march forward, proudly into our future and, hopefully, make a difference in this world.

Since I was a child I had wanted to leave something important behind for others to use when they might need it. I have, as a dancer, given of my art, as a teacher, of my knowledge and, as a friend, wife, mother and human being, I hope the very best that I have had in me. There is much still to give and I am writing this memoir to continue that dialogue. I thank LIFE for all it has given me and all that I continue to learn on a daily basis. I wish that all of us everywhere may be blessed with grace and humility.

I had heard Satoru sing before I heard him speak. At the end, unconsciously, I had given him the gift of hearing me sing to him alone as he was leaving this world. We had come full circle, and the song continues.

EPILOGUE

"Love, Dozo" was the telegram's message that gave me the name of my memoir and the love that held us together. Satoru asked me for "Love, please" and I answered "Love, thank-you." He asked me to love him and I thanked him for asking. Love was our grand theme on a daily basis. It was our never-ending commitment to fight for it no matter what. We felt it, we learned from it, and grew with it. It was what Christophe had lived with us and it would be what I would keep alive for him and me. There were no easy remedies or short cuts; I would be both Christophe's mother and father and a widow continuing to live the life that, on coming into the world, I had chosen. That it was a mystery, I was acutely aware, and that the challenge was great I had no doubt, but that I could meet the task, I was absolutely sure. I would slowly recover my emotional and physical strength and, with my indomitable spirit, forge on.

Life had offered me the supreme gift of all the experiences I had received and I was now much better equipped to move forward. I had survived my parents' sudden deaths with no preparation at all and lived Satoru's day-by-day for eight months in fear. I know one was not easier than the other. They were both enormous lessons. We stayed in Tuscany full-time until Christophe had to go to high school in Rome. During those last months of spring and summer, I plunged into our garden and buried my hands in its soil for reassurance, ripping up the weeds, the very weeds that reminded me that life, indeed, goes on; that their energy never dies, but continually renews itself. There, in my garden, I found a way to hold on, to have the courage to go into my soul, to delve in that place where the concentration of my gardening allowed me to begin to heal. It was a sort of purification, wherein my instincts were allowed to do as they wished. I just let go, and in my meanderings, I discovered by chance, places in my being that I had not looked into before. The garden became my teacher, my task-master, my exhausting and demanding healer.

The house Christophe and I were living in dated back to 1296 and I have often thought about all the sorrows and happiness that it stored within its walls. It had an air of great solidity; one was at peace there, yet it held all our secrets, all our wishes, our fears, our prayers to God, to the Universe, and all our dearly beloved.

In the twenty years that have elapsed since that awful day Satoru left us, Christophe and I have experienced many amazing events and continue to meet the many challenges that appear before us. It has not been easy; many times we have asked ourselves why we have had to keep surmounting the lessons thrown at us. But we are still here, stronger every day helping each other, and all who we can help along the way.

It is another story to tell, which I plan to do.

I end with a quote by James Joyce that I wrote out many, many years ago when I was growing up:

"History is a nightmare from which I am trying to awake and the way to awake from it is not to be afraid, and to recognize that all of this, as it is, is a manifestation of the horrendous power that is all creation. The ends of things are always painful. But the pain is part of there being a world at all. From this you come to the realization that you must do the best you can. Participate in the game. It is a wonderful, wonderful opera --- except that it hurts"

CPSIA information can be obtained at www.ICGtesting.com
Printed in the USA
LVOW121115230213

321364LV00003B/193/P